MARLBOROUGH

BY WINSTON S. CHURCHILL

The Story of the Malakand Field Force
The River War (2 volumes)
Savrola
London to Ladysmith via Pretoria
Ian Hamilton's March
Lord Randolph Churchill (2 volumes)
My African Journey
The World Crisis (4 volumes)
The Aftermath (volume V of *The World Crisis*)
The Unknown War (volume VI of *The World Crisis*)
A Roving Commission
Marlborough, His Life and Times (6 volumes)
Great Contemporaries
Step by Step, 1936–1939
Amid These Storms
Frontiers and Wars
Painting as a Pastime
The Second World War (6 volumes)
A History of the English-Speaking Peoples (4 volumes)

The Earl of Marlborough, by John Closterman. NATIONAL PORTRAIT GALLERY.

MARLBOROUGH

His Life and Times

Volume 1 of a 4-Volume Set

WINSTON S. CHURCHILL

ABRIDGED AND WITH AN INTRODUCTION BY
HENRY STEELE COMMAGER

New York

CHARLES SCRIBNER'S SONS

ε⊃ NOTE ⊂϶

In quoting from old documents and letters the original text has been preserved wherever it is significant. Letters of Marlborough and Sarah which enter directly into the narrative have been modernized in spelling, grammar, and punctuation so far as is convenient to the reader. But the archaic style and spelling has been preserved, and occasionally words are left in characteristic spelling.

Documents never made public [before the original six-volume edition] are distinguished by an asterisk (*) and left for the most part in their original form. In the case of unpublished letters to and from Marlborough preserved in the Blenheim collection no further reference is given.

In the diagrams, except where otherwise stated, fortresses held by the Allies are shown as black stars and those occupied by the French as white stars.

W. C.

METHOD OF DATING

Until 1752 dates in England and on the Continent differed owing to our delay in adopting the Reformed Calendar of Gregory XIII. The dates which prevailed in England were known as Old Style, those abroad as New Style. In the seventeenth century the difference was ten days, in the eighteenth century eleven days. For example, January 1,

NOTE

1601 (O.S.), was January 11, 1601 (N.S.), and January 1, 1701 (O.S.), was January 12, 1701 (N.S.).

The method used has been to give all dates of events that occurred in England in the Old Style, and of events that occurred abroad in New Style. Letters and papers are dated in the New Style unless they were actually written in England. In sea battles and a few other convenient cases the dates are given in both styles.

It was also customary at this time—at any rate, in English official documents—to date the year as beginning on Lady Day, March 25. What we should call January 1, 1700, was then called January 1, 1699, and so on for all days up to March 25, when 1700 began. This has been a fertile source of confusion. In this book all dates between January 1 and March 25 have been made to conform to the modern practice.

W. C.

❧ CONTENTS ☙

(xi)

CONTENTS

VOLUME 2

CONTENTS

(xiii)

CONTENTS

(xiv)

(Illustrations face or follow the page number given below; boldface numerals denote volume numbers)

LIST OF ILLUSTRATIONS

ஐ LIST OF MAPS ஐ

(xvii)

ᚷᛞ INTRODUCTION ᛞᚷ

WINSTON CHURCHILL is, beyond all doubt, that statesman who became the greatest historian, and that historian who became the greatest statesman, in the long annals of England. We do not say of him, had he not chosen to be a great public figure he would have been a great historian, for he was that, by every test. It is only because our gaze is fastened so continuously, and so intensely upon that career which has some claim to be the most splendid in two centuries of English history, that we do not concentrate more on that career which has some claim to be regarded as the most affluent in English historical literature.

Because, for half a century, Churchill played an active role in politics, we may be tempted to suppose that the writing of history was, with him, an avocation, and put him down as one of those glorious amateurs who are the specialty of English culture. There is of course some truth in this: doubtless Churchill preferred making history to writing it. The point is that he did both, and did them not as separate enterprises, but as instinctive expressions of a character of singular unity, harmony and consistency. There was no division, and certainly no conflict, between the two activities, the making and the writing of history: each nourished the other, and interacted on the other. For Churchill wrote history in order to mould it, and—so we sometimes suspect—he made history in order to write it. As he was a statesman in the familiar tradition of Cromwell, Chatham, Disraeli, and his own father, Lord Randolph, so he was an historian in the familiar tradition of Ralegh, Gibbon, Macaulay and Lecky, and to both enterprises, the political and the literary, he brought the same intellectual and moral qualities.

INTRODUCTION

It is the quality of Churchill's histories that assure them a permanent place in our literature, but the sheer bulk is no less impressive. What other major historian has written so much, so well: thirty-two volumes, no less, of history and biography, and another twenty volumes of speeches which add a not negligible dimension to historical literature. If this prodigious output had been achieved at the expense of scholarly accuracy, critical acumen, or literary polish, we might dismiss it as interesting chiefly for what it told us about Churchill himself, but the books do not shine in some borrowed light, but with their own. *The River War* is still far and away the best account of the struggle for the Sudan; *Lord Randolph Churchill* is one of the best biographies in English political literature; the *Marlborough* ranks with such biographies as Carlyle's *Frederick the Great* (a greatly under-valued work) and Freeman's *Lee*; the voluminous histories of two World Wars remain indispensable:—it is safe to say that no other leader of any of the warring nations has produced anything as sure of permanence.

We know that Churchill put a great deal of effort into his books, as he did into his speeches; but as they appear before us, they are shorn of all the machinery and all the scaffolding, and stand forth in their own comeliness and symmetry. They were, like his public papers, natural, though not spontaneous, expressions of his character. And that character was all of a piece: it is the same in whatever guise—soldier, journalist, politician, statesman, historian. Churchill wrote as he talked, and talked as he wrote; he took to the pen as he took to the sword or to the floor of the House of Commons.

As with most great historians, Churchill was self-taught and self-trained. Certainly he had no formal education for a career as historian —indeed it is accurate to say that he had no formal education for anything except soldiering. But his informal education was probably as good as that which any young man enjoyed in the whole of England. It was something to be born in Blenheim Palace, it was something to be heir to generations of Churchills, it was something to have the dazzling Lord Randolph for a father, to be connected with all the first families of politics and society, to be familiar with all the best drawing rooms—even those of royalty. As a boy he had not only read history, but seen it in the making. "I can see myself . . . sitting a little boy," he said to the students of Harrow, "always feeling the glory of England and its history, surrounding me and about me." Perhaps he did feel something of that at Harrow, but doubtless he felt even more of it in the spacious rooms and gardens of Blenheim, at the Vice-Regal Lodge in Dublin, at the house on St. James's Place. But even that was only the beginning. After Sandhurst, where he went because he was unable to pass "responsions" for Oxford, he continued his special preparation for History—and for life.

On distant Indian frontiers he immersed himself in history and philosophy. "All through the long, glistening, middle hours of the Indian day," he remembered, "from when we quitted stables till when the evening shadows proclaimed the hour of Polo, I devoured Gibbon." And not Gibbon alone, but Macaulay and Lecky and, for good measure, Plato and Aristotle too. "I approached it with an empty, hungry mind," he added, "and with fairly strong jaws, and what I got I bit." Indeed he did, and his bite left permanent marks! Circumstances, too, conspired to advance his education: he went as a journalist to Cuba, where there was a convenient revolution; he fought, and played polo, on the Indian frontier; he managed to get himself posted to the Sudan in time for the River War, whose history he wrote; he resigned from the Army, but not the military, and at twenty-one he was off to South Africa and the Boer War, a veteran now of four campaigns in four different quarters of the globe. Thus he learned of wars by fighting in them, as Herodotus had, and Thucydides, and Tacitus, and in time it came to seem that the wars were waged just so he could write the *Malakand Field Force*, and *The River War*, and *From London to Lady-smith*, to say nothing of his first, and only novel, *Savrola*.

All this preparation was, in a sense, fortuitous; the young Churchill was not really looking that far ahead. Fame was the spur, and necessity, too. Churchill had to make his way; he had to make his mark. The Army, for all its fascination, offered nothing permanent, nor assurance that it could satisfy Churchillian ambition. Torn between journalism, history, and politics, Churchill embraced all three and made them one. He was the most dashing of cavalrymen—and of polo players, too, which was important; he was the highest paid war correspondent in England; the *Malakand Field Force*, and then *The River War*, were acknowledged to be history of a high order, and if the success of *Savrola* did not beckon to a purely literary career, it was certainly nothing for a young man to be ashamed of. As early as 1898 he wrote his mother that he was planning a biography of Garibaldi, and a history of the

American Civil War, and for good measure he threw in a collection of short stories. Success intervened; he stood for Oldham, and won, and was launched on the turbulent seas of politics.

Churchill was never content to sail but one sea at a time. His father, whom he had worshipped from afar, rather than loved, had died in 1895; now that Churchill had proved himself in history, now that he had turned to politics, he launched himself upon a biography of Lord Randolph. "Once again," he said, "I lift the tattered flag lying on a stricken field." It was a splendid phrase for politics, but ominous for history. But astonishingly enough Churchill's biography of his father was not an essay in filiopietism, but judicious, comprehensive, and mature, penetrating not only to the realities of politics in those turbulent Victorian days, but of character.

It was, of course, more; it was a lifting of the tattered banner, and a mending of it, too. In a sense all of Churchill's histories were autobiographical: the early books which were history seen through the eyes of a young subaltern; the later books which were world history seen through the eyes of a world statesman; the biographies which were all family affairs. He lived a long life, every minute of it crammed with excitement, and he recorded all of it, for the benefit of posterity—and for his own benefit too, for he never overlooked that. The early books advertised his talent as a war correspondent; the books of the middle period testified to his role as a spokesman of the Churchill family; the later books were a monument to his genius as soldier and statesman. He was present in all of them: in the early histories as reporter; in the later as director. Never was there more personal history. It was Lord Balfour who called *The World Crisis*, "Winston's brilliant autobiography disguised as a history of the universe," and might not this have been said—with less justification for the touch of malice—of *The Second World War* too; while of *A History of the English-Speaking Peoples* it could be plausibly asserted that it was designed to make clear (or at any event did make clear) that the virtues which had for centuries exalted these peoples were precisely those which the whole world associated with Winston Churchill.

All of his life Churchill was fascinated with himself, and no wonder. He saw himself in his father—really a very different and much less stable character—and his description of the boy Randolph was autobiographical:

INTRODUCTION

This schoolboy, pausing unembarrassed on the threshold of life, has
made up his mind already. Nothing will change him much . . .
Lord Randolph's letters as a boy are his letters as a man. The same
vigour of expression; the same simple yet direct language; the same
odd, penetrating flashes; the same coolly independent judgments about
people and laws, and readiness to criticize both as if it were a right;
the same vein of humor and freedom from all affectation. . . .
[*Lord Randolph*, I, 13–14]

He saw himself in the great Duke, too; like Marlborough he loved the
sound of bullets, the clash of sabres, the crowded stage, the sense of
power, the sporting with destiny, the applause of nations and of
sovereigns, and of history, and his vindication of Marlborough from
neglect and contumely was in a sense a vindication of himself. As for
his histories of the two World Wars, he did not need to put himself
at the center of great affairs or make clear how many threads he held in
his own firm grip, for the world did that for him.

Most nearly autobiographical—and prophetic, too—was the first book
that Churchill wrote (not the first he published), the novel *Savrola*.
Youth excused the triteness and absurdity of its plot—it was another
Graustark, another *Prisoner of Zenda*—and of its philosophy, too, which
was half-baked Social Darwinism; but the vigorous style, the sharp
characterizations, and the curiously prophetic reflections on politics, do
not need excuses. The novel was about revolution, dictatorship, and,
rather awkwardly, platonic love; it was about power, which always
fascinated Churchill; it was about the ruthlessness and cruelty of war,
the fickleness of the mob, the brevity of fame. It was, above all, about
a young man who sounded and acted like Winston Churchill and who
foreshadowed what he was to become. Even the oratory was prophetic:

Amid the smoke he saw a peroration which would cut deep into the
hearts of a crowd; a high thought, a fine simile, expressed in that
correct diction which is comprehensible even to the most illiterate,
and appeals to the most simple; something to lift their minds from
the material cares of life and to awake sentiment. His ideas began to
take the form of words, to group themselves into sentences; he mur-
mured to himself; the rhythm of his own language swayed him; instinctively he alliterated. . . . The sound would please their ears, the
sense improve and stimulate their minds. What a game it was! His

brain contained the cards he had to play, the world the stakes he played for. [*Savrola*, p. 89]

The central figure of *Savrola* was a soldier who aspired to be a statesman, or a statesman who found he had to be a soldier. If there is a common denominator in all of Churchill's histories, except the *Lord Randolph*, it is the preoccupation with the military. And if Churchill had a specialty—and now-a-days all historians must—it was military history. He is, in all likelihood, the greatest of military historians writing in English, superior to Napier on the Peninsular Wars, to Oman who wrote on the history of war, to Fortescue whose history of the British Army is curiously parochial; and the peer of the three great American masters of the history of war, Francis Parkman, Douglas S. Freeman, and S. E. Morison. For consider Churchill's claim to preëminence in military history. His first books were about wars—frontier skirmishes, to be sure, but that can be said of Parkman's histories as well; his *Marlborough* can bear comparison with Freeman's seven volumes on *Lee* and his *Lieutenants*; his magisterial histories of two great world wars are still, for all the passage of time, the most comprehensive and scholarly available in English. No other major military historian covered so broad a territory—India, the Sudan, South Africa, western Europe, and eventually the globe; no other chronicled so many different wars, or wars so different; no other saw the wars he chronicled from such varied vantage points, from that of the cavalryman in the field to that of the Lord of the Admiralty and of the Supreme Commander; no other understood so fully the role of tactics, of strategy, and of grand strategy, of politics, diplomacy, and public opinion.

2.

WHAT philosophy suffused and illuminated these many histories, from *The River War* to *The Second World War?*—fifty years of history, fifty years of writing? No formal philosophy, certainly, for Churchill would have agreed with his friend George Macaulay Trevelyan, that philosophy was not something you took to history, it was something you carried away from history. Yet every historian takes some philosophy with him, inarticulate, or even unconscious—some concept of what life, and his-

tory, are about. Churchill matured early and, for all his political maneu-
vering, retained, to the end of his long life, a marvelous consistency.
He was, in manner, rhetoric, even in appearance, an eighteenth-century
figure; he combined, in himself, something of Chatham, of Burke and,
even more perhaps, of Charles James Fox; and he accepted, instinctively,
the attitude towards history which that century took for granted: that
history, in the words of Bolingbroke, was Philosophy teaching by examples. What is more, he was quite ready to stand there and point to
the examples. Indeed we can say of Churchill what he himself wrote
of Rosebery, that "the Past stood ever at his elbow and was the counsellor upon whom he most relied. He seemed to be attended by Learning
and History, and to carry into current events an air of ancient majesty."

Nowhere does this appear more simply than in the "Grand Theme"
which Churchill imposed upon his history of *The Second World War*:
"In War: Resolution; In Defeat: Defiance; In Victory: Magnanimity;
In Peace: Good Will." He read history as a stupendous moral scripture,
and for him the writing was, if not divinely inspired, at least authorita-
tive. More, it was straightforward and simple. History was a struggle
between the forces of right or wrong, freedom and tyranny, the future
and the past. By great good fortune Churchill's own people—"this island race," as he called them—were on the side of right, progress and
enlightenment; by great good fortune, too, it was given to him to buckle
these virtues onto him as armor in the struggle for a righteous cause.

If history was Philosophy teaching by examples, what lessons did it
teach?

The lessons that Churchill learned from history stare out at us from
a hundred aphorisms; no other modern historian has conjured up so
many aphorisms or coined so many epigrams. They are explicit in scores
of essays; they are implicit in fifty volumes of history and public argument. Let us summarize them.

First, History was not just the pursuit of idle hours but was, itself,
philosophy and, rightly read, furnished lessons which statesmen could
ponder and apply. Second, History was both memory and prophesy.
It provided the counsel and the solace of the long view both to the
past and to the future. The contemplation of the ages which mankind
had somehow endured, and survived, infused the student with patience,
with humility, and with courage; the prospect of a posterity which, a
thousand years hence, might pronounce the verdict that one generation

had given to a nation "its finest hour" encouraged resoluteness and hope, and strengthened the ability to confront crises that seemed insurmountable. Third, History followed great cycles: the same themes recurred, again and again, the same drama was played out, from age to age; and as men had somehow survived the vicissitudes of the past there was ground to hope that they might survive those of the present and the future. Thus four times Britain had fought to rescue Europe from the grip of a tyrant—Louis XIV, Napoleon, Kaiser William, and Hitler—and four times Britain had succeeded in saving Europe and, with it, the cause of liberty and justice. Here was a recurring pattern which augured well for the future of "this island race," and of mankind, for, as Churchill saw it, the welfare of mankind was inextricably intertwined with that of the English-speaking peoples. Fourth, History bore witness to the vital importance of national character, for character was as important to a people as to an individual, and every nation must be alert to defend and preserve it. That each nation had a special character Churchill did not doubt, and as he contemplated the long arch of centuries he was led to a fifth conclusion, that it was, above all, the English character which had lighted up the corridors of time, flickering now and then but mostly pure and clear and even luminous—the English character and that of England's daughter nations around the globe. For all his familiarity with the peoples of every continent, Churchill was the most parochial of historians. He looked out upon world history, but he looked through British spectacles, and his rallying cry was the familiar one from *King John:* "Come the three corners of the world in arms/And we shall shock them/Nought shall make us rue/if England to herself do rest but true." That was really the motto of all his histories—the *Marlborough,* when England did not stay true to herself; and the two World War histories, which recounted the famous story, how England did. All his life, Churchill's eyes were dazzled by the glory of England, and all of his writing was suffused by a sense of that glory. He never forgot that it was the English tongue that was heard in Chicago and Vancouver, Johannesburg and Sydney, Trinidad and Calcutta, or that it was English law that judges pronounced in Washington, Ottawa, Canberra and New Delhi, and English Parliamentary governments that flourished in scores of nations on every continent. It was this little island that had spread civilization throughout the globe, and what Churchill wrote, in *The River War*, could be inserted in almost all of his books:

> What enterprise that an enlightened community may attempt is more noble and more profitable than the reclamation from barbarism of fertile regions and large plantations? To give peace to warring tribes, to administer justice where all was violence, to strike the chains off the slave, to draw the richness from the soil, to plant the earliest seeds of commerce and learning, to increase in whole peoples their capacities for pleasure and diminish their chances of pain—what more beautiful ideal or more valuable reward can inspire human effort? [*The River War, 9*]

From all this flowed a sixth lesson, that the test of greatness was politics and war. Churchill knew something of the social and economic history of his people, he knew something of literature, for he had a great deal of it "by heart" which—as he said, was a good way to have it; and had he not chosen to be a soldier, a statesman, and an historian, he might have been a very considerable painter. But when he came to write history he put all this aside, and concentrated on the art of politics, the science of law, the beauty of justice, the power of government, the necessity of war.

Churchill knew the horrors of war, for he had experienced them, but he knew its exhilaration, too, and he might have said with General Lee that it is well that war is so terrible, else we might grow too fond of it. He had learned from history, and perhaps from Darwin, the law of the survival of the fittest, and he thought that England's capacity for survival was proof of her superiority. The call for "blood, toil, tears and sweat" was inspired not by the Blitz alone, but by a half century of conflict. "Battles," he wrote in the *Marlborough*, "are the principal milestones in secular history. . . . All great struggles of history have been won by superior will power wresting victory in the teeth of odds." And elsewhere he concluded flatly that "The story of the human race is War." Like those statesmen he most admired, Marlborough, Chatham, Wolfe, Clive, Washington, Lee, he was himself a war leader; alone of great war leaders he was a great war historian.

History—not least the history of war—taught a seventh lesson, and taught it not only *to* Churchill but *through* him: the vital importance of leadership. History, he asserted, was made "by those exceptional human beings whose thoughts, actions, qualities, virtues, triumphs, weaknesses and crimes have dominated the fortunes of the race." There is no record that he read Carlyle, but there is little doubt that he would have agreed with the philosopher from Cheyne Row that history "is the essence of innumerable biographies." This was the moral of the youthful *Savrola*, and it remained the moral of all Churchill's historical writing, and much of his political, for his volumes celebrated the "glorious few" who played, uncomplainingly, the role that History had assigned them—Lord Randolph, Marlborough, and that central and dominant figure of the two great war histories who so splendidly vindicated the principle of leadership.

Finally Churchill's reading of history reenforced his early education to exalt the heroic virtues. He was Roman rather than Greek, and as he admired Roman accomplishments in law, government, empire, so he rejoiced in Roman virtues of order, justice, fortitude, resoluteness, magnanimity. These were British virtues too, and, because he was the very symbol of John Bull, Churchillian. He cherished, as a law of history, the principle that a people who flout these virtues is doomed to decay and dissolution, and that a people who respect them will prosper and survive.

3.

DURING the dry years of forced retirement in the early twenties, Churchill wrote most of the volumes of *The World Crisis*. When the Conservatives were defeated again, in 1929, Churchill laid aside the scarlet robes of the Chancellor of the Exchequer which he had inherited from his father, and withdrew to Chartwell to launch himself upon an even more formidable historical enterprise, the biography of that famous Churchill who became the Duke of Marlborough. As with the *Lord Randolph* it was a filial, though not a filiopietistic work; as with the *Randolph*, too, it was a work of vindication and rehabilitation, for though Marlborough was recognized as a great soldier, his greatness of character was not acknowledged. As Churchill himself wrote, "Fame shines unwillingly upon the statesman and warrior whose exertions brought our island and all Europe safely through its perils and produced glorious results for Christendom. A long succession of the most famous writers of the English language have exhausted their resources of reproach and insult upon his name. Swift, Pope, Thackeray, Macaulay, in their different styles, have vied with one another in presenting an odious portrait to posterity."

The history of Marlborough was a theme worthy of Churchill's historical genius, and one which perhaps only he could have performed, combining as he did the advantages of access to the rich treasure of Marlborough archives at Blenheim and an experience in war and politics almost rivalling that of Marlborough himself. Churchill prepared himself for the enterprise, as he did for everything, with scrupulous care; studying all the voluminous sources, familiarizing himself with the terrain of battlefields and of marches, enlisting the aid of experts in political and diplomatic history, and deploying all his resources of narrative, eloquence, philosophy, and wit.

Here was indeed a subject worthy of the most eloquent pen in England. "It is my hope," he wrote,

> to recall this great shade from the past, and not only to invest him with his panoply, but make him living and intimate to modern eyes. I hope to show that he was not only the foremost of English soldiers, but in the first rank among the statesmen of our history; not only that he was a Titan . . . but that he was a virtuous and benevolent being, eminently serviceable to his age and country, capable of drawing harmony and design from chaos, and one who only needed an earlier and still wider authority to have made a more ordered and a more tolerant civilization for his own time and to help the future.

The hero was a man after Churchill's heart: the greatest soldier in the annals of the race, ever victorious and ever magnanimous; the statesman who welded together a continental alliance; the diplomat who mediated between the English, the Dutch, the Prussians and the Empire; the Captain loved by his soldiers, trusted by his allies, respected by his enemies. But the theme was more than biographical; it was nothing less than the theme of the struggle for Europe. The battlefield was more than Blenheim, Ramillies and Oudenarde; it stretched from England to the Mediterranean, from Sweden to Savoy and enlisted all the great sovereigns of Europe.

Churchill seized upon this heroic figure and this affluent theme, and discoursed upon it spaciously. He saw its almost limitless scope, its bewildering complexities, its mighty drama; and, like a master builder he fitted them all together into a structure that was coherent and symmetrical. He quarried his facts from rich deposits of material; he grounded his volumes on the solid foundations of scholarship; he familiarized himself with the terrain and provided a background of rich verisimilitude. He interwove, wth masterly skill, the tangled skeins of a dozen nations, armies, and courts—England, France, Holland, the Empire, Bavaria, Prussia, Sweden, Spain, Savoy, even Ireland, and imposed on it all an harmonious pattern. He told his story in a language strong, muscular, rich, and resourceful, one that did full justice to its splendid drama and its glittering actors, noble and mean alike. To the study and the record of these momentous years, to the untangling of intricate webs of battle, politics, diplomacy and personalities, he brought all that he had learned in a lifetime of war politics, study and reflection.

It is, to be sure, partisan history; it is almost family history. But how few great historians, from Clarendon to Rowse, from Bancroft to Douglas Freeman, have not been partisan? *Marlborough* is an argument for the defense, all the way; but an argument not fabricated by cleverness or insinuated by chicanery, or imposed by violence, but grounded on the solid rock of evidence. It is balanced, temperate, and fair; it carries conviction.

It cannot fairly be said that Churchill is blind to the weaknesses and the flaws in Marlborough's character, but it can be said that he regards the weaknesses as venial and the flaws as superficial, and that when he casts up the balance of weakness and strength, he is content with the result. He is a skillful attorney for the defense, and if he does not convince us that Marlborough is blameless, he does persuade us that a blameless Marlborough would be uninspiring. Was the young John Churchill kept by a beautiful mistress? No doubt—but what young man could have resisted Barbara, Duchess of Cleveland? And what impecunious young soldier could have resisted her money? Did he abandon his King, James II? Yes, but that was for the well-being of England. Did he negotiate secretly with the enemy over in Paris, or Versailles? No doubt, but only to deceive them, for he played a deeper game than they did. Was he governed in all things by Sarah—her vanity, her arrogance, her imperiousness? Possibly so, but was she not the most fascinating woman in England, and how delightful that the

Iron Duke should be so romantic! Was he parsimonious, and greedy of money? Yes, but how much better to be parsimonious than to be extravagant; and as for the money, it all went to larger ends, like the building of Blenheim!

But the reader can be trusted to judge for himself the success of Churchill's vindication of the great Duke, of the wars he waged and the politics, or intrigues, he pursued. Even if he is not won over to a verdict uncompromisingly favorable to Marlborough, he can still revel in the masterly portrayal of character, the vigorous narrative, the pageantry and the roar of battle, the skillful handling of diplomatic and court intrigue; he can still rejoice in one of the great monuments of our historical literature.

But the *Marlborough* has still another interest, one which is irresistible even to those who are unmoved by the drama of the War of Spanish Succession or the spectacle of the rivalry for the affection and confidence of a Queen. It looks forward as well as backward, it is not elegiac, but, in a sense, apocalyptic.

Rarely in the history of historical writing have author and subject seemed so made for each other as were Churchill and the Duke of Marlborough. Churchill's literary skill enables us to understand Marlborough, but *Marlborough*, in turn, contributed to and advanced the education of Churchill. Surely this historical investigation which for five years absorbed Churchill's energies, may be looked upon as a providential preparation for the years ahead when he was to stand, a greater Marlborough, surveying a greater scene, presiding over a greater battle, commanding a greater coalition, whose destinies were fraught with greater significance. It is not a distortion to see in Marlborough an embryonic Churchill acting out on what seems to us a more restricted scale the role Churchill was to play with such splendor and bravura on a global scale. Like Marlborough, Churchill was called upon to rescue Europe from the grasp of a tyrant, to preside over a prodigious political and military coalition, to sustain allies who faltered and drooped, to fire the spirits of those who were reluctant, to assuage those who thought they contributed more than their share, to persuade the British people to bear, over the cruel years, the blood, toil, tears and sweat of war. Like Marlborough, on him was imposed the direction of the military, the political, even the diplomatic campaigns. Like Marlborough he had endured in silence the slings and shafts of fortune, but only to prepare himself for duties which no other could perform, and like Marlborough, too, he had shifted from party to party, never confessing to fickleness but conscious only of devotion to his sovereign and his people. Like Marlborough he was called upon, in a solemn moment of history, to save his nation and when he had done this, was rejected, only to return, at the end, to the favor and love of his people. All this may push the parallels too far, but not for Churchill, who read History as Puritans read the Scriptures.

We cannot say that without the experience of writing the *Marlborough*—an experience which was deeply personal as well as public—Churchill would not have been prepared for the great ordeal of the forties. But we can say that the writing of *Marlborough* helped prepare him for the prodigious challenge which lay ahead. And we can say that the mind and character of the man who presided over the destinies of the western world when Hitler threatened its existence, and who won through to such triumph as no other English statesman has ever known, was himself a product of a half century of conflict in which the writing and the making of History were one.

ᛊᛞᛟᛞᛊ

THE only edition of the *Marlborough* heretofore available in America, is that published in the years 1933–38 in six volumes, and this has been for some time, out of print and unavailable. To make possible publication in one volume I have reduced the original text to approximately one-half its length, keeping, in the process, a large proportion of the original illustrations and maps. Nowhere, needless to say, have I taken liberties with the integrity of the text, which is precisely as Churchill wrote it. What I have done is to leave out such parts of the original as seemed to me less indispensable than others. Respect for Churchill's special talents dictated the selection of the chapters and passages included in this volume. In *Lord Randolph*, Churchill showed that he could deal, with firm hand and sure touch, with politics. But elsewhere, in his writings, he has preferred the annals of war to the story of peace, the battlefield to the cabinet, and in making the selections for this book I have very sensibly followed his preferences in the matter. Marlborough was a great political personality as he was a great warrior, but there is no doubt that in these volumes, at least, Churchill is at his best in telling the story of Marlborough the soldier rather than in unraveling the intricacies of Marlborough the politician or the courtier. I have therefore included almost the whole of the military narrative where Marlborough himself was in command, but merely enough of the political and the personal to brush in the background and keep the thread of the narrative, confident that while no one has told the military story in a more masterly fashion than has Churchill, others—notably George Macaulay Trevelyan—are fuller and doubtless more judicious in the analysis of the political story.

HENRY STEELE COMMAGER

Amherst, 1968

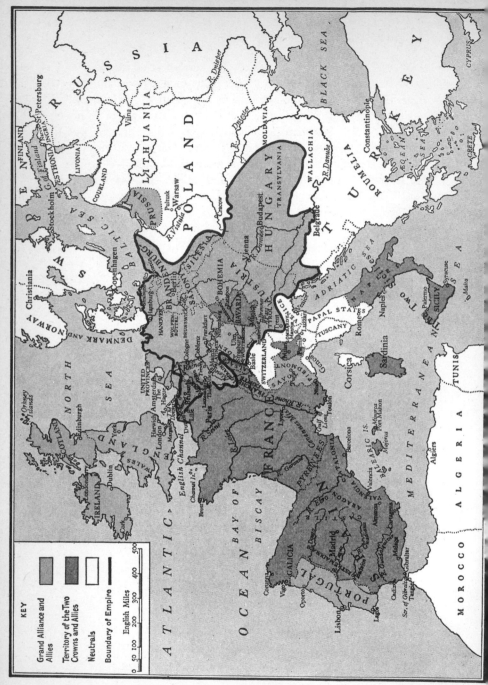

1. General Map of Europe

MARLBOROUGH

CHAPTER ONE

Ashe House

⧉ 1644-61 ⧉

In January 1644 a Devonshire lady, Eleanor (or Ellen), widow of Sir John Drake, alarmed by the Royalist activities in the West Country, had asked for a Roundhead garrison to protect her house at Ashe, near Axminster. She was "of good affection" to the Parliament, had aided them with money and provisions, and had "animated her tenants in seven adjoining parishes" to adhere to their cause. The troops were sent; but before they could fortify the place Lord Poulett, a neighbour who commanded for the King, marched upon it with his Irish soldiers, drove out the Parliamentarians, burned the house, and "stripped the good lady, who, almost naked and without shoe to her foot but what she afterwards begged, fled to Lyme for safety."

Here she encountered fresh hardships. The Roundhead seaport of Lyme Regis was soon attacked by the Royal forces. Early in April Prince Maurice, with six thousand men and "an excellent artillery," laid siege to the town. The story of its resolute defence is a cameo of the Civil War. For nearly three months a primitive, fitful, fierce combat was waged along and across the meagre ramparts and ditches which protected the townsfolk. Women aided the garrison in their stubborn resistance, relieving them in their watch by night and handing up the powder and ball in action. Colonel Blake, afterwards the famous Admiral of the Commonwealth, commanded the town. He several times offered the Royalists to open a breach in his breastworks and fight out the issue face to face on a front of twenty or on a front of ten men. His leadership, and twenty-six sermons by an eloquent Puritan divine, sustained the courage of the defenders. They depended for their supplies upon the sea. From time to time ships came in sight and aroused hopes and fears in both camps. Lady Drake was for a while in extreme distress. She must have watched the coming of ships with mingled feelings. The Royalist navy, such as it was, was commanded by her sister's grandson, James Ley, third Earl of Marlborough. Every week it was rumoured that her dreaded relation would arrive from the Channel Islands with reinforcements for the enemy. But he never came. The Parliament held the seas. Only Roundhead ships appeared. Eleanor endured privations, bombardments, and burnings for nearly three months. She was for her livelihood "reduced to the spinning and knitting of stockings, in which miserable condition she continued until the siege of Lyme was raised" by the arrival of a relieving Puritan army from London under the Earl of Essex, "whereof she got away and came to Parliament."

Her son John was no help to her in her misfortunes. We have been assured that he was "loyal to the King and on bad terms with his Puritan mother." But this seems incorrect. He was, on the contrary, at this time himself a prisoner of war in Prince Maurice's hands, and it was his mother who exerted herself on his behalf. Her sister, the Countess of Marlborough, stood high with the Royalists and appealed for the release of the captive. But the Parliamentary forces were now moving towards Axminster, and as the young Drake had said imprudently that he would get Lord Poulett's house burned in revenge for the burning of Ashe, his liberation was not unnaturally refused.

Lady Drake, though a resolute Puritan, continued to address herself to both sides, invoking with the Royalists her sister's, and with the Roundheads her own political merit. On September 28, 1644, Parliament ordered "that being wholly ruined by the enemy forces, she should have a furnished house in London rent free, £100 at once and £5 a week." The Westminster Commissioners accordingly four days later selected for her the house of a Royalist gentleman then still in arms—Sir Thomas Reynell; and she remained in these quarters for nearly four years, pursuing her claims for compensation through the slowly working mills of Westminster. Sir Thomas made his peace with Parliament and 'compounded for'—that is, ransomed—his house in

1646. He demanded reinstatement, as was his right; and he complained that Lady Drake during her tenancy "had digged up the ground and pulled up the floors in search of treasure." Nevertheless she continued to reside there in his despite, and perseveringly pursued her case against Lord Poulett for the burning of Ashe; and she had sufficient credit with the now irresistible Parliamentarians to carry it at last to a conclusion in the spring of 1648, when she was awarded £1500 compensation, to be paid out of Lord Poulett's estate.

It had taken Eleanor four years to secure the award. Two years more were required to extract the money from the delinquent, upon whose rents meanwhile she had a virtual receivership. In July 1650 she complained to Parliament that Lord Poulett still owed her £600. A further laborious investigation was set on foot. Six years passed after the burning of Ashe, which she claimed had lost her £6000, before Lady Drake recovered her £1500 compensation. She had need of it—and, indeed, of every penny. Hers was a family divided against itself by the wars. Her son fought for the Parliament; her son-in-law, Winston Churchill, fought for the King. Both he and his father had taken arms in the Royal cause from the early days. Both in turn—the father first —were drawn into the clutches of the Parliament. The Dorsetshire Standing Committee which dealt with the cases of the local Royalists reports in its minutes that in April 1646 John Churchill, a lawyer of some eminence, of Wootton Glanville, near Sherborne, had stated before them that he had formerly been nominated a Commissioner for the King; but he pleaded that in November 1645 he had taken the National Covenant and the Negative Oath. He had paid £300 for the Parliamentary garrison at Weymouth, and £100 on account of his personal estate. Moreover, reported the Committee, he was sixty years of age and unable to travel. In these circumstances in August 1646 he was fined £440, and a month later the sequestration of his estates was suspended.

The reckoning with his son Winston was delayed. Joining the King's army at twenty-two, he had made some mark upon the battlefields. He had become a captain of horse, and his bearing had been noted in the fights at Lansdowne Hill and Roundway Down. He was a youthful, staunch, and bigoted adherent of the King. Towards the end of 1645 he was wounded, and his plight amid the Roundheads now victorious throughout Dorset and Devon was most awkward. However, he had a refuge among the enemy. His father's house at Wootton Glanville was only a day's ride from Ashe. He was married to Lady Drake's third daughter, Elizabeth.

It is remarkable that such contracts should have been effected between persons so sharply divided by the actual fighting of the Civil Wars. We can see the stresses of the times from the fact that Winston's first child, Arabella, of whom more later, was not born till 1648, or more than five years after the date of the marriage, although thereafter children were born almost every year. No doubt the couple were parted by the severities of the war, and did not live regularly together till the struggle in the Western counties was ended. It was probable that Elizabeth lived with her mother during the whole of the fighting, and that from about the beginning of 1646 Winston joined her there. At any rate, from that time forward the two young people, wedded across the lines of civil war, lay low in the ruins of Ashe, and hoped to remain unnoticed or unpersecuted until the times should mend.

For a while all went well. But a regular system of informers had been set on foot, and, despite Winston's Roundhead connexions and Lady Drake's influence and record, the case against him was not allowed to lapse. At the end of 1649 he was charged with having been a captain in the King's army. According to the Dorsetshire records, witnesses, greedy, interested, but none the less credible, certified that as late as December 1645 Winston was still in the field against the Parliament, that he had been shot through the arm by the forces under Colonel Starr, and that he had resisted to the end with the royal garrison at Bristol. None of these facts could be rebutted.

However, the processes of law continued to work obstinately in spite of war and revolution. Beaten foes had rights which, unless specifically abolished by statute, they could assert. The delinquent captain fell back upon the law. He sought to collect debts owing to him from others. He claimed that a thousand marks given to his wife by her father, the late Sir John Drake, could not be sequestered. He laboured to put off the day when the final sentence would be pronounced. Long delays resulted. By August 1650 the Parliamentary authorities had lost patience. "Some cases," say their records,

> are sued out for no other end but to protract time, as that of Winston Churchill, who, it seems by his order, pretended his father (John

Churchill) and Lady Ellen Drake had an interest in his portion, whereas he has still a suit depending against Colonel William Fry and Sir Henry Rosewell in his own name, only for his wife's portion; had anybody else a title to it, he would not have commenced such a suit. As to his being in arms, he will surely not so far degenerate from his principles as to deny it.

The penalty was severe for a man whose estate seems to have been worth only £160 a year. Although Winston paid his fine at the end of 1651, he did not attempt to keep an independent home. Nor did he live with his father at Wootton Glanville. There may have been other reasons besides impoverishment for this. His father had married a second time about 1643; Winston was apparently on bad terms with his stepmother, and it was to his mother-in-law rather that he turned for aid. When the ultimate judgment and compassion of the Almighty, as the victors would have expressed it, had become fully manifest throughout the West Country, Lady Drake sate indignant on the winning side amid her ruins, and Ashe House continued to be a refuge from poverty, if not from destitution, for the broken Cavalier, his young wife, and growing family. They do not seem to have returned home till Winston's father died in the year before the Restoration. Thus they lived at Ashe for thirteen years, and hard must those years have been. The whole family dwelt upon the hospitality or charity of a mother-in-law of difficult, imperious, and acquisitive temper; a crowded brood in a lean and war-scarred house, between them and whose owner lay the fierce contentions of the times.

No record is in existence of the daily round of the composite Drake household. We must suppose from its long continuance that family affection and sheer necessity triumphed over unspeakable differences of sentiment and conviction. Lady Drake did her duty faithfully to her daughter's family. She fed, clothed, and sheltered them in such portions of her house as their partisans had left her. They, having scarcely any other resources, accepted her bounty. While Lady Drake, vaunting her fidelity, pursued her claims for compensation from the Parliament, Winston, with her aid and collusion, sought to escape its exactions. It may be that in this prolonged double effort to save as much as possible from the wreck of their affairs a comradeship of misfortune was added to family ties. It must, none the less, have been a queer and difficult home. We may judge of their straitened means by the fact that they could not afford to put a fresh roof over the burned-out parts of the house until after the Restoration. They huddled together all these years in the one remaining wing. The war had impoverished the whole West countryside, and to keep up the style of gentlefolk and educate children must have imposed a severe frugality on all at Ashe.

To the procreation of children and the slow excitements of frequent litigation Winston added the relief of writing and the study of heraldry. In a substantial and erudite volume, *Divi Britannici*, still widely extant and universally unread, he explored from "the Year of the World 2855" downwards those principles of the Divine Right of Kings for which he had fought and suffered. He went so far in doctrine as to shock even Royalist circles by proclaiming the right of the Crown to levy taxation by its mere motion.

He cherished the theory that all nations derived their names from their food, dress, appearance, habits, etc. He thinks, therefore, the Britons got their name from a drink which the Greeks called "bruton or bruteion, which Athinæus defined as *ton krithinon oinon*—i.e., *Vinum hordeaceum*, Barley Wine."

The preface to *Divi Britannici*, which was not published till 1675, contains in its dedication a sentence the force and dignity of which may justify the book. It was, wrote the author, "begun when everybody thought that the monarchy had ended and would have been buried in the same grave with your martyred father," and "that none of us that had served that blessed Prince had any other weapons left us but our pens to show the justice of our zeal by that of his title."

Since Arabella had been born on February 23, 1648, births and deaths swiftly succeeded one another with almost annual regularity. Mrs. Winston Churchill had twelve children, of whom seven died in infancy. The third child of these twelve and the eldest son to live is the hero of this account. It is curious that no previous biographer—among so many—should have discovered the entry of his birth. A mystery has been made of it, which Coxe and other writers have used devious methods to solve. It is still often wrongly given. We therefore offer the evidence from the parish register of St. Michael's, Musbury, in facsimile. The infant was baptized in the tiny private chapel of Ashe House seven days later.

[John the Sonne of Mr Winston Churchill,
Born the 26 Day of May, 1650.]

The first ten years of his life were lived in the harsh conditions which have been suggested. We are here in the region of surmise. Facts are vague and few; but it seems easy to believe that the child grew up in a home where wants were often denied, and feelings and opinions had nearly always to be repressed. Public affairs marched forward, and their course was viewed at Ashe from standpoints separated by deep and living antagonisms. Blood and cruel injuries lay between those who gathered around the table. Outraged faith, ruined fortunes, and despairing loyalties were confronted by resolute, triumphant rebellion, and both were bound together by absolute dependence. It would be strange indeed if the children were not conscious of the chasm between their elders; if they never saw resentment on the one side, or felt patronage from the other; if they were never reminded that it was to their grandmother's wisdom and faithful championship of the cause of Parliament they owed the bread they ate. It would be strange if the ardent Cavalier then in his prime, poring over his books of history and heraldry, watching with soured eyes the Lord Protector's victories over the Dutch or the Spaniards and the grand position to which England seemed to have been raised by this arch-wrongdoer, and dreaming of a day when the King should enjoy his own again and the debts of Royalist and regicide be faithfully and sternly settled, should not have spoken words to his little son revealing the bitterness of his heart. The boy may well have learned to see things through his father's eyes, to long with him for a casting down of present pride and power, and have learned at the same time—at six, seven, and eight years of age—not to flaunt these opinions before half at least of those with whom he lived.

The two prevailing impressions which such experiences might arouse in the mind of a child would be, first, a hatred of poverty and dependence, and, secondly, the need of hiding thoughts and feelings from those to whom their expression would be repugnant. To have one set of opinions for one part of the family, and to use a different language to the other, may have been inculcated from John's earliest years. To win freedom from material subservience by the sure agency of money must have been planted in his heart's desire. To these was added a third: the importance of having friends and connexions on both sides of a public quarrel. Modern opinion assigns increasing importance to the influences of early years on the formation of character. Certainly the whole life of John Churchill bore the imprint of his youth. That impenetrable reserve under graceful and courteous manners; those unceasing contacts and correspondences with opponents; that iron parsimony and personal frugality, never relaxed in the blaze of fortune and abundance; that hatred of waste and improvidence in all their forms —all these could find their roots in the bleak years at Ashe.

We may also suppose that Winston Churchill concerned himself a good deal with the early education of his children. For this he was not ill qualified. He had gathered, as his writings show, no inconsiderable store of historical knowledge. He presented in these years the curious figure of a cavalry captain, fresh from the wars, turned perforce recluse and bookworm. Time must have hung heavy on his hands. He had no estates to manage, no profession to pursue. He could not afford to travel; but in the teaching of his children he may well have found alike occupation and solace. Or, again, he may have loafed and brooded, leaving his children to play in the lanes and gardens of that tranquil countryside. The only information we have on John's education is provided by the unknown author of *The Lives of the Two Illustrious Generals* (1713):

He was born in the Time of the grand Rebellion, when his Father for Siding with the Royal Party against the Usurpers, who then prevailed, was under many Pressures, which were common to such as adher'd to the King. Yet, notwithstanding the Devastations and Plunderings, and other nefarious Practices and Acts of Cruelty which were daily committed by the licentious Soldiery, no Care was omitted on the Part of his tender Parents for a Liberal and Gentile Education. For he was no sooner out of the hands of the Women but he was given into those of a sequestered Clergyman, who made it his first concern to instil sound Principles of Religion into him, that the Seeds of humane Literature might take the deeper Root, and he from a just

Knowledge of the Omnipotence of the Creator, might have a true
Sense of the Dependence of the Creature.

It is said that famous men are usually the product of unhappy childhood. The stern compression of circumstances, the twinges of adversity,
the spur of slights and taunts in early years, are needed to evoke that
ruthless fixity of purpose and tenacious mother-wit without which great
actions are seldom accomplished. Certainly little in the environment of
the young John Churchill should have deprived him of this stimulus;
and by various long-descending channels there centred in him martial
and dangerous fires.

Besides attending to his son's education Winston in his studious leisure bethought himself often of his pedigree and his arms. His re-
scarches into genealogy have produced as good an account of the origin
of the Churchills as is likely to be required.

Students of heredity have dilated upon this family tree. Galton cites
it as one of the chief examples on which his thesis stands. Winston
himself has been accounted one of the most notable and potent of
sires. Had he lived the full span, he would have witnessed within the
space of twelve months his son gaining the battle of Ramillies and his
daughter's son that of Almanza; and would have found himself acknowledged as the progenitor of the two greatest captains of the age at
the head of the opposing armies of Britain and of France and Spain.
Moreover, his third surviving son, Charles, became a soldier of well-
tried distinction, and his naval son virtually managed the Admiralty
during the years of war. The military strain flowed strong and clear
from the captain of the Civil Wars, student of heraldry and history,
and champion of the Divine Right. It was his blood, not his pen, that
carried his message.

Although in this opening chapter we have set the reader in these bygone times, eleven years of our hero's life have already been accomplished. Ashe House, still unroofed, passes from the scene.

These scenes certainly played a curiously persistent part in John
Churchill's life. It was on the very soil of his childhood, in sight almost
of his birthplace, that he was in 1685 to lead the Household Cavalry,
feeling their way towards Monmouth's army; and three years later on
the hill across the river he was to meet the Prince of Orange after deserting James II. So much for Ashe!

But now the times are changed. Oliver Cromwell is dead. General Monk has declared for a free Parliament. His troops have marched from Coldstream to Hounslow. The exiled Charles has issued the Declaration of Breda. The English people, by a gesture spontaneous and almost unanimous, have thrown off the double yoke of military and Puritan rule. Amid bonfires and the rejoicings of tumultuous crowds they welcome back their erstwhile hunted sovereign, and by one of those intense reactions, sometimes as violent in whole nations as in individuals, change in a spasm from oppressive virtue to unbridled indulgence. On April 23, 1661, Charles II was crowned at Westminster, and the restoration of the English monarchy was complete.

These memorable events produced swift repercussions at Ashe House. Winston Churchill passed at a stroke from the frown of an all-powerful Government to the favour of a King he had faithfully served. The frozen years were over, and the Cavaliers, emerging from their retreats, walked abroad in the sun, seeking their lost estates. We need not grudge him these good days. He had acted with unswerving conviction and fidelity. He had drunk to the dregs the cup of defeat and subjugation. Its traces can be seen in his anxious eyes. Now was the time of reward. Instantly he sprang into many forms of activity. In 1661 he entered Parliament for Weymouth. In 1664 he became one of the original members of the Royal Society. Although his fortunes were much depleted, he regained his independence and a hearth of his own. More important than this, he stood in a modest way high in the favour of the new régime. He was received with consideration and even intimacy at Court. The terms under which Charles had returned to his kingdom were not such as to allow him to bestow wealth upon his humbler adherents. His sovereignty rested on a compromise between rebels and Royalists, between Anglicans and Presbyterians, between those who had seized estates and those who had lost them, between the passions of conflicting creeds and the pride of lately hostile regiments. He had no means of meeting even the just claims which faithful subjects might urge, still less could he satisfy the ravenous demands of long-nursed grievances or blatant imposture.

It is remarkable that amid the crowds of hungry and often deserving suitors who thronged the antechambers of Whitehall so much attention should have been paid to the merits and services of Winston Churchill. Far more was done for him than for most. There was one cheap, sure way to please him. It was apparently well known. Accordingly an augmentation of arms and a crest unusual in a family of such standing was offered to his heraldic propensities. Nevertheless, this evidence of royal favour and affection was not in itself sufficiently substantial, in Winston's opinion at least, to repair the injuries he had suffered in pocket and skin. He remained cherished but disconsolate, blazoning on his new coat of arms an uprooted oak above the motto *Fiel pero desdichado* ("Faithful but unfortunate"). More practical reliefs, as will be shown in the next chapter, were however in store.

CHAPTER TWO

The Jovial Times

ᚨ 1661-69 ᚪ

Our readers must now brace themselves for what will inevitably be a painful interlude. We must follow the fortunes or misfortunes of a maiden of seventeen and her younger brother as they successively entered a dissolute Court. The King was the fountain not only of honour, but of almost every form of worldly success and pleasure. Access to his presence, intimacy with his family or favourites, were the sole pathway even of modest and lawful ambition. An enormous proportion of the amenities and glories of the realm was engrossed in the narrow family circle of royal personages, friends, dependants, and important Ministers or agents of the Crown. Nearly all chances of distinction and solid professional advancement went by favour. An officer well established at Court was a different kind of officer from one who had nothing but the merits of his sword. The success of jurists and divines was similarly determined. The royal light shone where it listed, and those who caught its rays were above competition and almost beyond envy, except—an important exception—from rivals in their own select sphere.

If those were the conditions which ruled for men, how much more compulsive was the environment of the frailer sex. To sun oneself in the royal favour, to be admitted to the charmed circle, to have access to a royal lady, to be about the person of a queen or princess, was to have all this exclusive, elegant, ambitious, jostling world on one's doorstep and at one's footstool. Aged statesmen and prelates; eager, ardent, attractive youths; the old general, the young lieutenant—all produced whatever treasure they had to bestow to win the favour of the sovereign's mistress, or of his relations' mistresses, and of his important friends or servants. That nothing should be lacking to frame the picture of privilege and indulgence, it must be remembered that all this was dignified by the affairs of a growing state, by the presence of upright and venerable men and formidable matrons, providing the counterpoise of seriousness and respectability. Scientists, philosophers, theologians, scholars; the mayors of cities, rugged sea-captains, veteran colonels, substantial merchants—all pressed forward on the fringes of the parade in the hope of being gratified by some fleeting glint of the royal radiance.

Such ideas seem remote to the English-speaking nations in these times. We must make allowances for the backward conditions which prevailed in England and France, to say nothing of the barbarous countries, when Charles II and Louis XIV sat upon their thrones. There was undoubtedly an easy commerce of the sexes, marked at times by actual immorality. Men and women who had obtained power were often venal, and insolent besides, to those whom they dubbed their inferiors. Even judges were occasionally, and members of the legislature frequently, corrupt. Generals and admirals were usually jealous of each other, and sometimes stooped to intrigue to gain promotion. Even brilliant writers and pamphleteers, the journalists of those primitive times, wrote scurrilous gossip to please their patrons and employers. We in this happy and enlightened age must exercise our imagination to span the gulf which separates us from those lamentable, departed days. Securely established upon the rock of purity and virtue, ceaselessly cleansed by the strong tides of universal suffrage, we can afford to show tolerance and even indulgence towards the weaknesses and vices of those vanished generations without in any way compromising our own integrity.

It is strange indeed that such a system should have produced for many generations a succession of greater captains and abler statesmen than all our widely extended education, competitive examinations, and democratic system have put forth. Apart from the Church and the learned professions, the area of selection was restricted entirely to the circles of rank, wealth, and landed property. But these comprised several thousand families within which and among whom an extremely searching rivalry and appraisement prevailed. In this focus of the nation men were known and judged by their equals with intimate knowledge and a high degree of comprehension. There may be more truth than paradox in Lord Fisher's brutal maxim, "Favouritism is the secret of efficiency." There was, of course, great need to seek out ability. Appointments and promotions went largely by favour: but favour went largely by merit.

The English Court under Charles II was no Oriental scene of complete subservience, where women were secluded and where men approached the supreme figures with bated breath. It had not the super-centralization of the French Court under Louis XIV. The nobility and wealthy gentlefolk could live on their estates, and though excluded from the fame of national employment, had effective rights which they used frequently against the Crown. There were always independent powers in England. This counterpoise enhanced the strength of the central institution. There were degrees, values, and a hierarchy of considerable intrinsic virtue. A great society, sharply criticized, but accepted as supreme, indulging every caprice and vanity, and drawing to itself the chief forms of national excellence, presided at the summit of the realm.

It is important to remember also the differences of feeling and outlook which separate the men and women of these times from ourselves. They gave a very high—indeed, a dominating—place in their minds to religion. It played as large a part in the life of the seventeenth century as sport does now. One of their chief concerns was about the next world and how to be saved. Although ignorant compared with our standards, they were all deeply versed in the Bible and the Prayer Book. If they read few books, they studied them and digested them thoroughly. They had settled opinions on large questions of faith and doctrine, and were often ready to die or suffer on account of them.

Rank and breeding were second only to religion in their esteem. Every one in Court or county society was known, and all about them. Their forbears for many generations were carefully scrutinized. The coat of arms which denoted the family's achievements for hundreds of years was narrowly and jealously compared. It was not easy to get into the great world in those days, if one did not belong to it. A very clear line was drawn between 'gentles' and 'simples,' and the Church and the Law were almost the only ladders by which new talent could reach the highest positions. Indeed, religion and family pride together absorbed much of the sentiment now given to nationalism. The unity of Christendom had been ruptured at the Reformation, but strong cosmopolitan sympathies prevailed among the educated classes in all the Western countries.

Although the administration of England had not attained to anything like the refined and ordered efficiency of France, there was already a strong collective view about fundamental dangers. There was already a recognizable if rudimentary Foreign Office opinion. And there were in every capital grave, independent men who gave lifelong thought to doctrine and policy. Their business was transacted by long personal letters, laboriously composed, in which every word was weighed, and conversations, few and far between, the purport of which was memorable. Government was then the business of sovereigns and of a small but serious ruling class, and, for all their crimes, errors, and shortcomings, they gave keen and sustained attention to their task.

In these days society was callous about prisoners and punishments, and frightful forfeits were senselessly exacted. But these were the ages of Pain. Pain, when it came, was accepted as a familiar foe. No anæsthetic robbed the hospital of all the horrors of the torture-chamber. All had to be endured, and hence—strangely enough—all might be inflicted. Yet in some ways our forerunners attached more importance to human life than we do. Although they fought duels about women and other matters of honour, instead of seeking damages from the courts, and although death sentences were more numerous in those days, they would have recoiled in lively horror from the constant wholesale butcheries of scores of thousands of persons every year by motor-cars, at which the modern world gapes unconcernedly. Their faculties for wonder and indignation had not been blunted and worn away by the catalogues of atrocities and disasters which the advantages of the electric telegraph and the newspaper press place at our disposal every morning and evening. Above all, they were not in a hurry. They made fewer speeches, and lived more meditatively and more at leisure, with companionship rather than motion for their solace. They had far fewer facilities than we have for the frittering away of thought, time, and life. Altogether they were primitive folk, and we must make allowances for their limitations. The one trait which they shared in common with the twentieth century was the love of money, and respect and envy for its fortunate possessors. But, then, money in those days was still mainly derived from land, and the possession of land usually denoted ancient lineage.

The Convention Parliament of the Restoration was dissolved in 1660, and the so-called Cavalier, or Pensionary, Parliament met in May 1661. This was "a parliament full of lewd young men, chosen by a furious people in spite to the Puritans, whose severity had distasted them." They were "of loyal families, but young men for the most part, which being told the King, he replied that there was no great fault, for he could keep them till they got beards." So in fact he did; for this Parliament continued to sit for eighteen years. In it Winston Churchill represented the constituency of Weymouth. During its first two sessions he was an active Member; he served on various committees, and as late as May 10, 1662, he was sent by the Commons to request the participation of the Lords in a joint committee to discuss questions arising out of an Army Bill.

Meanwhile the Restoration settlement in Ireland was proceeding very slowly. Thirty-six commissioners had been appointed and had set up an office in Dublin in May 1661. But after nearly a year's work only one claim had been settled. The King had himself blamed the commissioners, and seven new commissioners were now chosen to go over to Ireland and reopen the Court of Claims.

Among these latter Winston Churchill was named and probably sailed to Ireland to carry out his new duties in July.

Throughout 1663 Winston Churchill and his fellow-commissioners remained in Ireland. Their task was a difficult one. On March 25 they wrote to Whitehall affirming that

> Since our coming into this Kingdom, we have found so many unexpected discouragements, from those whose security and settlement was and is a powerful part of our care, that we confess we were much dejected. . . . But we have now received new life from his sacred Majesty's most gracious letters to us, by which we understand that neither our sufferings, nor our innocence, were hid from, or unconsidered by his Majesty.

Nevertheless, in December Churchill begged Arlington for leave to return home for just two months, so desirous was he of a rest from his labours. A month later his wish was gratified, for the King summoned him back to England on January 10, 1664, and twelve days later rewarded his services with a knighthood. If Winston brought his eldest son with him from Dublin on this occasion, as there is every reason to suppose, it must have been at this date that John Churchill became one of the 153 scholars of St Paul's School. His father bought a house somewhere in the City, where the fourteen-year-old boy lived while he attended school; but on September 13, 1664, Winston was appointed Junior Clerk Comptroller to the Board of Green Cloth, a minor post in the royal household, and moved into Whitehall.

About 1665 the Duchess of York was graciously pleased to offer Winston's eldest daughter, Arabella, a coveted appointment as maid of honour. Historians have inquired in wonder how a strict and faithful husband, a devoted father, and a God-fearing Anglican Cavalier could have allowed his well-loved daughter to become involved in a society in which so many pitfalls abounded. In fact he was delighted, and so was his wife, and every one whom they knew and respected hastened to congratulate the family upon an auspicious and most hopeful preferment. Who should say what honours might not flow from such propinquity to the King's brother and heir to the throne? The sanction of Divine Right descended not only on all around the sovereign, but upon all within the sacred circle of the blood royal. Power, fame, wealth, social distinction, awaited those who gained the royal favour. The association was honourable and innocent, and should any mishap occur, Church and State stood attentive to conceal or vindicate the damage. Thus it was thought a splendid advantage for a young girl to be established at Court and take her fortune there as it came.

Arabella after some delays prospered in the Duke of York's household. Anthony Hamilton, who is famous for the authorship of Grammont's memoirs, has penned some mischievous pages from which historians diligently fail to avert their eyes. There is a tale of a riding-party to a greyhound-coursing near York, and of Arabella's horse running away in a headlong gallop; of a fall and a prostrate figure on the sward; of the Royal Duke to the rescue, and of a love born of this incident. Hamilton declares that, while Arabella's face presented no more than the ordinary feminine charms, her figure was exceedingly beautiful, and that James was inflamed by the spectacle of beauty in distress and also in disarray. It is, however, certain that some time before 1668 Arabella became the mistress of the Duke of York, and that in the next seven or eight years she bore him four children, of whom the second was James Fitz-James, afterwards Duke of Berwick, Marshal of France and victor of Almanza. There is no disputing these facts, and historians may rest upon them with confidence.

Among the many stains with which John Churchill's record has been darkened stands the charge that he lightly and even cheerfully acquiesced in his sister's dishonour—or honour, as it was regarded in the moral obliquity of the age. Why did he not thus early display the qualities of a future conqueror and leader of men? Why did he not arrive hotfoot at Whitehall, challenge or even chastise the high-placed seducer, and rescue the faltering damsel from her sad plight? We must admit that all researches for any active protest upon his part have been fruitless. Nearly sixty years afterwards the old Duchess, Sarah, made her comments upon this default in terms certainly not beyond the comprehension of our own day.

By January 1666 Sir Winston was back again in Dublin, but he had left his wife and family behind him in England. By this date his eldest son, John, had left school and had been made page to James, Duke of York. The author of *The Lives of the Two Illustrious Generals* relates that James had been struck by the beauty of the boy, whom he had often seen about the Court. It may be, however, that the influence of Sir Winston's patron, the Earl of Arlington, had effected this choice. The father was well content with this: he thought it the best opening he could find for any of his sons. Shortly afterwards Arlington obtained a similar, if not so exalted, position for John's brother George, to accompany the famous Earl of Sandwich, late commander-in-chief of the Navy, to the Court of Madrid. In writing from dismal Ireland to thank the Secretary of State for this attention Sir Winston, now a civil servant, observed, "though (as times go now) it is no great preferment to be a Page, yet I am not ignorant of the benefit of disposing him (in such a Juncture of time as this) into that country where all the Boys seem Men, and all the men seem wise." And he concluded his letter by hoping that "my Sons may with equal gratitude subscribe themselves as I do," his faithful servant.

Meanwhile the annals of John are even more scanty than those of his father. Marlborough is, indeed, the last of the great commanders about whose early life practically nothing is recorded. That he was born in 1650, that he lived in his grandmother's house for nine years, that he went with his father to Dublin, that he attended St Paul's School, and that he went to Court as page to the Duke of York at about the age of sixteen and later entered the army, sums the total of our information. We know as much of the early years of Alexander the Great, Hannibal, and Julius Cæsar as we do of this figure separated from us by scarcely a couple of centuries.

CHAPTER THREE

Barbara

⟡ 1667-71 ⟡

JOHN served the Duke of York as page, and, like his sister, dwelt happily in the royal household. His duties were neither onerous nor unpleasant. He had no money; but he lived in comfort and elegance. He knew all the great people of the English world, and many of its prettiest women. No one was concerned to be disagreeable to this attractive, discreet, engaging youth, who moved gaily about the corridors and anterooms of Whitehall with a deft, decided step, and never slipped or slid on those polished floors where a clumsy fall may so easily be final. He must have met about this time one of the King's pages, a young man five years his senior—Sidney Godolphin. There is a gulf between youths of sixteen and twenty-one. It soon narrowed. The two became friends; and their unbroken association runs through this story.

The Duke of York was a resolute and experienced commander. After religion the art of war claimed the foremost place in his thoughts. As Lord High Admiral he knew the service of the sea. His interest in the land forces was no less keen. It was his custom to spend a part of many days in reviewing and drilling the troops. He would frequently muster two battalions of the Guards in Hyde Park, and have them put through their elaborate exercises in his presence. His page accompanied him on these occasions.

At these parades the Duke of York noticed the interest of his page. He saw the boy following with gleaming eyes the warlike ceremonial. One day after a review he asked him what profession he preferred.

Whereupon John fell upon his knees and demanded "a pair of colours in one of these fine regiments." The request was not denied.

Besides his sister Arabella John had a tie of kinship and acquaintance with another favourite of high importance. On the eve of his restoration Charles II met at The Hague Barbara Villiers, then newly married to Roger Palmer, afterwards Earl of Castlemaine. She became his mistress; she preceded him to England; she adorned the triumphs and enhanced for him the joys of the Restoration. She was a woman of exceeding beauty and charm, vital and passionate in an extraordinary degree. In the six years that had passed she had borne the King several children. At twenty-four, in the heyday of her success, this characteristic flower of the formidable, errant Villiers stock was the reigning beauty of the palace. She held Charles in an intense fascination. Her rages, her extravagances, her infidelities seemed only to bind him more closely in her mysterious web. She was John Churchill's second cousin once removed. His mother's sister, a Mrs Godfrey, was her closest confidante. The young page, it is said, was often in his aunt's apartments eating sweets, and there Barbara soon met and made friends with this good-looking boy. Very likely she had known him from his childhood. Naturally she was nice to him, and extended her powerful protection to her young and sprightly relation. Naturally, too, she aroused his schoolboy's admiration. There is not, as we shall hope to convince the reader, the slightest ground for suggesting that the beginning of their affection was not perfectly innocent and such as would normally subsist between a well-established woman of the world and her cousin, a boy of sixteen, newly arrived at the Court where she was dominant.

John was certainly a success at Court, and his favour was not diminished by his smart uniform. Still, adolescence is a trying period both for the victim and his companions. In those days there was a feeling that young men about the Court should take their turn of service with the fleet or Army as gentlemen-volunteers. Still more was this opinion effective upon a young officer. Leave to serve abroad would readily be granted by his regiment, and all his friends and well-wishers would give their cordial approval. John found doctrine and prospect alike congenial.

Some time in 1668 he quitted the Court and sailed for Tangier. The gossip-mongers suggest that the Duchess of York herself had begun to show him undue attention: or, again, that he was getting rather old to be on such privileged terms with Lady Castlemaine. But there is no excuse for looking beyond the reasons which have been set forth. Such evidence as exists shows that his departure and prolonged absence were entirely in accordance with his own inclination. He went to Tangier, or at any rate he stayed there and in the Mediterranean for nearly three years, because he liked the life of adventure, and because the excitement of the petty warfare was refreshing after the endless glittering ceremonial of the Court. Few youths of spirit are content at eighteen with comforts or even caresses. They seek physical fitness, movement, and the comradeship of their equals under hard conditions. They seek distinction, not favour, and exult in manly independence.

He seems to have lived from eighteen to twenty the rough, care-free life of a subaltern officer engaged in an endless frontier guerrilla. That the conditions were by no means intolerable is shown by the following letter, written from Madrid in March 1670 to the Earl of Arlington by the Earl of Castlemaine, on his way back from Tangier.

> * At my arrival, I was never so surprized than to find so many officers so very well clad and fashioned that though I have been in most of the best garrisons of Europe I do not remember I ever yet saw the like, and which added to my admiration was that though necessaries are a great deal dearer, and all superfluities there four times the value of what they are in England, yet the Generality both of our Commanders and Soldiers lay up something, which argues much industry.
> . . .
> For the Town itself (if the Mole be made) all the world sees it will, as it were, command the Mediterranean, by stopping its mouth; how quick a receipt it is for the Merchants with [in] any War with Spain, what a Bridle it will be of the Pirates of Barbary, as a Constant place of our own, for our men of War, with opportunities also of revictualling and fitting as if we were at home; which bears now no small proportion with the expense of an expedition; neither is it a little honour to the Crown to have a Nursery of its own for soldiers, without being altogether beholding to our Neighbours for their Education and breeding.

The English fleet in the Mediterranean was in 1670 engaged in an intermittent blockade of Algiers. Sir Thomas Allin was setting out with a squadron of fourteen ships to renew his blockade. An Admiralty regiment, or, as we should say, a 'Naval Brigade' or Division, was being recruited and embarked as marines for the operation. It seems certain that John obtained permission to exchange his service of the land for that of the sea, and was attached to the Algiers expedition of 1670. We know that he required an outfit for the campaign and that his father bought it for him.

John's experiences with the fleet are unrecorded. All we know is that in August 1670 Admiral Allin defeated a number of Algerian corsairs, and was afterwards relieved of his command. Surveying all the facts we have been able to marshal, we may accept the following conclusions: that Churchill, still penniless and heart-whole, quitted the Court in 1668, that he served at Tangier till 1670, that early in that year he sailed with the fleet against the pirates, and served for some months in the Mediterranean. Eagerly seeking adventure by land or sea, he pulled all the strings he could to convey him to the scenes of action, and his zeal was noticed and well regarded in the highest circles.

So far all is well, and the conduct of our hero will command general approbation. We now approach a phase upon which the judgment of individuals and periods will vary. In all his journey Marlborough found two, and only two, love-romances. Two women, both extraordinary beings, both imperious, tempestuous personalities, both well-known historical figures, are woven successively into his life. Here and now the first appears. We have already made her acquaintance.

At the beginning of 1671 John Churchill, grown a man, bronzed by African sunshine, close-knit by active service and tempered by discipline and danger, arrived home from the Mediterranean. He seems to have been welcomed with widespread pleasure by the Court, and by none more than by Barbara, now become Duchess of Cleveland. She was twenty-nine and he twenty. They were already affectionate friends. The distant degree of cousinly kinship which had hitherto united them had sanctioned intimacy, and did not now prohibit passion. Affections, affinities, and attractions were combined. Desire walked with opportunity, and neither was denied. John almost immediately became her lover, and for more than three years this wanton and joyous couple shared pleasures and hazards. The cynical, promiscuous, sagacious-indulgent sovereign was outwitted or outfaced. Churchill was almost certainly the father of Barbara's last child, a daughter, born on July 16, 1672, and the ties between them were not severed until the dawn of his love for Sarah Jennings in 1675.

It is an exaggeration to speak of Churchill as "rivalling the King in his nearest affection." After ten years Charles II was already tiring of the tantrums and divagations of the Duchess of Cleveland, and other attractions made their power felt. From 1671 onward the bonds which were to bind the King and the Duchess were their children, most of whom were undoubtedly his own. None the less, the intimacy of John and Barbara continued to cause Charles repeated annoyance, and their illicit loves, their adventures and escapades, were among the most eminent scandals of the English Court at this period.

We have some indication of John's whereabouts during this year.

News-letter from London

February 6, 1671

Yesterday was a duel between Mr Fenwick and Mr Churchill esquires who had for their seconds Mr Harpe and Mr Newport, son to my Lord Newport; it ended with some wounds for Mr Churchill, but no danger of life.

Two of the adventures of the lovers are well known. The first—described by Burnet—is that, being surprised by Charles in the Duchess's bedroom, John saved her honour—or what remained of it—by jumping from the window, a considerable height, into the courtyard below. For this feat, delighted at his daring and address, she presented him with £5000.

The second anecdote is attributed to the French Ambassador, Barillon. The Duke of Buckingham, he says, gave a hundred guineas to one of his waiting-women to be well informed of the intrigue. He knew that Churchill would be one evening at a certain hour in Barbara's apartments. He brought the King to the spot. The lover was hidden in the Duchess's cupboard (she was not Duchess till 1670). After having prowled about the chamber the King, much upset, asked for sweets and liqueurs. His mistress declared that the key of the cupboard was lost. The King replied that he would break down the door. On this she opened the door, and fell on her knees on one side while Churchill, discovered, knelt on the other. The King said to Churchill, "Go; you are a rascal, but I forgive you because you do it to get your bread."

BARBARA

It is a good story, and the double-barrelled insult is very character-istic of Charles. But is it true? Barillon, who did not himself arrive in England till September 1677, probably got it from his predecessor, Courtin. He fixes the date as 1667. Burnet's story belongs to 1670. Here is a fine exposure of these gossips. There can be little doubt, as we have shown, that nothing of this kind can have occurred before 1671. It is therefore one of those good stories invented long afterwards and fas-tened, as so many are, on well-known figures.

We are on much firmer ground when we come to money matters. The famous Lord Halifax in the intervals of statecraft conducted a rudi-mentary form of life insurance. The rates were attractive, for the lives of young gallants and soldiers—the prey of wars, duels, adventures, and disease—were precarious. At twenty-four John purchased from Lord Halifax for £4500 an annuity of £500 a year for life. It was a profitable investment. He enjoyed its fruits for nearly fifty years. It was the foun-dation of his immense fortune. Where did the money come from? No one can suggest any other source than Barbara. Was this, then, the £5000 that she had given him when he leaped from the window, and if so what are we to think of the transaction? Some of Marlborough's de-fenders have disputed the facts. They point to the scanty evidence—contemporary gossip and a passing reference in one of Lord Chester-field's letters. The Blenheim papers contain the actual receipt.

The code of the seventeenth century did not regard a man's taking money from a rich mistress as necessarily an offence against honour. It was no more a bar to social success and worldly regard than are mar-riages for money in these modern times. But every one has been struck by the judicious foresight of the investment. Moralists have been shocked by the fact that John did not squander Barbara's gift in riotous living. Cards, wine, and other women would seem to be regarded by these logicians as more appropriate channels for the use of such funds. They treat the transaction as the aggravation of an infamy. It may well be true that no other man of twenty-four then alive in England would have turned this money into an income which secured him a modest but lifelong independence. The dread of poverty inculcated in his early days at Ashe may be the explanation. It may be that Barbara, knowing his haunting prepossession, resolved to free him from it, and that an annuity was the prescribed purpose of the gift. However this may be, there is the bond.

Barbara Duchess of Cleveland. BY PERMISSION OF VISCOUNT DILLON.

Sarah Jennings before she married, by Simon Verelst. This portrait always hung in her dressing-room at Holywell. BY PERMISSION OF EARL SPENCER.

CHAPTER FOUR

The Europe of Charles II

⟨ 1667-72 ⟩

Iτ is fitting to turn from the scraps and oddities which, pieced together, form our only record of Churchill's youth to survey the vast, stately European scene wherein he now began to move and was one day to shine.

The supreme fact upon the Continent in the latter half of the seventeenth century was the might of France. Her civil wars were over. All internal divisions had been effaced, and Louis XIV reigned over a united nation of eighteen or nineteen million souls possessed of the fairest region on the globe. Feudalism, with its local warriors and their armed retainers, had at length been blown away by gunpowder, and as wars were frequent, standing armies had arisen in all the states of Europe. The possession of organized regular troops, paid, disciplined, trained by the central Government, was the aim of all the rulers, and in the main the measure of their power. This process had in the course of a few generations obliterated or reduced to mere archaic survivals the Parliamentary and municipal institutions of France. In different ways similar effects had followed the same process in other Continental countries. Everywhere sovereignty had advanced with giant strides. The peoples of Europe passed out of a long confusion into an age of autocracies in full panoply against all foes from within or from without.

But for the storm-whipped seas which lapped the British islands, our fortunes would have followed the road upon which our neighbours had started. England had not, however, the same compulsive need for a standing army as the land Powers. She stood aloof, moving slowly and lagging behind the martial throng. In the happy nick of time her Parliament grew strong enough to curb the royal power and to control the armed forces, and she thus became the cradle, as she is still the citadel, of free institutions throughout the world.

There she lay, small, weak, divided, and almost unarmed. The essence of her domestic struggle forbade a standing army. Scotland and Ireland lay, heavy embarrassments and burdens, on her shoulders or at her flank. Although there was much diffused well-being throughout the country, very little money could be gathered by the State. Here again the conditions of the internal struggle kept the executive weak. The whole population of England—their strength thus latent and depressed, their energies dispersed, their aim unfocused—attained little more than five millions.

Yet upon the other side of the Channel, only twenty-one miles across the dancing waves, rose the magnificent structure of the French monarchy and society. One hundred and forty thousand soldiers in permanent pay, under lifelong professional officers, constituted the peacetime force of France. Brilliant, now famous, captains of war or fortification, Turenne, Condé, Vauban; master organizers like Louvois; trainers like Martinet (his name a household word)—forged or wielded this splendid instrument of power. Adroit, sagacious, experienced Foreign Ministers and diplomatists urged the march of French aggrandisement. Financiers and trade Ministers as wise and instructed as Colbert reached out for colonies bound by exclusive commercial dealings, or consolidated the expanding finances of the most modern, the most civilized, and the strongest society.

Nor were the glories of France confined to the material sphere. The arts flourished in a long summer. In the latter half of the century French was becoming not only the universal language of diplomacy outside the Holy Roman Empire, but also that of polite society and even of literature. The French drama was performed and French poetry read, the names of Molière, Racine, Boileau were honoured, throughout the cultured cities of the world. French styles of architecture, of painting, even of music, were imitated in every Court in Germany. Even the Dutch, who were contributing notably to the progress of civilization in the financial, industrial, and domestic arts, accused themselves under William of Orange of being "debauched by French habits and customs." French Court theologians, their wits sharpened first by the Jansenist and secondly by the Gallican controversy, rivalled those of Rome. French Catholicism, adorned by figures like Fénelon or Bossuet, was the most stately, imposing, and persuasive form of the Old Faith which had yet confronted the Reformation. The conquest, planned and largely effected, was not only military and economic, but religious, moral, and intellectual. It was the most magnificent claim to world dominion ever made since the age of the Antonines. And at the summit there reigned in unchallenged splendour for more than half a century a masterful, competent, insatiable, hardworking egoist, born to a throne.

Since the days of Queen Elizabeth and the Spanish Armada Spain had been the bugbear of Protestant England. Many devout families, suffering all things, still adhered to the Catholic faith. But deep in the hearts of the English people from peer to peasant memories of Smithfield burned with a fierce glow which any breeze could rouse into flame. And now Spain was in decrepitude, insolvent, incoherent, tracing her genealogies and telling her beads. Her redoubtable infantry, first conquered nearly thirty years ago by Condé at Rocroi, had vanished. In their place, alike in the Spanish Netherlands, which we now know as Belgium and Luxembourg, and in the New World, stood decaying garrisons, the mockery of soldiers. The Spanish harbours were filled with rotting ships; the Spanish treasury was bare. The once proud empire of Charles V, irreparably exhausted by over a century of almost continuous war, had fallen a victim to religious mania. Layer upon layer of superstition and ceremonial encrusted the symbols of departed power. Cruelties ever more fantastic enforced a dwindling and crumbling authority. There remained an immense pride, an ancient and secure aristocracy, the title-deeds of half the outer world, a despotic Church, and a throne occupied by a sickly, sterile child who might die any day, leaving no trace behind.

Gradually the fear of Spain had faded from the English mind. In Oliver Cromwell, a man of conservative temperament, born under Queen Elizabeth, the old prejudice obstinately survived. But when, in 1654, he proposed to join France in war against Spain, his council of Roundhead generals surprised him by their resistance. Left to themselves, they would probably have taken the opposite side. The authority of the Lord Protector prevailed, and his Ironside redcoats stormed the Spanish positions upon the sand-dunes by Dunkirk. Wide circles of instructed English opinion regarded these antagonisms as old-fashioned and obsolete. To them the new menace to English faith, freedom, and trade was France. This Battle of the Dunes marked the end of the hundred years' struggle with Spain. Henceforth the dangers and difficulties of England would not arise from Spanish strength, but from Spanish weakness. Henceforth the mounting power of France would be the main preoccupation of Englishmen.

Nearest akin in race, religion, and temperament to the English, the Dutch were their sharpest rivals upon the seas, in trade and colonization. It is said that at this time one-half of the population of Holland gained their livelihood from commerce, industry, and shipping. A tough, substantial race, welded by their struggles against Spanish tyranny, dwelling, robust and acquisitive, under embattled oligarchies, the Dutch clashed with the English at many points. There was the Dutch navy, with its memories of Tromp and his broom "to sweep the English from the seas." There were the dangers of Dutch competition in the colonies and in trade as far as the coasts of India, in the East, and as far as New Amsterdam, since 1664 renamed New York, across the Atlantic. Thus the war which Cromwell had waged against Holland had broken out again in the earlier years of Charles II. Its course was ignominious to England. The sailors of the Royal Navy were in those days paid only at the end of a three or four years' commission. The crews who came home in 1666 received their pay warrants, called tickets, for three years' hard service. Such was the poverty of the Crown that when these were presented at the Naval Pay Office no payment could be made. Conceiving themselves intolerably defrauded, some of the sailors committed an unpardonable crime. They made their way to Holland and piloted the Dutch fleet through the intricate approaches of the Thames estuary. Several of the laid-up English ships in the Medway and the Thames were burned, and the rumble of the Dutch guns was plainly heard in London. But the lack of money forbade effectual reprisals. Charles and his subjects swallowed the insult, and peace was made in 1667. A great bitterness continued between the countries, and the claim of England to the unquestioned sovereignty of the Narrow Seas, though recognized by the peace treaty, accorded ill with the actual incidents of the naval war. "With the Treaty of Breda," says the historian of the United Netherlands, "began the most glorious period of the Republic."

The relations between England and Holland followed a chequered course, and many years were to pass before their grievous quarrels about trade and naval supremacy were finally thrust into the background before the ever-growing French power. It is easy nowadays to say that Charles "should have marched with the Dutch and fought the French" or "marched with the Protestants and fought the Papists." But the Dutch attitude was oblique and baffling, and many great Catholic states were opposed to France. Holland was then ruled by John de Witt and his brother Cornelius. The De Witts were friendly to France. John de Witt believed that by astute conciliation he could come to terms with Louis XIV. Louis had always a potent bribe for the Dutch in the carrying trade of France, on which they thrived. Had not France been the friend, and even champion, of the Republic during its birth-throes? And what was Belgium, that fief of Spain, but a convenient, useful buffer-state whose partition, if inevitable, offered large, immediate gains to both its neighbours? There were, indeed, two Hollands—the pacific, and at times the Francophile, Holland of John de Witt and Amsterdam, and the Holland which adhered to the memory and lineage of William the Silent, and saw in his frail, spirited, already remarkable descendant the prince who would sustain its cause. No Government, French or English, could tell which of these Hollands would be supreme in any given situation.

These uncertainties arose in part from the dubious, balancing attitude of what we now call Prussia. The Great Elector of Brandenburg ruled the main northern mass of Protestant Germany. But upon his western bounds along the whole course of the Rhine, and stretching southward to Bavaria and the Danube, lay a belt of powerful minor states, partly Protestant, partly Catholic in sympathy, whose accession to the one side or the other might be decisive in the balance of power. Beyond Prussia, again, lay Poland, a large, unkempt, slatternly kingdom, ranging from the Baltic to the Ukraine, still partly in feudalism, with an elective monarchy, the trophy of foreign intrigue, and a constitution which might have been designed for a cauldron of domestic broil. "Ceaselessly gnawed by aristocratic lawlessness," its throne a prey to all the princes and adventurers of Europe, its frontiers ravaged, its magnates bribed, Poland was the sport of Europe. There was to be an interlude of glorious independence under John Sobieski; but for the rest Louis XIV, the Emperor, and the Great Elector tirelessly spun their rival webs about the threatened state, and with each candidature for its throne put their competing influences to the test. No wonder the Great Elector, until a final phase which we shall presently reach, had to follow an equivocal policy.

On the eastern flank of Poland lay the huge, sprawling Muscovy Empire, until recent times called Russia, still almost barbarous and perpetually torn by the revolt of the Cossacks against the Tsar. Moscow was ravaged by the Cossack Hetman Stenka, who also brought "unspeakable horrors" upon an "oppressed peasantry." The possibilities of contact with Western civilization were blocked by Sweden and Poland, which together also impeded Russia from any outlet on to the Baltic. In the south the Turks shut it out from the Black Sea. The Tsar Alexis (1645–76), a peace-loving and conscientious man, entrusted a reforming patriarch, the monk Nikon, with most of the affairs of State during the early part of his reign. Later, in 1671, Stenka was captured and quartered alive, and when Alexis died, although no one yet foresaw the emergence of these eastern barbarians as a Western Power, the way lay open for the work of Peter the Great.

In the north of Europe Sweden, the ancient rival of Denmark, was the strongest Power, and aimed at making the Baltic a Swedish lake. At this time the Swedish realm included Finland, Ingria, Esthonia, Livonia, and West Pomerania; and the house of Vasa had traditional designs on Denmark and parts of Poland. The hardy, valiant race of Swedes had impressed upon all Europe the startling effects of a well-trained, warlike professional army. For a spell in the Thirty Years War Gustavus Adolphus had overthrown the troops of every Central European state. But Gustavus and his victories now lay in the past. The chief desire of Prussia was to win Pomerania from the Swedish Crown. Soon, in the battle of Fehrbellin (1675), the Great Elector with his Prussian troops was to overthrow the famous army of Sweden. The antagonism between the two countries was keen and open. Only the unfailing strength of France saved Pomerania for a time from Prussian absorption. Although the bias of Sweden was towards Protestantism, no Dutch or German statesman in the last quarter of the seventeenth century could ever exclude the possibility that her doughty soldiery would be bought by France, or rallied to her cause. All these baffling potential reactions were well comprehended at Whitehall in the closet of King Charles II.

Continuing our progress, we reach the domains of the Holy Roman Empire. This organism of Central Europe, "the survival of a great tradition and a grandiose title," signified not territory but only a sense of membership. The member states covered roughly modern Germany, Austria, Switzerland, Czecho-Slovakia, and Belgium. The ruler was chosen for life by the hereditary Electors of seven states. The Hapsburgs, as sovereigns of Austria, laying claim to Silesia, Bohemia, and Hungary, were the most powerful candidates, and in practice became the hereditary bearers of the ceremonial office of Emperor.*

Austria proper and the Hapsburg dynasty were deeply Catholic; not violent, aggressive, or, except in Hungary, proselytizing, but dwelling solidly and sedately in spiritual loyalty to the Pope. Then, as in our own age, the Hapsburgs were represented by a sovereign who reigned for fifty troublous years over an empire already racked by the stresses which two centuries later were, amid world disaster, to rend it in pieces. Confronted and alarmed by the growing power and encroachments of France, at variance often with Prussia, Vienna had fearful preoccupations of its own. The Turk under fanatical Sultans still launched in the south-east of Europe that thrust of conquest which in earlier periods had been successively hurled back from France and Spain. At any time the Ottoman armies, drawing recruits and supplies from all those subjugated Christian peoples we now call the Balkan States, might present themselves in barbaric invasion at the gates of Vienna. And there were always the Magyars of Hungary, always in revolt. In general, the divided princes of Germany faced the united strength of France, and Austria struggled for life against the Turk; but the whole vague confederacy recognized common dangers and foes, and the majestic antagonisms of Bourbons'and Hapsburgs were the main dividing line of Europe.

Italy in the seventeenth century was merely a geographical expression. In the north Savoy (Piedmont) was brought out of its obscurity at the beginning of the century by the genius of Charles Emmanuel I (1580–1630). Afterwards it poised precariously between France and the Empire, deserting them both in turn according to the apparent fortunes of war. It has been said that the geographical position of Savoy, "the doorkeeper of the Alps," made its rulers treacherous. At best

* In this account we shall use 'the Empire,' 'Austria,' and 'the Court at Vienna' as more or less interchangeable terms.

they could only preserve themselves and their country from ruin by miracles of diplomatic alternation.

Such were the unpromising and divided components of a Europe in contrast with which the power and ambitions of France arose in menacing splendour. Such were the factors and forces amid which Charles II had to steer the fortunes of his kingdom.

The politics of a weak and threatened state cannot achieve the standards open to those who enjoy security and wealth. The ever-changing forms of the dangers by which they are oppressed impose continuous shifts and contradictions, and many manœuvres from which pride and virtue alike recoil. England in the seventeenth century was little better placed than were Balkan states like Roumania or Bulgaria, when in the advent or convulsion of Armageddon they found themselves bid for or struck at by several mighty empires. We had to keep ourselves alive and free, and we did so. It is by no means sure that plain, honest, downright policies, however laudable, would have succeeded. The oak may butt the storm, but the reeds bow and quiver in the gale and also survive.

It is a mistake to judge English foreign policy from 1667 to 1670, from the Triple Alliance with Holland against France to the Secret Treaty of Dover with France against Holland, as if it meant simply alternating periods of good and evil, of light and darkness, and of the influence of Sir William Temple as against that of the Duchess of Orleans. In fact, both the problems and the controls were continuous and the same, and our policy rested throughout in the same hands, in those of Charles II and his Minister Arlington. Although devoid of both faith and illusions, they were certainly not unintelligent, nor entirely without patriotic feeling. The invasion of Belgium by Louis XIV in the late summer of 1667 confronted them both with a situation of the utmost perplexity. At this stage in his life, at any rate, Charles desired to play an independent part in Europe, while Arlington, with his Spanish sympathies and training and his Dutch wife, was positively anti-French. Their first impulse was to resist the invasion of Belgium.

Strange indeed why this patch of land should exercise such compelling influence upon our unsophisticated ancestors! Apparently in 1667 they forgot or expunged the burning of their battleships in the Medway and Thames and all the passions of hard-fought naval battles because France was about to invade Belgium. Why did Belgium count so much with them? Two hundred and fifty years later we saw the manhood of the British Empire hastening across all the seas and oceans of the world to conquer or die in defence of this same strip of fertile, undulating country about the mouth of the Scheldt. Every one felt he had to go, and no one asked for logical or historical explanations. But then, with our education, we understood many things for which convincing verbal arguments were lacking. So did our ancestors at this time. The Court, the Parliament, the City, the country gentlemen, were all as sure in 1668 that Belgium must not be conquered by the greatest military power on the Continent as were all parties and classes in the British Empire in August 1914. A mystery veiling an instinct!

If resistance to France were possible, still more if it were profitable, the King and Arlington were prepared to make an effort. They sounded the Courts of Europe: but the replies which they received from every quarter were universally discouraging. Spain was utterly incapable of defending her assaulted province. Without English or Dutch shipping she could not even reach it. Yet voluntarily Spain would not yield an inch. The Dutch would not attack France. If strongly supported, they would seek to limit the French territorial gains, but would agree to many of them, and all at the expense of Spain. The Emperor, whatever his Ambassador in London might say, seemed curiously backward. He would make no offensive alliance, least of all with heretics. In fact, as we now know, he was during these very months framing a secret treaty with France for the future partition of the whole Spanish Empire. The Great Elector would not move without subsidies which the Dutch would not and the Spanish could not give him. He was nervous of Sweden, and if the French gave him a free hand in Poland he would not oppose their progress in the west. Truly a depressing prospect for a coalition against the dominating, centralized might of France, wielded by a single man.

In a spirit which it is easy to call 'cold-blooded' and 'cynical' Charles and Arlington next examined the possibility of persuading France to let England share in her winnings, in return for English support in a war against Holland. Here they encountered a sharp rebuff. Louis, who hoped to obtain Belgium without coming to actual war with Holland, was not prepared to barter Spanish colonies against an English alliance, or still less against English neutrality. Both alternatives having thus been unsentimentally explored, Charles, with natural and obvious misgivings, took his decision to oppose France. He sent Sir William Temple to The Hague to make the famous Triple Alliance between England, Holland, and Sweden. The two Governments—for Sweden was a mere mercenary—entered upon it with limited and different objectives, but both sought to extort the favour of France by the threat of war. The English ruling circle hoped to win the French alliance by teaching Louis XIV not to despise England; the Dutch thought they could still retain the friendship of France by compelling Spain to a compromise. Perverse as were the motives, flimsy as was the basis, the result emerged with startling force. Louis saw himself confronted by a Northern league, and simultaneously Arlington brought about a peace between Spain and Portugal which freed the Spanish forces for a more real resistance. The consequences were swift and impressive. The shadow of the Spanish succession fell across the world. Louis, by his aggression upon the Belgian soil so strangely sacred, had called into being in phantom outline that beginnings of the Grand Alliance which was eventually to lay him low. He recoiled from the apparition. By his Partition Treaty of 1668 with the Emperor he had assured himself by merely waiting future gains throughout the whole Spanish Empire incomparably greater than those which might now be won by serious war. He could afford to be patient. Recalling his armies, silencing the protests of his generals, he retreated within his bounds, content for the time being with the acquisition of Lille, Tournai, Armentières, and other fortresses that put Belgium at his mercy. In April 1668, under the pressure and guarantee of the Triple Alliance, France and Spain consequently signed the peace of Aix-la-Chapelle.

We now approach days fatal to the house of Stuart. The national foreign policy attempted in 1668 rested upon diverse motives and paper guarantees. The Triple Alliance must succumb to any strain or temptation. Its partners were bound to protect the *status quo* in Belgium by expeditionary forces in the event of aggression; for this they looked, and in vain, to Spanish subsidies. They were still divided by their old hatreds and recent injuries, by their ceaseless hostilities in the East Indies and in Guiana, and in their rivalry of the Channel. Charles, whatever his subjects might feel, had never forgiven the burning of his ships in the Medway. He hated the Dutch, and though he had been forced by events to side with them for a while and they with him, he yearned for a day when he could unite himself to France. In 1669 he began with Croissy, the French Ambassador, negotiations which reached their fruition in 1670.

Louis's sister-in-law, Duchess of Orleans—the "Madame" of the French Court—was also Charles's sister and his "beloved Minette." She was in the final phase the agent of France. Romance, as well as history, had played around this delightful, tragic figure, so suddenly decisive, so swiftly extinguished. No one stood so high in the love and respect of both monarchs. They cherished her personality: they admired her mind. She was to Charles the purest and deepest affection of his life. Louis realized only too late what he had lost in not making her his Queen. Minette loved both her native and adopted countries, and longed to see them united; but her heart was all for England's interests, as she misunderstood them, and for the Old Faith, to which she was devoutly attached. She presented and pleaded with all her wit and charm the case for an accommodation—nay, an alliance with the Sun King. Why condemn England to an endless, desperate struggle against overwhelming force? Why not accept the friendly hand sincerely, generously extended, and share the triumph and the prize? With France and England united, success was sure, and all the kingdoms of the world would lie in fee. It often happens that when great projects have been brought to maturity, personal touch is needed to set them in action. Minette came to England in the summer of 1670, bringing in her train another charmer, who also was destined to play her part—Louise de Kéroualle. "Madame's" husband, jealous of her political power and of his own eclipse, grudged every day of the Princess's absence from the home he had made odious with his minions. But Charles welcomed her with unrestrained joy. He met her with his Navy, and for a few sunlit days the English Court made picnic revel at Dover. Louis awaited results in eager suspense. They were all he could desire. Minette bore with her back to France—signed, sealed, and delivered—the Secret Treaty. She returned to perish almost immediately of a mysterious illness. She left as her legacy and life's achievement an instrument ruinous to all she prized.

By the Secret Treaty of Dover Charles agreed to join with Louis in an attack on Holland which aimed at nothing less than the destruction of the United Provinces as a factor in Europe, and to take all measures needful to that end. Louis agreed to respect the integrity of Belgium; to place in British keeping much of the coastline of conquered Holland, including the isle of Walcheren, with its valuable ports of Sluys and Cadsand, and the mouths of the Scheldt. Every safeguard was furnished to English naval requirements and colonial ambition. The mastery of the seas, the command of the Dutch outlets, and the exploitation of Asia and the Americas were inestimable temptations. For the young Stadtholder, William of Orange, a prince of Stuart blood, now just twenty, a dignified, if restricted, sphere would be reserved. He might reign as hereditary sovereign over the truncated domains of the former Dutch Republic, for which his great-grandfather William the Silent had battled with all that his life could give. Next there was to be money. Large subsidies, sufficient to make King Charles with his hereditary revenues almost independent in times of peace of his contumacious Parliament, would be provided. Money, very handy for mistresses and Court expenses, but also absolutely necessary to restore and maintain the strength of the Royal Navy, now decaying in its starved dockyards! Such were the secular clauses. But the pact contained what in those days was even graver matter. Charles was to try persistently and faithfully, by every means at his disposal, to bring his subjects back to the Catholic faith. Full allowance would be made for the obvious difficulties of such a task; but the effort was to be continuous and loyal. In any case, not only French money, but French troops were to be available to secure the English monarchy against the anger of Parliament or the revolt of the nation.

Such was the hideous bargain, struck by so fair a hand, upon which the execration of succeeding generations has fastened. Far be it from us to seek to reverse that verdict of history which every British heart must acclaim. It would not, however, have been difficult to state a case at Charles II's council board against any whole-hearted espousal of Dutch interests, nor to have pleaded and even justified a temporizing opportunist policy towards France, deceitful though it must be. "We cannot commit ourselves to Holland; at any moment she may outbid us with France. Spain is futile and penniless. Alone we cannot face the enmity of the Great King. Let us take his money to build our fleet, and wait and see what happens." As for religion, Charles had learned in a hard school the willpower of Protestant England. Whatever his own leanings to the Catholic faith, all his statecraft showed that he would never run any serious risk for the sake of reconverting the nation. Manœuvre, fence, and palter as he might, he always submitted, and always meant to submit, with expedition to the deep growl of his subjects and to the authority of their inexpugnable institutions.

The Secret Treaty of Dover was handled personally by Louis, Charles, and their intermediary, Minette. But, of course, Colbert and Croissy had long studied its terms, and in England Arlington's support was soon found indispensable. As the protocol began to take shape first Arlington and then Clifford and the rest of the Cabal were invited to approve its secular provisions. It was perhaps less of a turn-about for Arlington than it appeared on the surface, and we cannot measure the slow, persistent pressures to which he yielded. Ministers in those days considered themselves the servants of the King, in the sense of being bound to interpret his will up to the point of impeachment, and sometimes beyond it. The whole Cabal endorsed such parts of the treaty as were communicated to them. The religious plot—it deserves no other name—was locked in the royal breast. James had not been much consulted in the negotiations, but he learned all that had been done with an inexpressible joy. Most especially he admired the religious clauses. Here more clearly than ever before he saw the blessed hands of the Mother of God laid upon the tormented world.

If anyone in 1672 computed the relative forces of France and England, he could only feel that no contest was possible; and the apparent weakness and humiliation of the pensioner island was aggravated by the feeble, divided condition of Europe. No dreamer, however romantic, however remote his dreams from reason, could have foreseen a surely approaching day when, by the formation of mighty coalitions and across the struggles of a generation, the noble colossus of France would lie prostrate in the dust, while the small island, beginning to gather to itself the empires of India and America, stripping France and Holland of their colonial possessions, would emerge victorious, mistress of the Mediterranean, the Narrow Seas, and the oceans. Aye, and carry forward with her, intact and enshrined, all that peculiar structure of law and liberty, all her own inheritance of learning and letters, which are to-day the treasure of the most powerful family in the human race.

This prodigy was achieved by conflicting yet contributory forces, and by a succession of great islanders and their noble foreign comrades or guides. We owe our salvation to the sturdy independence of the House of Commons and to its creators, the aristocracy and country gentlemen.

We owe it to our hardy tars and bold sea-captains, and to the quality of a British Army as yet unborn. We owe it to the inherent sanity and vigour of the political conceptions sprung from the genius of the English race. But those forces would have failed without the men to use them. For the quarter of a century from 1688 to 1712 England was to be led by two of the greatest warriors and statesmen in all history: William of Orange, and John, Duke of Marlborough. They broke the military power of France, and fatally weakened her economic and financial foundations. They championed the Protestant faith, crowned Parliamentary institutions with triumph, and opened the door to an age of reason and freedom. They reversed the proportions and balances of Europe. They turned into new courses the destinies of Asia and America. They united Great Britain, and raised her to the rank she holds today.

CHAPTER FIVE

Arms

❧ 1672-74 ❧

THERE are two main phases in the military career of John, Duke of Marlborough. In the first, which lasted four years, he rose swiftly from ensign to colonel by his conduct and personal qualities and by the impression he made on all who met him in the field. In the second, during ten campaigns he commanded the main army of the Grand Alliance with infallibility. An interval of more than a quarter of a century separates these two heroic periods. From 1671 to 1675 he exhibited all those qualities which were regarded as the forerunners in a regimental officer of the highest military distinction. He won his way up from grade to grade by undoubted merit and daring. But thereafter was a desert through which he toiled and wandered. A whole generation of small years intervened. His sword never rusted in its sheath. It was found bright and sharp whenever it was needed, at Sedgemoor, at Walcourt, or in Ireland. There it lay, the sword of certain victory, ready for service whenever opportunity should come.

"Everybody agreed," wrote Anthony Hamilton, "that the man who was the favourite of the King's mistress and brother to the Duke's was starting well and could not fail to make his fortune." But the influence of royal concubines was not the explanation of the rise of Marlborough. That rise was gradual, intermittent, and long. He was a professional soldier. "And," wrote the old Duchess at the end of her life,

> I think it is more Honour to rise from the lowest Step to the greatest, than, as is the fashion now, to be Admirals without ever having seen Water but in a Bason, or to make Generals that never saw any action of war.

By the time he arrived at the highest command he was passing the prime of life, and older than many of the leading generals of the day. The early success and repeated advancement which this chapter records were followed by lengthy intervals of stagnation. Arabella and Barbara had long ceased to count with him or anyone else, while he was still regarded as a subordinate figure, when he had yet to make and remake his whole career. Continual checks, grave perplexities, extreme hazards, disgrace and imprisonment, constant skilful services, immense tenacity, perseverance and self-restraint, almost unerring political judgment, all the arts of the courtier, politician, and diplomatist, marked his middle life. For many long years his genius and recognized qualities seemed unlikely to carry him through the throng of securely established notabilities who then owned the fulness of the earth. At twenty-four he was a colonel. He was fifty-two before he commanded a large army.

In 1672 the slumbering Treaty of Dover awoke in the realm of action. Louis, having perfected his plans to the last detail, suddenly, without cause of quarrel, made his cavalry swim the Rhine and poured his armies into Holland. At the same time England also declared war upon the Dutch. The States-General, de Witt and his Amsterdammers, taken by surprise, were unable to stem the advance of 120,000 French troops, armed for the first time with the new weapon of the bayonet. Cities and strongholds fell like ninepins. The Dutch people, faced with extermination, set their despairing hopes upon William of Orange. The great-grandson of William the Silent did not fail them. He roused and animated their tough, all-enduring courage. John de Witt and his brother were torn to pieces by a frenzied mob in the streets of The Hague. William uttered the deathless battle-cry, "We can die in the last ditch." The sluices in the dykes were opened; the bitter waters rolled in ever-widening deluge over the fertile land. Upon the wide inundation the fortified towns seemed to float like arks of refuge. All military operations became impossible. The French armies withdrew in bewilderment. Holland, her manhood, her navy, and her hero-Prince preserved their soul impregnable.

Meanwhile the French and English fleets united had set themselves to secure the mastery of the Narrow Seas. A contingent of six thousand English troops under Monmouth's command served with the French armies. Lediard and other early writers suppose that Churchill was among them. In fact he took part in a deadlier struggle afloat. The sea fighting began on March 13, before the declaration of war, with the surprise attack of Sir Robert Holmes's English squadron upon the Dutch Smyrna fleet while at anchor off the Isle of Wight. This treacherous venture miscarried, and the bulk of the Dutch vessels escaped. The companies of the Guards in which Churchill and his friend George Legge were serving were embarked for the raid and took part in the action.

The handling of the Dutch navy under De Ruyter in this campaign commands lasting admiration. He pressed into the jaws of the Channel to forestall the concentration of the French and English fleets. But the Duke of York, setting sail from the Thames in good time, made his junction with the French fleet from Brest, and De Ruyter was glad to extricate himself from the Channel and return safely to the North Sea. The combined fleets proceeded through the Straits of Dover to Sole Bay (or Southwold), on the Suffolk coast. This was the opportunity which De Ruyter sought. On the morning of May 28/June 7 a French frigate, hotly pursued, brought the news that the whole Dutch fleet was at her heels. Every one scrambled on board, and a hundred and one ships endeavoured to form their line of battle. The French division, under D'Estrées, whether from policy or necessity or because James's orders were lacking in precision, sailed upon a divergent course from the English fleet. De Ruyter, playing with the French and sending Van Ghent to attack the ships of Lord Sandwich, fell himself upon the Duke of York's division, of which at first not more than twenty were in their stations. In all he had ninety-one vessels and a superiority of at least two to one in the first part of the battle.

Grievous and cruel was the long struggle which ensued. The Suffolk shores were crowded with frantic spectators, the cannonade was heard two hundred miles away. From noon till dusk the battle raged at close quarters. The Dutch desperately staked their superiority with cannon and fire-ships against the English, tethered upon a lee shore. The captain of the ship and more than two hundred men, a third of the complement, were killed or wounded. Both sides fought with the doggedness on which their races pride themselves. Sunset and the possible return of the French ended a battle described by De Ruyter as the hardest of his thirty-two actions, and the Dutch withdrew, having destroyed for many weeks the offensive power of the superior combined fleets.

Not one single word has come down to us of John's part in this deadly business, through which he passed unscathed. No reference to it exists in his correspondence or conversation. This was before the age when everybody kept diaries or wrote memoirs. It was just in the day's work. All we know is that his conduct gained him remarkable advancement. No fewer than four captains of the Admiralty Regiment had been killed, and he received double promotion from a Guards ensign to a Marine captaincy.

Lieutenant Edward Picks complained to Sir Joseph Williamson, Arlington's Under-Secretary, that:

> Mr Churchill, who was my ensign in the engagement, is made a Captain and I, without my Lord Arlington's kindness and yours, I fear may still continue a lieutenant, though I am confident my greatest enemies cannot say I misbehaved myself in the engagement. . ,

We do not know the details of the action. Favouritism there may have been in the double step, but it was favouritism founded upon exceptional conduct. In such rough times, when chiefs and subalterns faced the fire together, many wholesome correctives were at work. The Duke of York, coming himself out of heavy battle, would have acted in accordance with what he had seen and with what men said of Churchill's conduct.

Sole Bay for the time being knocked out the fleet, and only meagre funds were found to refit and repair it. The infantry and gentlemen volunteers came ashore, and the Guards were ordered to France. The courtiers forgathered at Whitehall to celebrate their experiences in revel and carouse, and John, fresh from danger and in the flush of promotion, was welcomed, we doubt not, in the arms of Barbara. It is believed that at this time she paid the purchase money which enabled him to take up the captaincy his sword had gained. We apologize for mentioning such shocking facts to the reader; but it is our duty, for such was the depravity of these fierce and hectic times.

In 1673 Louis XIV again made war in person. Condé with weak forces occupied the Dutch in the north. Turenne similarly engaged the Imperialists in Alsace. The Great King advanced in the centre with the mass and magnificence of the French Army. All the world wondered where he would strike. It soon appeared that he had honoured Maestricht, a strong Dutch fortress garrisoned by about five thousand men, as the scene of his intended triumph. He felt his military qualities more suited to sieges than to battles; and "Big sieges," he remarked, "please me more than the others." Maestricht was accordingly invested on June 17.

We do not know precisely what happened to Captain Churchill between the battle of Sole Bay and the siege of Maestricht. The Admiralty Regiment in which he now held a company went to France in December. Various English contingents were serving in Alsace or in garrison with the French. It seems probable that once it became clear that the centre of the war was to be in Flanders and that the Great King would be there himself, Monmouth allowed or encouraged a handful of swells and their personal attendants to leave the different units of the army and come to the bull's-eye of the fighting under his personal direction. At any rate, England was represented at Maestricht only by the Duke of Monmouth with a score of gentlemen volunteers, prominent among whom was Churchill, and an escort of thirty gentlemen troopers of the Life Guards. Louis XIV treated the distinguished delegation with the ceremony due to the bastard son of his royal brother. Monmouth was assigned his turn as 'General of the Trenches,' and ample opportunity was offered to him and his friends of winning distinction before the most critical and fashionable military assemblage of the period. Every one of them was on his mettle, eager to hazard his life in the arena and wrest renown from beneath so many jealous and competent eyes. Little did this gay company trouble themselves about the rights and wrongs of the war, or the majestic balance of power in Europe; and we cannot doubt that our young officer shared their reckless mood to the full. Comradeship and adventure and the hopes of glory and promotion seemed all-sufficing to the eyes and sword of youth.

The trenches were opened ten days after the investment, and a week later the siege works justified an attempt to break in upon the fortress. The attack, timed for ten o'clock at night, was arranged to fall in Monmouth's tour of duty. Picked detachments from the best regiments, including the King's Musketeers, formed the storming forces. The King came and stood at the end of the trenches to watch. The signal was given, and Monmouth, with Churchill and his Englishmen at his side, led the French assault. With heavy losses from close and deadly fire, amid the explosion of two mines and of six thousand grenades, the counterscarp galleries were occupied, and a half-moon work in front of the Brussels gate was attacked. Three times the assailants were driven partly out of their lodgments and three times they renewed the assault, until finally Churchill is said to have planted the French standard on the parapet of the half-moon. The rest of the night was spent in consolidating the defence and digging new communications, and at daylight Monmouth handed over the captured works to supporting troops. The Englishmen were resting in their tents, and Monmouth was about to dine, when near noon of the next day the dull roar of a mine and heavy firing proclaimed the Dutch counter-stroke. The governor, M. de Fariaux, a Frenchman in the service of the States-General, gallantly leading his men, had sallied out upon the captured works.

The episode which followed belongs to romance rather than to history or war, but the most detailed and authentic records exist about it.

Monmouth sent appeals to a company of musketeers at hand. Their officer, a certain M. d'Artagnan, then famous in the Army and since deathless in Dumas's fiction, responded instantly. There was no time to go through the zigzags of the communication trenches. De Fariaux was already in the half-moon. Monmouth, fleet of foot, led straight for the struggle across the top of the ground. With him came Churchill, twelve Life Guardsmen, and a handful of Englishmen of quality, with some valiant pages and servants. They reached the half-moon from an unexpected direction at the moment when the fighting was at its height. D'Artagnan and his musketeers joined them. The Life Guards threw away their carbines (twelve were subsequently reissued from the English ordnance stores) and drew their swords. Monmouth, Churchill, and d'Artagnan forced their way in.

Churchill, who was wounded at Monmouth's side, was also held to have distinguished himself. He was, in fact, publicly thanked upon a great parade by Louis XIV, who assured him that his good conduct would be reported to his own sovereign. Another subaltern fought in this attack whose name will recur in these pages: Louis Hector de Villars against orders joined the assault. His gallantry won forgiveness for his disobedience. We do not know whether he and Churchill became acquainted at Maestricht. They certainly met at Malplaquet.

The governor of Maestricht, satisfied with the resistance he had made and strongly pressed by the townsfolk to capitulate while time remained, beat a parley, and was allowed to march out with the honours of war. The severity of the losses, especially among persons of note in the storming troops, made a strong impression throughout the camps and the Courts concerned. Monmouth was praised and petted by Louis not only from policy, but on the undoubted merit of his performance. He and his English team received the unstinted tributes of "the finest army in the world." The brief and spectacular campaign was soon brought to a close. Louis XIV rejoined his anxious Court, who burned before him the incense of flattery with all the delicate address of which the French are peculiarly capable. The armies retired into winter quarters, and Monmouth and his hunting party were welcomed again into the bosom of Whitehall.

Meanwhile Captain Churchill and the Duchess of Cleveland continued to make the running at the Court. That a virile young officer should be the lover of a beautiful, voluptuous, and immoral woman is not inexplicable to human nature. The fact that she was a few years his senior is by no means a bar. On the contrary, the charms of thirty are rarely more effective than when exerted on the impressionable personality of twenty-three. No one is invited to applaud such relationships, but few, especially in time of war, will hold them unpardonable, and only malignancy would seek to score them for ever upon a young man's record. How disgusting to pretend, with Lord Macaulay, a filthy, sordid motive for actions prompted by those overpowering compulsions which leap flaming from the crucible of life itself! Inconstant Barbara loved her youthful soldier tenderly and followed with eager, anxious eyes his many adventures and perils from steel and fire. He returned her love with the passion of youth. She was rich and could have money for the asking. He had no property but his sword and sash. But they were equals, they were kin, they lived in the same world. She was now the mother of his child.

He was back at the front in the early autumn. The Admiralty Regiment was now with Turenne in Westphalia. There is little doubt that Churchill served as a captain with them during the rest of 1673. Although no great operations were in progress, he made his way in the Army. There is always the story of Turenne wagering, when some defile had been ill defended, that the "handsome Englishman" would retake it with half the number of troops used when it was lost; and how this was accordingly and punctually done. No one has been able to assign the date or the place, but at any rate the newly made captain in the Admiralty Regiment was a figure well known in Turenne's army and high in the favour of the Marshal himself before the year closed.

Stern, curious eyes were now turned upon the Duke of York. Rumours of his conversion to Rome had long been rife. How would he stand the Test, administered according to the Act which excluded Papists from all offices of State? The answer was soon forthcoming. The heir to the throne renounced all his offices, and Prince Rupert succeeded him in the command of the fleet. So it was true, then, that James was a resolute Papist, ready to sacrifice all material advantages to the faith his countrymen abhorred. And now there came a trickle of allegations and disclosures about the Secret Treaty of Dover. Rumours of decisions taken by the King, by his brother, and his Ministers to convert England to Rome were rife during all the summer and autumn of 1673.

Moreover, the war went ill. Like so many wars, it looked easy and sure at the outset. There is always the other side, who have their own point of view and think, often with surprising reason, that they also have a chance of victory. The cutting of the dykes had marred the opening French campaign. The Dutch defensive at sea in 1672 and 1673 was magnificent. Rupert's battles against De Ruyter were bloody and drawn. The situation of Holland had vastly improved. The Prince of Orange, Stadtholder and Captain-General, stood at the head of truly 'United Provinces,' and in August both the Empire and Spain entered into alliance with the Dutch to maintain the European balance. Diplomatically and militarily the Anglo-French compact had failed. On top of all this came the news that Charles had allowed a most obnoxious marriage between the Duke of York and the Catholic princess Mary of Modena.

A new scene, and, indeed, a new era, now opened.

Through Spanish mediation peace was signed with Holland on February 19, 1674. The Dutch, stubborn though they were, gave in their sore straits the fullest satisfaction to English naval pride. Within six years of the Medway, within two years of Sole Bay, and within a year of De Ruyter's proud encounters with Rupert, Holland accepted with every circumstance of humility the naval supremacy of England. The States-General confirmed the agreement of the Treaty of Breda (1667) that all Dutch ships should dip their flag and topsails whenever, north of Cape Finisterre, they sighted an English man-of-war. Not only were

Dutch fleets and squadrons to make their salute to similar forces of the Royal Navy, but even the whole of the Dutch fleet was to make its submission to a single English vessel, however small, which flew the royal flag. The history books which dwell upon our shame in the Medway and the Thames do not do justice to this turning of the tables. Callous, unmoral, unscrupulous as had been Charles's policy, he might now on this account at least exclaim, "He laughs best who laughs last."

There were in 1674 five or six thousand English troops in French pay; but these had to be reduced after the Anglo-Dutch treaty, and as many of the men returned home and no drafts were sent out, the strength of the various regiments soon fell, and it became necessary to amalgamate units. Thus Skelton's regiment became merged with Peterborough's. Peterborough resigned. Who was to take his place? Who should command the combined regiment but the brilliant officer who had planted the lilies of France on the parapet of the Maestricht half-moon, whose quality was known throughout the French Army, who had been thanked by Louis in the field, and whose advancement was so entirely agreeable to Charles II, to the Duke of York, and to both their lady-loves? A news-letter from Paris on March 19, 1674, says:

> Lord Peterborough's regiment, now in France, is to be broken up and some companies of it joined to the companies that went out of the Guards last summer, and be incorporated into one regiment, and to remain there for the present under the command of Captain Churchill, son of Sir Winston.

But before Churchill could receive the colonelcy he had to be presented at Versailles and receive the personal approval of the Great King. On March 21 Louvois wrote to thank Monmouth for his letter, to announce that Churchill had been accepted as a colonel in the French service by Louis XIV, and to suggest that companies not merely from Skelton's, but also from Sackville's and Hewetson's regiments, should be included in his command. On April 3 the commission was granted, and John Churchill found himself Colonel in the service of France and at the head of a regiment of English infantry. He was just twenty-four. He had skipped the rank of lieutenant after Sole Bay; he now, in the French service, skips the ranks of Major and Lieutenant-Colonel at a bound. He retained his substantive rank of Captain in the

English Army until January 1675, when he was promoted Lieutenant-Colonel in the Duke of York's regiment. He had evidently at this time impressed his personality on the French Court. He had been there a year before with half a dozen English officers on the way to the Maestricht campaign. Once again the Great King acknowledged the bows of the young Adonis in scarlet and gold, of whose exploits under the planets of Mars and Venus he had already been well informed through the regular channels. He would certainly not have allowed the royal radiance to play upon this elegant, graceful figure if there were not veils which shroud the future.

On the 16th of June the whole army marched on Sinzheim, on the left bank of the Elsatz. The battle began with Turenne's seizure of the town and the forcing of the stream. The fighting lasted for seven hours and ended in the retreat of the enemy with heavy loss. Although unaccompanied by strategic results, it is claimed as a perfect example in miniature of Turenne's handling of all three arms. Turenne after various manœuvres received reinforcements, and proceeded to ravage the Palatinate, partly to fill his own magazines and partly to impede its reoccupation by a still unbeaten enemy. This military execution of the province dictated by the needs of war must be distinguished from the systematic devastation of the same region ordered by Louis XIV seven years later as a measure of policy.

We have a letter from an old lady—the widow Saint-Just—one of the few residents who did not suffer from Turenne's severities in 1674, written to the Duke of Marlborough from Metz on July 16, 1711, in which she says:

> It would be indeed difficult for me to forget you, Monseigneur, and I have an indispensable duty to remember all my life the kindness which you showed me in Metz *thirty-four years ago*. You were very young then, Monseigneur, but you gave already by your excellent qualities the hope of that valour, politeness and conduct which have raised you with justice to the rank where you command all men. And what is more glorious, Monseigneur, is that the whole world, friends and enemies, bear witness to the truth of what I have the honour to write; and I have no doubt that it was your generosity on my account which [then] made itself felt, because the troops who came and burnt everything around my land at Mezeray in the plain spared my estate, saying that they were so ordered by high authority.

Whether this letter stirred some scented memory, long cherished in Churchill's retentive mind, which after the lapse of thirty-four years would make the shielding of this little plot and homestead from the ravages of war an incident he would not forget, we cannot tell. We think, however, that the widow is wrong in her dates. It is, of course, possible—though the evidence is against it—that Churchill was in Metz on some military duty in 1677. But it is far more likely that the letter refers to the year 1674, when indeed the troops "came and burnt everything around . . . Mezeray."

There is no dispute, however, about Churchill's presence at the head of his regiment in the battle of Enzheim in October. Here all is certain and grim. We have one of his matter-of-fact letters written to Monmouth about the action. We have also a much fuller account by the future Lord Feversham. Turenne had ten thousand horse and twelve thousand foot against enemy forces almost double. Nevertheless, he crossed the Breusch river and attacked the Imperialists by surprise. All turned upon what was called the 'Little Wood,' which lay on the French right between the armies. The development of the main action depended on who held the wood, and the fight for it constituted the crux of the battle. A competent French colonel, Boufflers by name, whom we shall meet several times in higher situations later, was sent to clear the wood with his dragoons. He could make no headway, and resigned his effort to the infantry. Both sides began to cram battalions into the wood. The French rarely stint their own, and never their allies' blood; and the brunt of Turenne's battle was borne by the hired troops. Dongan's battalion of Hamilton's Irish regiment, the third battalion of Warwick's Loyal English, and Churchill's battalion were successively thrown into the struggle. Duras (Feversham) wrote, "One and all assuredly accomplished marvels." They certainly suffered most severe losses. Churchill's battalion, which was the last to engage, had half its officers killed or wounded in the Little Wood. The rest of the island mercenaries suffered almost as heavily in this and other parts of the field. The three squadrons of Monmouth's horse charged the Imperialists who were attacking the French left and centre at a critical moment, and won much honour with almost total destruction. Turenne bivouacked on the field, claiming a victory at heavy odds, and his strategic theme was vindicated. But the battle must take its place in that large category 'bloody and indecisive.'

Feversham, reporting to the Government, wrote, "No one in the world could possibly have done better than Mr Churchill has done and M. de Turenne is very well pleased with all our nation." Turenne also mentioned Churchill and his battalion in his despatches. It was a very rough, savage fight in a cause not reconcilable with any English interest.

Even before the battle it seems likely that Churchill was well esteemed in the army. We find him selected by Turenne with five hundred picked men for an attack upon the Imperialist rearguard at a moment when it was recrossing the Rhine. But only here and there does his figure catch a fleeting gleam. Lots of others, for whom no one has rummaged, did as well. All that can be said is that he did his duty and bore a solid reputation in this hard-pressed, over-weighted, and yet victorious army. There is no doubt that he fought too in the midwinter attack on Turckheim. In those days the armies reposed from October till April, the condition of such roads as there were alone imposing immobility upon them; but Turenne, starting from Haguenau on November 19, broke into the Imperialist cantonments, and after cutting up various detachments gained a considerable success on Christmas Day. Churchill's regiment marched with him. Duras and other English officers had already been given leave to Paris, it being essential to Turenne's design to pretend that the year's campaign was over. Although a letter on December 15 states that Churchill was daily expected in Paris, he was certainly with the troops.

It is customary to say that he learned the art of war from Turenne. This is going too far. No competent officer of that age could watch the composed genius of Turenne in action without being enriched thereby. But no battle ever repeats itself. The success of a commander does not arise from following rules or models. It consists in an absolutely new comprehension of the dominant facts of the situation at the time, and all the forces at work. Cooks use recipes for dishes and doctors have prescriptions for diseases, but every great operation of war is unique. The kind of intelligence capable of grasping in its complete integrity what is actually happening in the field is not taught by the tactics of commanders on one side or the other—though these may train the mind—but by a profound appreciation of the actual event. There is no surer road to ill-success in war than to imitate the plans of bygone heroes and to fit them to novel situations.

CHAPTER SIX

Sarah

♔ 1675-76 ♕

IN the early seventies a new star began to shine in the constellations of the English Court. Frances Jennings—"la belle Jenyns" of Grammont —beautiful as "Aurora or the promise of Spring," haughty, correct, mistress of herself, became a waiting-woman of the Duchess of York. She soon had no lack of suitors. The Duke himself cast favourable glances towards her, which were suavely but firmly deflected. Fair and impregnable, she shone upon that merry, easy-going, pleasure-loving society.

Her father, Richard Jennings, of Sandridge, came of a Somersetshire family who, though long entitled to bear arms, had no crest before the reign of King Henry VIII. For some time they had been settled in Hertfordshire, near St Albans, at Holywell House, on the banks of the Ver. Her grandfather was High Sheriff of Herts in 1625, and, like his son Richard, was repeatedly returned to the House of Commons as Member for St Albans. Their property also included land in Somersetshire and Kent, and may have amounted at this period to about £4000 a year. Curiously enough—in after-light—the Manor of Churchill, in Somersetshire, was, as we have seen, in the possession of the Jennings family for a hundred years.

About Frances Jennings' widowed mother various reports exist. We find references in Somersetshire letters to "your noble mother." In *The New Atalantis* she is described as a sorceress: "the famous Mother Shipton, who by the power and influence of her magic art had placed her daughter in the Court." She certainly bore a questionable reputation, suffered from a violent temper, and found in St James's Palace, where she had apartments, a refuge from hungry creditors who, armed with the law, bayed outside.

In 1673 Frances brought her younger sister Sarah, a child of twelve, into the Court circle. She too was attached to the household of the Duke of York. There she grew up, and at the mature age of fifteen was already a precocious, charming figure. She was not so dazzling as her sister, but she had a brilliancy all her own; fair, flaxen hair, blue eyes sparkling with vivacity, a clear, rosy complexion, firm, engaging lips, and a nose well chiselled, but with a slightly audacious upward tilt. She also, from her tenderest years, was entirely self-possessed and self-confident, and by inheritance she owned, when roused, the temper of the devil.

Towards the end of 1675 she began to dance with John Churchill at balls and parties. He, of course, must have been acquainted with her ever since she arrived at St James's, but after one night of dancing at the end of that year they fell in love with each other. It was a case of love, not at first sight indeed, but at first recognition. It lasted for ever; neither of them thenceforward loved anyone else in their whole lives, though Sarah hated many. The courtship was obstructed and prolonged. Meanwhile Sarah grew to her beauty and power, and her personality, full of force, woman's wiles, and masculine sagacity, became manifest.

At Blenheim Palace there is a bundle of thirty-seven love-letters of John and Sarah covering a period of about three years, from 1675 to 1677. All are unsigned and all are provokingly undated. All but eight are his. Her contributions are short, severe, and almost repellent. She must have written many more letters, and it is surmised that these were in a more tender vein. She seems, however, only to have kept copies of her warlike missives. She asked him to destroy all her letters, and he must have done so, for none survives except this bundle of thirty-seven, of which hers are copies and his only are originals. In her old age the Duchess several times fondled and reread this correspondence. Her own letters are endorsed in her handwriting, "Some coppys of my letters to Mr Churchill before I was married & not more than 15 years old." She left a request that her chief woman-in-waiting, or secretary, Grace Ridley, should after her death be given the letters in order that she might "burn without reading them." There is an endorsement in the quivering hand of age stating that she had read over all these letters in 1736. Finally, the year before her death, "Read over in 1743 desiring to burn them, but I could not doe it."

The reader shall be the judge of the correspondence. The first batch consists entirely of John's letters.

John to Sarah

* My Soul, I love you so truly well that I hope you will be so kind as to let me see you somewhere to-day, since you will not be at Whitehall. I will not name any time, for all hours are alike to me when you will bless me with your sight. You are, and ever shall be, the dear object of my life, for by heavens I will never love anybody but yourself.

* I am just come and have no thought of any joy but that of seeing you. Wherefore I hope you will send me word that you will see me this night.

* My head did ache yesterday to that degree and I was so out of order that nothing should have persuaded me to have gone abroad but the meeting of you who is much dearer than all the world besides to me. If you are not otherwise engaged, I beg you will give me leave to come at eight o'clock.

* I fancy by this time that you are awake, which makes me now send to know how you do, and if your foot will permit you to give me the joy of seeing you in the drawing-room this night. Pray let me hear from you, for when I am not with you, the only joy I have is hearing from you.

* My Soul, it is a cruel thing to be forced in a place when I have no hopes of seeing you, for on my word last night seemed very tedious to me; wherefore I beg you will be so kind to me as to come as often as you can this week, since I am forced to wait [to be in waiting]. I hope you will send me word that you are well and that I shall see you here to-night.

* I did no sooner know that you were not well, but upon my faith without affectation I was also sick. I hope your keeping your bed yesterday and this night has made you perfectly well, which if it has, I beg that I may then have leave to see you to-night at eight, for believe me that it is an age since I was with you. I do love you so well that I have no patience when I have not hopes of seeing my dear angel, wherefore pray send me word that I shall be blessed and come at eight, till when, my Soul, I will do nothing else but think kindly of you.

I hope your sitting up has done you no harm, so that you will see me this afternoon, for upon my soul I do love you with all my heart and take joy in nothing but yourself. I do love you with all the truth imaginable, but have patience but for one week, you shall then see that I will never more do aught that shall look like a fault.

If your happiness can depend upon the esteem and love I have for you, you ought to be the happiest thing breathing, for I have never anybody loved to that height I do you. I love you so well that your happiness I prefer much above my own; and if you think meeting me is what you ought not to do, or that it will disquiet you, I do promise you I will never press you more to do it. As I prefer your happiness above my own, so I hope you will sometimes think how well I love you; and what you can do without doing yourself an injury, I hope you will be so kind as to do it—I mean in letting me see that you wish me better than the rest of mankind; and in return I swear to you that I never will love anything but your dear self, which has made so sure a conquest of me that, had I the will, I have not the power ever to break my chains. Pray let me hear from you, and know if I shall be so happy as to see you to-night.

I was last night at the ball, in hopes to have seen what I love above my own soul, but I was not so happy, for I could see you nowhere, so that I did not stay above an hour. I would have written sooner, but that I was afraid you went to bed so late that it would disturb you.

Pray see which of these two puppies you like best, and that keep; for the bitch cannot let them suck any longer. They are above three weeks old, so that if you give it warm milk it will not die. Pray let me hear from you, and at what time you will be so kind as to let me come to you to-night. Pray, if you have nothing to do, let it be the latest [earliest], for I never am truly happy but when I am with you.

We now see the falling of shadows upon the sunlit path. We cannot tell their cause, whether they come from passing clouds or from some solid obstruction. We do not know the reason, nor even the year. We must realize that these written fragments, luckily preserved, represent only a tiny part of all that happened in nearly a thousand days of two young lives.

* I stayed last night in the drawing-room expecting your coming back, for I could have wished that we had not parted until you had given me hopes of seeing you, for, my soul, there is no pain so great to me, as that when I fear you do not love me; but I hope I shall never live to see you less kind to me than you are. I am sure I will never deserve it, for I will by all that is good love you as long as I live. I beg you will let me see you as often as you can, which I am sure you ought to do if you care for my love, since every time I see you I still find new charms in you; therefore do not be so ill-natured as to believe any lies that may be told you of me, for on my faith I do not only now love you but do desire to do it as long as I live. If you can have time before you go to church, pray let me hear from you.

* I was last night above an hour in the Bedchamber still expecting every one that came in it should be you, but at last I went to Mrs Brownley's, where I found Mrs Mowdie, who told me that you were with your sister, so that you would not be seen that night; so I went to Whitehall to find out the Duke, for when I know that you will not appear I do not care to be at St James's. For 'tis you and you only I care to see, for by all that is good I do with all the truth imaginable love you. Pray let me hear from you, and I beg that I may be blessed this night in being with you. I hope you will like the waistcoat; I do assure you there is not such another to be had in England.

* My Soul, I go with the heaviest heart that ever man did, for by all that is good I love you with all my heart and soul, and I am sure that as long as I live you shall have no just reason to believe the contrary. If you are unkind, I love [you] so well that I cannot live, for you are my life, my soul, my all that I hold dear in this world; therefore do not make so ungrateful a return as not to write. If you have charity you will not only write, but you will write kindly, for it is on you that depends the quiet of my soul. Had I fitting words to express my love, it would not then be in your power to refuse what I beg with tears in my eyes, that you would love me as I will by heavens do you.

To show you how unreasonable you are in accusing me, I dare swear you yourself will own that your going from me in the Duchess's drawing-room did show as much contempt as was possible. I may grieve at it, but I will no more complain when you do it, for I suppose it is what pleases your humour. I cannot imagine what you meant by your saying I laughed at you at the Duke's side, for I was so far from that, that had it not been for shame I could have cried. And

[as] for being in haste to go to the Park, after you went, I stood near a quarter of an hour, I believe, without knowing what I did. Although at Whitehall you told me I should not come, yet I walked twice to the Duke's back-stairs, but there was no Mrs Mowdie; and when I went to my Lord Duras's, I would not go the same way they did but came again down the back-stairs; and when I went away, I did not go in my chair, but made it follow me, because I would see if there was any light in your chamber, but I saw none. Could you see my heart you would not be so cruel as to say I do not love you, for by all that is good I love you and only you. If I may have the happiness of seeing you to-night, pray let me know, and believe that I am never truly pleased but when I am with you.

Thus time slipped by, and ardent courtship must have lasted far into its second year. Sarah's sister Frances, after rejecting so many suitors, royal or honourable, was already married to Lord Hamilton, a man of charm and distinction, but of no great wealth. Sarah, approaching seventeen, was alone. She had chased away her mother, and the man she loved and who loved her so well had not yet spoken the decisive word.

Meanwhile the war continued; but such few records of John Churchill as exist for the years 1675, 1676, and 1677 are conclusive against his having fought any more on the Continent. His name is never mentioned in any of the operations. The regiment which he had formerly commanded, withering for lack of drafts, was incorporated in Monmouth's Royal English regiment in May 1675. It is therefore almost certain that he took no part in this year's campaign either with Turenne or elsewhere.

In August we read of him hastening to Paris. We can but guess at his mission. Since 1673 he had been Gentleman of the Bedchamber to the Duke of York. On August 9, 1675, the French Ambassador in England wrote to Louis XIV describing an interview with James at which the Duke had asked for an immediate subsidy from the French King to free his brother from the need of summoning Parliament. In view of the fact that four years later James was to send Churchill over to Paris to make a similar request for a subsidy, and that he was already well known at Versailles, it is not unlikely that he was sent to Paris to reinforce his master's petition. A warrant showing that in October he had permission to import from France free of duty his silver plate seems to mark the end of his stay abroad. In September 1676 he was a member of a court-martial convened in London to try an officer for an assault on the governor of Plymouth. There is therefore no doubt that he spent these years mainly at Court, and that he was increasingly employed in diplomatic work and at his ordinary duties in the Duke of York's household.

Towards the end of this year the Duke of Monmouth expressed his dissatisfaction with the Lieutenant-Colonel of his Royal English regiment, which was serving with the French Army against the Dutch, and proposed to Louis XIV that the command should be transferred to Churchill. Justin MacCartie, a nephew of the Duke of Ormonde, who when an ensign had accompanied Feversham to the siege of Maestricht, also sought this appointment. Courtin, the French Ambassador, laid the situation before Louvois, together with elaborate and scandalous accounts of John's love-affairs. Louvois replied that Churchill appeared to be too much taken up with the ladies to devote his whole-hearted affection to a regiment. He would give, Louvois said, "more satisfaction to a rich and faded mistress, than to a monarch who did not want to have dishonourable and dishonoured carpet knights in his armies." Courtin, however, considered Churchill a far abler officer than his competitor, and the post was undoubtedly offered him. It was Churchill who refused. "Mr Churchill," reported the Ambassador, whose news was now certainly up to date, "prefers to serve the very pretty sister [Sarah Jennings] of Lady Hamilton than to be lieutenant-colonel in Monmouth's regiment." Mars was quite decidedly set aside for Venus. However, the estrangement was not final.

During the same year, 1676, Sir Winston Churchill and his wife became concerned at the attachment of their son to Sarah Jennings. They did not see how he could make a career for himself unless he married money. To this, with his looks and prowess, he might well aspire. They fixed their eyes upon Catharine Sedley, daughter and heiress of Sir Charles Sedley, a man renowned for his wit and his wealth. Catharine Sedley was also of the household of the Duke of York. She exerted her attractions in her own way, and, though not admired, was both liked and feared. Ultimately, after the parental hopes had failed to unite her to John Churchill, she became, in what seemed almost rotation for the maids of honour, the Duke of York's mistress.

The news of these parental machinations must have been swiftly carried to Sarah. How far, if at all, John lent himself to them, at what point they begin to darken the love-letters, we cannot tell. Certainly the arguments which Sir Winston and his wife could deploy were as serious and matter-of-fact as any which could ever be brought to bear upon a son. We may imagine some of them.

"You have your foot on the ladder of fortune. You have already mounted several important rungs. Every one says you have a great future before you. Every one knows you have not got—apart from the annuity or your pay—a penny behind you. How can you on a mere whim compromise your whole future life? Catharine Sedley is known to be a most agreeable woman. She holds her own in any company. The Duke listens to all she says, and the whole Court laughs at her jests. She is asked everywhere. Women have beauties of mind quite as attractive, except to enamoured youth, as those of body. Sir Charles is a really wealthy man, solid, long-established, with fine houses, broad acres, and failing health. She is his only child. With his fortune and her humour and sagacity behind you, all these anxieties which have gnawed your life, all that poverty which has pursued us since your infancy, would be swept away. You could look any man in the face and your career would be assured.

"Moreover, do you really think this little Jennings could be a companion to you? Although she is only a child, little more than half your age, she has proved herself a spitfire and a termagant. Look at the way she treats you—as if you were a lackey. You have told us enough of your relations with her—and, indeed, it is the talk of the Court—to show that she is just humiliating you, twirling you round her finger for her own glorification. Did she not say only last week to So-and-so how she could make you do this, that, or anything? Even if she had all Catharine's money we would beg you for your peace of mind, with all the experience of the older generation, not to take this foolish step. It would be a decision utterly out of keeping with your character, with your frugal life—never throwing any expense on us, always living within your income—with all your prudence and care for the future. You would be committing a folly, and the one kind of folly we were always sure you would never commit.

"Lastly, think of her. Are you really doing her justice in marrying her? She has come to Court under good protection. She could never hold a candle to her sister, but she may well hope to marry into the peerage. There is the Earl of Lindsay, who could give her a fine position. He is paying her a great deal of attention. Would she ever be happy with love in a cottage? Would she not drag you down and sink with you?" "Believe me, my son, I, your father," Sir Winston might have said, "pillaged by the Roundheads, uprooted from my lands for my loyalty, have had a hard time. I can give nothing to you or your bride but the shelter of my roof at Mintern. You know how we live there. How would she put up with that? We have never been able to do more than hold up our heads. These are rough times. They are not getting better. By yielding to this absurd fancy you will ruin her life as well as your own, and throw a burden upon us which, as you know, we cannot bear. I am to meet Sir Charles next week. He is a great believer in you. He has heard things about you from the French. It is said that among the younger men none is your master in the land service. I never commanded more than a cavalry troop, but you at half my age are almost a general. But are you not throwing away your military career as well?"

How far did John yield to all this? He was no paragon. All around was the corrupt, intriguing Court with its busy marriage market. In those days English parents disposed their children's fortunes much as the French do now. Winston himself had perhaps been betrothed at fourteen or fifteen, and had made a happy, successful family life. We do not believe that John ever weakened in his purpose. Certainly he never wavered in his love. No doubt he weighed with deep anxiety the course which he should take. All the habit of his mind was farsighted. "In the bloom of his youth," says Macaulay, "he loved lucre more than wine or women." However, he loved Sarah more than all. But how were they to live? This was the cold, brutal, commonplace, inexorable question that baffled his judgment and tied his tongue.

Her situation, as she learned about the family negotiations and saw her lover oppressed and abstracted, was cruel. Already, with discerning feminine eye, she had marked him for her own. Now wealth and worldly wisdom were to intervene and snatch him from her. Already barriers seemed to be growing between them, and it was here that the vital truth of her purpose saved all. Weakness on her part in dealing with him might perhaps have been fatal. She maintained towards him a steady, bayonet-bristling front. Between perfect love, absolute unity, and scorn and fury such as few souls are capable of, there was no middle choice. Sometimes, indeed, her ordeal in public was more than she could bear. Scores of peering, knowing eyes were upon her. Her tears were seen at some revel, and the French Ambassador wrote a sneering letter about them for the gossips of Versailles.

* There was a small ball last Friday at the Duchess of York's where Lady Hamilton's sister who is uncommonly good-looking had far more wish to cry than to dance. Churchill who is her suitor says that he is attacked by consumption and must take the air in France. I only wish I were as well as he. The truth is that he wishes to free himself from intrigues. His father urges him to marry one of his relations who is very rich and very ugly, and will not consent to his marriage with Miss Jennings. He is also said to be not a little avaricious and I hear from the various Court ladies that he has pillaged the Duchess of Cleveland, and that she has given him more than the value of 100,000 livres. They make out that it is he who has quitted her and that she has taken herself off in chagrin to France to rearrange her affairs. If Churchill crosses the sea, she will be able to patch things up with him. Meanwhile she writes agreeably to the Duchess of Sussex conjuring her to go with her husband to the country and to follow her advice but not her example.

Thus Courtin. We must make allowance for his own love of scandal, and for the palates he sought to spice: but here, at any rate, we have a definite situation. Courtin's letter is dated November 27, 1676. We see that John's relations with Barbara have ended; that his father is pressing him to marry Catharine Sedley; that he is deeply in love with Sarah, but does not feel justified in his poverty in proposing marriage; that she is indignant at his delay and miserable about the other women and all the uncertainty and the gossip. We see her magnificent in her prolonged ordeal. We see John for the only time in these pages meditating flight from a field the difficulties of which seemed for the moment beyond his sagacious strength. Well is it said that the course of true love never did run smooth. The next chapter will, however, carry the lovers to their hearts' desire.

CHAPTER SEVEN

Marriage

⌖ 1676-78 ⌖

WE now approach the delicate question of how John freed himself from the Duchess of Cleveland. Unquestionably towards the end of 1676 he quitted Barbara for Sarah. Was he "off with the old love before he was on with the new"? Or was it one of those familiar dissolving views, where one picture fades gradually away and the other grows into gleaming, vivid life? Gossip and scandal there is a-plenty; evidence there is none. Of course, a married woman separated from her husband, unfaithful to him, notoriously licentious, who has a young man in the twenties as her lover, must expect that a time will come when her gay companion will turn serious, when all the charms and pleasures she can bestow will pall and cloy, and when he will obey the mysterious command of a man's spirit to unite himself for ever, by every tie which nature and faith can proffer, to a being all his own. But Barbara took it very ill, and after a brief attempt to console herself with Wycherley, the playwright, she withdrew from England altogether and took up her abode in Paris. Here she became intimate with Montagu, the English Ambassador to Paris, with results which after a while emerged upon the stage of history.

Let us turn to the love-letters, which plead John's cause to posterity, as well as to Sarah. The deadlock in their affairs continued, and she rightly challenged him to end it or to leave her.

MARRIAGE

Sarah to John

If it were true that you have that passion for me which you say you have, you would find out some way to make yourself happy—it is in your power. Therefore press me no more to see you, since it is what I cannot in honour approve of, and if I have done too much, be so just as to consider who was the cause of it.

John to Sarah

As for the power you say you have over yourself, I do no ways at all doubt of it, for I swear to you I do not think you love me, so that I am very easily persuaded that my letters have no charms for you, since I am so much a slave to your charms as to own to you that I love you above my own life, which by all that is holy I do. You must give me leave to beg that you will not condemn me for a vain fool that I did believe you did love me, since both you and your actions did oblige me to that belief in which heaven knows I took so much joy that from henceforward my life must be a torment to me for it. You say I pretend a passion to you when I have other things in my head. I cannot imagine what you mean by it, for I vow to God you do so entirely possess my thoughts that I think of nothing else in this world but your dear self. I do not, by all that is good, say this that I think it will move you to pity me, for I do despair of your love; but it is to let you see how unjust you are, and that I must ever love you as long as I have breath, do what you will. I do not expect in return that you should either write or speak to me, since you think it is what may do you a prejudice; but I have a thing to beg which I hope you will not be so barbarous as to deny me. It is that you will give me leave to do what I cannot help, which is to adore you as long as I live, and in return I will study how I may deserve, although not have, your love. I am persuaded that I have said impertinent things enough to anger you, for which I do with all my heart beg your pardon, and do assure you that from henceforward I will approach and think of you with the same devotion as to my God.

John to Sarah

You complain of my unkindness, but would not be kind yourself in answering my letter, although I begged you to do it. The Duchess goes to a new play to-day, and afterwards to the Duchess of Monmouth's, there to dance. I desire that you will not go thither, but make an excuse, and give me leave to come to you. Pray let me know what you do intend, and if you go to the play; for if you do, then I will do what I can to go, if [although] the Duke does not. Your not writing to me made me very uneasy, for I was afraid it was want of kindness in you, which I am sure I will never deserve by any action of mine.

Sarah to John

As for seeing you I am resolved I never will in private nor in public if I could help it. As for the last I fear it will be some time before I can order so as to be out of your way of seeing me. But surely you must confess that you have been the falsest creature upon earth to me. I must own that I believe that I shall suffer a great deal of trouble, but I will bear it, and give God thanks, though too late I see my error.

Here the door is firmly closed, and then opened with a chink again.

John to Sarah

It is not reasonable that you should have a doubt but that I love you above all expression, which by heaven I do. It is not possible to do anything to let you see your power more than my obedience to your commands of leaving you, when my tyrant-heart aches me to make me disobey; but it were much better it should break than to displease you. I will not, dearest, ask or hope to hear from you unless your charity pities me and will so far plead for me as to tell you that a man dying for you may hope that you will be so kind to him as to make a distinction betwixt him and the rest of his sex. I do love and adore you with all my heart and soul—so much that by all that is good I do and ever will be better pleased with your happiness than my own; but oh, my soul, if we might be both happy, what inexpressible joy would that be! But I will not think of any content but what you shall think fit to give, for 'tis you alone I love, so that if you are kind but one minute, that will make me happier than all the world can besides. I will not dare to expect more favour than you shall think fit to give, but could you ever love me, I think the happiness would be so great that it would make me immortal.

MARRIAGE

Sarah to John

I am as little satisfied with this letter as I have been with many others, for I find all you will say is only to amuse me and make me think you have a passion for me, when in reality there is no such thing. You have reason to think it strange that I write to you after my last, where I protested that I would never write nor speak to you more; but as you know how much kindness I had for you, you can't wonder or blame me if I try once more, to hear what you can say for your justification. But this I must warn you of—that you don't hold disputes, as you have done always, and to keep me from answering of you, and yourself from saying what I expect from you, for if you go on in that manner I will leave you that moment, and never hear you speak more whilst I have life. Therefore pray consider if, with honour to me and satisfaction to yourself, I can see you; for if it be only to repeat those things which you said so oft, I shall think you the worst of men, and the most ungrateful; and 'tis to no purpose to imagine that I will be made ridiculous in the world when it is in your power to make me otherwise.

John to Sarah

I have been so extreme ill with the headache all this morning that I have not had courage to write to know how you do; but your being well is what I prefer much above my own health. Therefore pray send me word, for if you are not in pain I cannot then be much troubled, for were it not for the joy I take in the thought that you love me, I should not care how soon I died; for by all that is good I love you so well that I wish from my soul that that minute that you leave loving me, that I may die, for life after that would be to me but one perpetual torment. If the Duchess sees company, I hope you will be there; but if she does not, I beg you will then let me see you in your chamber, if it be but for one hour. If you are not in the drawing-room, you must then send me word at what hour I shall come.

Sarah to John

At four o'clock I would see you, but that would hinder you from seeing the play, which I fear would be a great affliction to you, and increase the pain in your head, which would be out of anybody's power to ease until the next new play. Therefore, pray consider, and without any compliment to me, send me word if you can come to me without any prejudice to your health.

This unkind sarcasm drew probably the only resentful reply which John ever penned in all his correspondence with Sarah. The letter does not exist; but we can judge its character by his covering note to her waiting-woman, whose support he had doubtless enlisted.

Colonel John Churchill to Mrs Elizabeth Mowdie

Your mistress's usage to me is so barbarous that sure she must be the worst woman in the world, or else she would not be thus ill-natured. I have sent a letter which I desire you will give her. It is very reasonable for her to take it, because it will be then in her power never to be troubled with me more, if she pleases. I do love her with all my soul, but will not trouble her, for if I cannot have her love, I shall despise her pity. For the sake of what she has already done, let her read my letter and answer it, and not use me thus like a footman.

This was the climax of the correspondence. Sarah's response shows that she realized how deeply he was distressed and how critical their relations had become. She held out an offended hand, and he made haste to clasp it. Some days evidently passed before he wrote again, and this time his rebellious mood had vanished.

Sarah to John

I have done nothing to deserve such a kind of letter as you have writ to me, and therefore I don't know what answer to give; but I find you have a very ill opinion of me, and therefore I can't help being angry with myself for having had too good a one of you; for if I had as little love as yourself, I have been told enough of you to make me hate you, and then I believe I should have been more happy than I am like to be now. However, if you can be so well contented never to see me as I think you can by what you say, I will believe you; though I have not other people; and after you are satisfied that I have not broke my word, you shall have it in your power to see me or not—and if you are contented without it I shall be extremely pleased.

MARRIAGE

John to Sarah

It would have been much kinder in you, if you had been pleased to have been so good-natured to have found time to have written to me yesterday, especially since you are resolved not to appear when I might see you. But I am resolved to take nothing ill but to be your slave as long as I live, and so to think all things well that you do.

This was the only surrender to which the Duke of Marlborough was ever forced. It was to the fan of a chit of seventeen. Moreover, so far as we have been able to ascertain, his courtship of Sarah affords the only occasions in his life of hazards and heart-shaking ordeals when he was ever frightened. Neither the heat of battle nor the long-drawn anxieties of conspiracy, neither the unsanctioned responsibilities of the march to the Danube nor the tortuous secret negotiations with the Jacobite Court, ever disturbed the poise of that calm, reasonable, resolute mind. But in this love-story we see him plainly panic-stricken. The terror that he and Sarah might miss one another, might drift apart, might pass and sail away like ships in the night, overpowered him. A man who cared less could have played this game of love with the sprightly Sarah much better than he. A little calculation, a little adroitness, some studied withdrawals, some counter-flirtation, all these were the arts which in every other field he used with innate skill. He has none of them now. He begs and prays with bald, homely, pitiful reiteration. We see the power of the light which sometimes shines upon the soul. These two belonged to one another, and, with all their faults, placarded as we know them, their union was true as few things of which we have experience here are true. And at this moment in the depth of his spirit, with the urge of uncounted generations pressing forward, he feared lest it might be cast away.

We now reach at least the year 1677, and with it the final phase of the correspondence. It seems plain that they are engaged. The difficulties that remain are only those of time and means. He writes of an interview with his father, of the importance of Sarah not angering the Duchess of York, and of business arrangements for their future.

Frances, Lady Hamilton, had now arrived upon the scene, and Sarah seems to have threatened him with plans for going abroad with her.

John to Sarah

When I writ to you last night I thought I writ to the one that loved me; but your unkind, indifferent letter this morning confirms me of what I have before been afraid of, which is that your sister can govern your passion as she pleases. My heart is ready to break. I wish 'twere over, for since you are grown so indifferent, death is the only thing that can ease me. If that the Duchess could not have effected this, I was resolved to have made another proposal to her, which I am confident she might have effected, but it would not have brought so much money as this. But now I must think no more on it, since you say we cannot be happy. If they should do the first I wish with all my soul that my fortune had been so considerable as that it might have made you happier than your going out with your sister to France will do; for I know 'tis the joy you propose in that, that makes you think me faulty. I do, and must as long as I live, love you to distraction, but would not, to make myself the happiest man breathing, press you to ought that you think will make you unhappy. Madame, methinks it is no unreasonable request to beg to see you in your chamber to-night. Pray let me hear presently two words, and say I shall; and, in return, I swear to you if you command my death I will die.

One by one, as in a methodical siege, he had removed the obstacles which had barred the way. He had put aside his military prospects. Barbara was gone. Catharine was gone. The parents, still perhaps protesting, had given way. Evidently he had now in sight some means of livelihood sufficient for him and Sarah. Even now she did not soften her hectoring tone. But everything was settled.

Sarah to John

If your intentions are honourable, and what I have reason to expect, you need not fear my sister's coming can make any change in me, or that it is in the power of anybody to alter me but yourself, and I am at this time satisfied that you will never do anything out of reason, which you must do if you ever are untrue to me.

Sarah to John

I have made many reflections upon what you said to me last night, and I am of the opinion that could the Duchess obtain what you ask her, you might be more unhappy than if it cannot be had. Therefore, as I have always shown more kindness for you than perhaps I ought, I am resolved to give you one mark more—and that is, to desire you to say nothing of it to the Duchess upon my account; and your own interest when I am not concerned in it, will probably compass what will make you much happier than this can ever do.

We now come to the marriage. No one knows exactly or for certain when or where it took place. For several months it was kept secret. That poverty rather than parental opposition was the cause is proved by a remarkable fact. John's grandfather had strictly entailed his estates, and Sir Winston was only tenant for life. He was heavily in debt, and was now forced to appeal to his son for help. Just at the moment when some assured prospects were most necessary to his heart's desire, John was asked to surrender his inheritance. He did so for his father's sake. Part of the property was realized, and Sir Winston's debts were paid. At his death the remnant went to the other children. John, therefore, by his own act disinherited himself. This was a singular example of filial duty in a young man desperately in love and longing to marry.

He could not keep his wife in any suitable conditions at the Court. Once the marriage was announced all sorts of things would be expected. Mary of Modena, "the Dutchesse" of the letters, was the good fairy. She was the partisan of this love-match; she used all her power to help the lovers. Evidently something had to be done to provide them with some means of living. Although Sarah had expectations, and John had his pay and, of course, his £500 a year, "the infamous wages," these were very small resources for the world in which they lived. The future Queen threw herself into the marriage, and her generous, feminine, and romantic instincts were stirred. "None but the brave," she might well have exclaimed, "deserves the fair." We have seen in the letters traces of various plans which the Duchess favoured or tried to order to make some provision for the lovers. We do not know what arrangements were made. Something, at any rate, was assured. Some time in the winter of 1677–78, probably in Mary of Modena's apartments, the sacred words were pronounced, and John and Sarah were man and wife. There is a strong local tradition at Newsells Park, Royston, Hertfordshire, then in the possession of a branch of the Jennings family, that the dining-room had been specially built for the festivities of Sarah Jennings' marriage. Probably they passed their honeymoon here.

After nearly a quarter of a century of married life Churchill, sailing for the wars from Margate quay, wrote to his wife:

> It is impossible to express with what a heavy heart I parted with you when I was at the waterside. I could have given my life to have come back, though I knew my own weakness so much I durst not, for I should have exposed myself to the company. I did for a great while have a perspective glass looking upon the cliffs in hopes I might have had one sight of you.

Sarah, in a letter certainly later than 1689, and probably when he was in the Tower, wrote:

> Wherever you are, whilst I have life, my soul shall follow you, my ever dear Lord Marl and wherever I am I should only kill the time wishing for night that I may sleep and hope the next day to hear from you.

Finally when, after his death, her hand was sought by the Duke of Somerset:

> If I were young and handsome as I was, instead of old and faded as I am, and you could lay the empire of the world at my feet, you should never share the heart and hand that once belonged to John, Duke of Marlborough.

These are tremendous facts, lifting the relations of men and women above the human scene with all its faults and cares. They rekindle in every generous bosom the hope that things may happen here in the life of the humblest mortals which roll round the universe and win everlasting sanction

> Above Time's troubled fountains
> On the great Atlantic mountains,
> In my golden house on high.

Mrs Manley, the French Ambassador Courtin, and other scurrilous writers have dwelt upon the enormous wealth which John had extracted from the Duchess of Cleveland. However, it was five years after he had married the girl he loved before he could buy her a house of his own. They shifted from one place to another according as his duties or employment led him. They followed the Duke or the drum. For five years Churchill kept on his bachelor lodgings in Germaine Street (Jermyn Street), five doors off St James's Street, and here they stayed during their rare visits to town. Meanwhile at first she lived at Mintern with Sir Winston and his wife, both now getting on in years and increasingly impoverished.

It must have been a very sharp descent for the glittering blade, lover of the King's mistress, daring Colonel of England and France, and friend or rival of the highest in the land, and for the much-sought-after Sarah, to come down to the prosaic, exacting necessities of family life. However, they loved each other well enough not to worry too much about external things. This was a strange beginning for the life of a man who "in the bloom of youth loved lucre more than wine or women."

CHAPTER EIGHT

The Unseen Rift

ᘒ 1679-82 ᘓ

THIS chapter is gloomy for our tale. While the French power grew and overhung Europe, the political and religious storms which raged in England from 1679 to 1683 concentrated their fury upon the Duke of York. His change of religion seemed to be the origin of the evils that had fallen upon the realm. There was impatience with individual conscientious processes which disturbed the lives of millions of people. That one man should have it in his power, even from the most respectable of motives, to involve so many others in distress and throw the whole nation into disorder, weighed heavily on the minds of responsible people. Even the most faithful servants of the King, the most convinced exponents of Divine Right, looked upon James with resentment. They saw in him the prime cause of the dangers and difficulties which his loving royal brother had to bear. There he was, a public nuisance, the Papist heir whose bigotry and obstinacy were shaking the throne. His isolation became marked; the circle about him narrowed severely. Forced into exile in Belgium and now to be marooned in Scotland, his lot was cast in dismal years. With all the strength and obstinacy of his nature he retorted scorn and anger upon his innumerable foes—the subjects he hoped to rule. The ordeal left a definite and ineffaceable imprint upon his character. He felt some of the glories of martyrdom. Henceforward he would dare all and inflict all for the faith that was in him.

It was in the household of this threatened, harassed, and indignant Prince that the first four or five years of the married life of John and

Sarah were to lie. The wars had stopped, and with them for John not only pay and promotion, but all chance to use that military gift of which he had become conscious. He must follow a master, united to him by many ties, but a man unlovable, from whom his whole outlook and nature diverged—nay, if the truth be told, recoiled; a master who was at times an outcast, and whose public odium his personal servants to some extent shared. Between him and that master opened the almost unbridgeable gulf which separated Protestant and Catholic. Faithful and skilful were the services which Churchill rendered to James. Many a secret or delicate negotiation with the French King or with Charles II and the Court or with English political parties was entrusted to the discreet and persuasive henchman. The invaluable character of these services and the sense of having been his patron from boyhood onwards were the bonds which held James to him. But no services, however zealous and successful, could fill the hiatus between contrary religions.

However, the joys and responsibilities of the early years of married life redeemed for John and Sarah their harsh, anxious, and disturbed surroundings. They had in their family life an inner circle of their own, against which the difficulties of the Duke's household and the nation-wide hostility with which that household was regarded, might beat in vain.

John's earnest wish was to return from Scotland to England to see his wife and baby. His hopes of coming south were not ill-founded, for on January 29, 1680, Charles sent a welcome command to his brother to return. James lost no time in taking leave of his Scottish Government, and at the end of February transported himself and his household in the royal yachts from Leith to Deptford.

Churchill on the eve of the voyage begged his wife to

> pray for fair winds, so that we may not stay here, nor be long at sea, for should we be long at sea, and very sick, I am afraid it would do me great hurt, for really I am not well, for in my whole lifetime I never had so long a fit of headaching as now: I hope all the red spots of the child will be gone against I see her, and her nose straight, so that I may fancy it be like the Mother, for as she has your coloured hair, so I would have her be like you in all things else.

The family were united in Jermyn Street in the beginning of March, and John saw his child for the first time. We do not know how long the infant lived. It may well be that the sorrow of her death came upon them almost as soon as they were together again.

James spent the summer of 1680 in England, and hoped, with the King, that the new Parliament summoned for October might be more tolerant to him. He favoured Churchill's fitness to be Ambassador either to France or to Holland. In the latter case he was warmly seconded by William. Barillon's account of May 20, 1680, may serve.

> Mr Sidney [the English Minister at The Hague] will come home soon. It is believed he will not return and I am told that Mr Churchill [*le sieur Chercheil*] may well succeed him. If this is done, it will be to satisfy the Duke of York and to reassure him on all possible negotiations with the Prince of Orange. He [James] distrusts Mr Sidney, and has hated him for a long time. Mr Churchill on the contrary has the entire confidence of his master, as your Majesty could see when he had the honour of presenting himself to you last year. He is not a man who has any experience of affairs. It is also said that the Prince of Orange has declared that there should be no other Ambassador of England in Holland but him, and that it is only necessary to send docile personages who let themselves be led.

But all these hopes and projects, real or shadowy, came to naught. The new Parliament was fiercer than its predecessor. Shaftesbury was at the head of a flaming Opposition. A fresh Exclusion Bill advanced by leaps and bounds. The ferocity of the Whigs knew no limit, and their turpitude lay not far behind. Their cause was the cause of England, and is the dominant theme of this tale. Their conduct was sullied by corruption and double-dealing unusual even in that age. Their leaders without exception all took for either personal or party purposes French gold, while they shouted against Papist intrigues and denounced all arrangements with France. Upon this squalid scene Louis XIV gloated with cynical eyes. His agent Barillon, presiding over the dizzy whirlpools of Westminster and Whitehall, bribed both sides judiciously to maintain the faction fight. Thus Louis stoked the fires which burned away the English strength.

One name is conspicuous in its absence from the lists of shame— Churchill's. Yet how glad Barillon would have been to have slipped a thousand guineas into the palm of this needy Colonel and struggling family man! The artful Ambassador, as we see by his correspondence, was no friend to John. Any tittle of spiteful gossip or depreciatory opinion which he could gather he sedulously reported. Churchill, this influential, ubiquitous go-between, the Protestant agent of the Duke of York, was well worth tainting, even if he could not be squared. Sarah long afterwards wrote, "The Duke of Marlborough never took a bribe." Think how these lists have been scanned by the eyes of Marlborough's detractors. See how every scrap of fouling evidence has been paraded and exploited. Yet nothing has been found to challenge Sarah's assertion.

The approaching assembly of this hostile Parliament was sufficient to force the King again to expatriate the brother of whom he was so fond. On October 20 James and his household most reluctantly again set out by sea for Edinburgh. This time both the Churchills could go together. They endured a rough voyage of five days. James was received in Scotland with due ceremony; but the famous cannon known as 'Mons Meg' burst in firing its salute, and many were the superstitious head-waggings which followed the occurrence. This time James seriously undertook the government of Scotland, and set his seal upon a melancholy epoch.

Now, embittered by ill-usage, emboldened by anger, his thorough-going temperament led him to support the strongest assertions of authority. When, in June 1681, Churchill brought him from London his patent as Royal Commissioner he decided to make use of the Scottish Parliament to obtain an emphatic and untrammelled assertion of his right of succession. He summoned the first Parliament held in Scotland since 1673. He set himself to demonstrate here on a minor scale the policy which he thought his brother should follow in England. He passed through the Parliament of 1681 an anti-Exclusion Bill. He developed with care the anti-national Scottish army. He used the wild Highlanders, the only Catholics available, to suppress the contumacy of the Lowlanders. The torture of the boot was inflicted freely upon Covenanters and persons of obstinate religious opinions. On these occasions most of the high personages upon the Privy Council would make some excuse to leave the room. But accusing pens allege that the Duke of York was always at his post. Dark and hateful days for Scotland!

Churchill, apart from his aversion from cruelties of all kinds, was now placed in a most difficult and delicate position. James relied on him to make every effort to secure his return to Court, and to support his claims against Monmouth and the Exclusionists; while, on the other hand, Churchill's powerful friends in London, Sunderland, Halifax, Godolphin, and Hyde, told him to keep James in Scotland at all costs. Amid these conflicting currents no man was more capable of steering a shrewd and sensible course. He carried out his instructions from James with proper diligence and discretion; but, on the other hand, his cautious temper prevented the wilder threats of his master (about raising the Scots or the Irish in his own defence) from being "attended with consequences"; for he "frankly owned" to the French Ambassador that James "was not in a condition to maintain himself in Scotland, if the King his brother did not support him there."

In August 1681 the Duke of York's affairs in England were going from bad to worse, and the King was in desperate grapple with his brother's pursuers. An intense effort was concerted to persuade James to conform at least in outward semblance to the religion of his future subjects. His appeals to be recalled to England were made use of against him. The King offered to allow him to return if he would but come to church. Every one could see what a simplification his assent would make; and what a boon to all! His first wife's brother, Laurence Hyde, afterwards Earl of Rochester, was entrusted with the difficult task of his conversion to conformity, upon which the strongest family, social, and State pressures were engaged. Hyde, Churchill, and Legge were James's three most intimate personal servants. They had been with him for many years. His partiality for them had long been proved. Legge was absent, but we cannot doubt that Churchill supported Hyde with any influence he could command. Nothing availed. James was advised by his confessor that there could be no paltering with heresy. Such advice was decisive.

This incident deserves prominence because it evoked from Churchill one of those very rare disclosures of his political-religious convictions in this period which survive. He wrote to Legge the following letter:

Sept. 12, 1681, Berwick

Dear Cousin,

I should make you both excuses and compliments for the trouble you have been at in sending my wife to me, but I hope it is not that time of day between you and I, for without compliment as long as I live I will be your friend and servant. My Lord Hyde, who is the best man living, will give you an account of all that has passed. You will find that nothing is done in what was so much desired, *so that sooner or later we must be all undone.* As soon as Lewen has his papers the Duke would have [wish to] take the first opportunity by sea and come from Scotland. My heart is very full, so that should I write to you of the sad prospect I fear we have, I should tire your patience; therefore I refer myself wholly to my Lord Hyde and assure you that wherever I am, you and my Lord Hyde have a faithful servant of [in] me.

This letter, written so secretly to his intimate friend and kinsman seven years before the revolution of 1688, must not be forgotten in the unfolding of our story.

On December 12, 1681, the somewhat lackadaisical ninth Earl of Argyll was brought to trial for treason for explaining that he took the Oath of Allegiance "as far as it was consistent with the Protestant religion," and "not repugnant to it or his loyalty." By the authority of James he was condemned to death. On the eve of his execution he escaped by a romantic artifice and for a time lay hidden in London. When the news of his refuge was brought to the King by officious spies, the tolerant Charles brushed them away with the remark, "Pooh, pooh, a hunted partridge!" His brother had a different outlook.

Churchill had deplored Argyll's sentence. He wrote to Sir John Werden, the Duke of York's secretary, and told him he hoped on account of their old friendship that Argyll would receive no punishment; and he wrote to George Legge that he trusted Argyll's escape from prison would be looked on as a thing of no great consequence.

The leaders of Scottish society were not men of half-measures. Affronted to the core by the ill-usage of their country as it continued year after year, they devoted their lives to practical schemes of vengeance, and they turned resolutely to the Prince of Orange. The flower of the Scottish nobility emigrated to Holland with deep, bitter intent to return sword in hand. All became unrelenting enemies of the House of Stuart. In the revolution of 1688 Lowland Scotland swung to William as one man.

In 1682 the long-sought permission to come to London was granted. James, with a considerable retinue of nobles and servants, embarked in the frigate *Gloucester* on May 4, 1682, to wind up his affairs in Scotland and bring his household home.

The catastrophe which followed very nearly brought this and many important tales to an end. But another revealing beam of light is thrown by it upon Churchill's attitude towards his master. The royal vessel was accompanied by a small squadron and several yachts, on one of which was Samuel Pepys himself. Two days out the *Gloucester* grounded in the night upon a dangerous sandbank three miles off Cromer, on the Norfolk coast, known as the 'Lemon and Ore.' After about an hour she slipped off the bank and foundered almost immediately in deep water. Although the sea was calm and several ships lay in close company, scarcely forty were saved out of the three hundred souls on board.

Numerous detailed and incompatible accounts of this disaster from its survivors and spectators have been given. Some extol the Duke of York's composure, his seamanship, his resolute efforts to save the vessel, and the discipline and devotion of the sailors, who, though about to drown, cheered as they watched him row away. Others dwell on the needless and fatal delays in abandoning the ship, on the confusion which prevailed, on the ugly rushes made for the only available boat, and finally portray James going off with his priests, his dogs, and a handful of close personal friends in the longboat, which "might well have held fifty," leaving the rest to perish miserably. Catholic and Tory writers, naturally enough, incline to the former version, and Protestants and Whigs to the latter. We have no concern with the merits of the controversy. What is important is Churchill's view of it. He, like Legge, was one of the favoured few invited into the boat by James, and to that he owed his life. One would therefore have expected that he would instinctively have taken the side of his master and, in a sense, rescuer, and would have judged his actions by the most lenient standards. Instead, he appears to have been the sternest critic. Sixty years later Sarah, in her illuminating comments on Lediard's history, writes as follows:

* Since my last account of Mr Lediard's Book, I have read the account of the shipwreck of the *Gloucester* (page 40). The Truth of which I had as soon as the Duke [of Marlborough] came to Scotland from his own Mouth: (for I was there) who blamed the Duke [of York] to me excessively for his Obstinacy and Cruelty. For if he would have been persuaded to go off himself at first, when it was certain the Ship could not be saved, the Duke of Marlborough was of

the Opinion that there would not have been a Man lost. For tho'
there was not Boats enough to carry them all away, all those he men-
tions that were drowned were lost by the Duke's obstinacy in not
coming away sooner; And that was occasioned by a false courage to
make it appear, as he thought he had what he had not; By which he
was the occasion of losing so many Lives. But when his own was in
danger, and there was no hope of saving any but those that were
with Him, he gave the Duke of Marlborough his Sword to hinder
Numbers of People that to save their own Lives would have jumped
into the Boat, notwithstanding his Royal Highness was there, that
would have sunk it. This was done, and the Duke went off safe; and
all the rest in the Ship were lost, as Mr Lediard gives an account, except my Lord Griffin, who had served the Duke long, who, when the
Ship was sinking, threw himself out of a Window, and saved himself
by catching hold of a Hen Coop. . . . All that Lediard relates to fill-
ing the boat with the priests and the dogs is true. But I don't know
who else went in the boat or whether they were of the same religion.

There can be no doubt that this is the real story which John told Sarah
in the deepest secrecy as soon as he and the other woebegone survivors
from the shipwreck arrived in Edinburgh. That no inkling of his servant's opinion ever came to James seems almost certain. We in this
afterlight can see quite plainly where the Churchills stood in relation·
to James. It is not merely want of sympathy, but deep disapproval.
They served him because it was their duty and their livelihood. He
retained them because better servants could not be found elsewhere.
But all this lay far below the surface. The whole ducal household arrived at Whitehall, for good or ill, in the summer of 1682, and
Churchill was rewarded on December 21, 1682, for his patient, astute
diplomacy and invaluable services of the past three years with the
barony of Churchill of Aymouth, in the peerage of Scotland, and the
command of the second troop of the Life Guards.

CHAPTER NINE

The Princess Anne

ᚦᚲ 1679-85 ᚦᚲ

FEW stories in our history are more politically instructive than the five years' pitiless duel between King Charles II and his ex-Minister Shaftesbury. The opposing forces were diversely composed, yet, as it proved, evenly balanced; the ground was varied and uncertain; the conditions of the combat were peculiarly English, the changes of fortune swift and unforeseeable, the issues profound and the stakes mortal. For the first three years Shaftesbury seemed to march with growing violence from strength to strength. Three separate Parliaments declared themselves with ever-rising spirit for his cause. London, its wealth, its magistrates, its juries, and its mob, were resolute behind him. Far and wide throughout the counties and towns of England the fear of "Popery and Slavery" dominated all other feelings and united under the leadership of the great Whig nobles almost all the sects and factions of the Centre and of the Left, as they had never been united even at the height of the Great Rebellion. Thus sustained, Shaftesbury set no limits to his aims or conduct. He exploited to the last ounce alike the treacheries of Montagu and the perjuries of Oates. He watched with ruthless eye a succession of innocent men, culminating in Lord Stafford, sent to their deaths on the scaffold or at Tyburn upon false testimony. He held high parley with the King, as if from power to power, demanded the handing over of Portsmouth and Hull to officers approved by Parliament, indicted the Duke of York before a London Grand Jury as a Popish recusant, threatened articles of impeachment against the Queen, and made every preparation in his power for an eventual resort to arms. This was the same Shaftesbury who, as a Minister in the Cabal, had acquiesced only four years before in the general policy of the Secret Treaty of Dover, and only two years before had been a party to the Declaration of Indulgence—which in the name of toleration gave to Catholics the freedom they were denying to Protestants in every country where they were in the ascendant—and the acceptance of subsidies from France.

The King, on the other hand, seemed during the first three years to be almost defenceless. His weakness was visible to all. He was forced to leave Danby, his faithful agent, for whose actions he had assumed all possible responsibility, whom he had covered with his royal pardon, to languish for five years in the Tower. He dared not disown the suborned or perjured Crown witnesses brought forward in his name to prove a Popish plot, nor shield with his prerogative of mercy their doomed victims. He had to suffer the humiliation of banishing his brother and the insult of hearing his Queen accused of plotting his murder. He had to submit to, or perhaps even connive at his beloved son Monmouth joining the leaders of his foes.

All the while he lay in his voluptuous, glittering Court, with his expensive mistresses and anxious courtiers, dependent upon the dear-bought gold of France. And meanwhile behind the wrathful proceedings of justly offended faction-fanned Parliaments, Puritan England was scandalized, Cromwellians who had charged at Marston Moor or Naseby prayed that old days might come again, and the common people were taught to believe that the Great Plague and Fire had fallen upon the land as God's punishment for the wickedness of its ruler. Vulnerable in the last degree, conscious of his peril, and yet superb in patient courage, the profound, imperturbable, and crafty politician who wore the challenged crown endured the fury of the storm and awaited its climax. And in the end triumph! Triumph in a completeness and suddenness which seemed incredible to friends and enemies alike.

The turning-point of the conflict was the King's sudden dissolution of the Parliament of 1680. After the third election both Houses were convened at Oxford in March 1681, to avoid the violent pressures which the citizens, apprentices, and the mass of London could exert. Shaftesbury, after the Royal Speech, handed the King what was virtually an ultimatum in favour of the succession of Monmouth. "My lord, as I grow older I grow more steadfast," replied the King. Confronted with the attitude of the assembly, and finding that Oxford was a camp of armed bands whom a word might set at each other's throats, Charles proclaimed the dissolution, and lost no time in withdrawing under strong escort to Windsor.

Stripped of their Parliamentary engines, the Whigs turned to conspiracy, and beneath conspiracy grew murder. Their declared purpose to exclude James from the succession broadened among many into naked republicanism. "Any design but a commonwealth," said Shaftesbury to Lord Howard, "would not go down with my supporters now." There can be no doubt that schemes and even preparations for an armed national rising were afoot; nor that some of the greatest Parliamentary personages were active in them. Behind the machinations of the famous Whig leaders darker and even more violent forces stirred. Rumbold and other grim Cromwellian figures stalked the streets of London. A design to assassinate the King and the Duke where the road from Newmarket passed Rumbold's home, the Rye House, was discussed, and to some extent concerted, by a group of plotters in a London tavern. But while projects, general and particular, germinated in the soil, the mood of the nation gradually but decisively changed; its anti-Catholic rage had exhausted itself in the shedding of innocent blood, and public sympathy gradually turned to the sufferers and against their loud-mouthed, hard-swearing, vainglorious, implacable pursuers.

By 1683 the King was as safe on his throne as on the morrow of his coronation, nearly a quarter of a century before. He had come through an ordeal which few British sovereigns, certainly neither his father nor his brother, could have survived. For all his cynicism and apparent indolence and levity he had preserved the hereditary principle of the monarchy and its prerogative inviolate. He had successfully defended his brother's right to the throne; he had championed the honour of his Queen; he had obtained a more complete control of the national and municipal organs of government and of the judiciary than had existed since the days of his grandfather. He had never lost the support of the Episcopacy. He was poor, he was a pensioner of France, he was powerless on the Continent; but as long as he avoided the expenses of a foreign war he was master in his own house.

The next three years, 1683–85, form an interlude of peace and domestic sunshine in John Churchill's anxious, toilsome, exciting life. He was reabsorbed into the heart and centre of the Court he knew so well, and in which he had lived from childhood. He enjoyed the accustomed intimate favour of the King and the Duke. We read of his being one of Charles's two or three regular tennis partners—with Godolphin and Feversham, "all so excellent players that if one beat the other 'tis alternatively"—and of accompanying the royal party on various progresses or excursions. He was promoted to the colonelcy of the King's Own regiment of Dragoons. This improved the family income, but gave rise to jealous carpings.

> Let's cut our meat with spoons!
>   The sense is as good
>   As that Churchill should
> Be put to command the Dragoons.

The appointment was, however, not ill justified by events. Otherwise no important office or employment fell to his lot. It was perhaps the only easy, care-free time he ever had. No tortuous channels to thread, no intricate combinations to adjust, no doubtful, harassing, dire choices to take! Peace and, if not plenty, a competence. But as the dangers of the State and the need for action or manoeuvre ceased, he subsided into the agreeable obscurities of home and social life. Charles seems to have regarded him as a well-liked courtier and companion whom he had long been used to have about him, as a military officer of a certain standing, as a discreet, attractive, experienced figure, a cherished piece of furniture in the royal household, but not at this time at all considered in the larger sphere of public affairs. Indeed, when he heard Churchill's name mentioned as one who might be Sunderland's Ministerial colleague the King said lightly that "he was not resolved to have two idle Secretaries of State." The Court subsequently explained the rumour by cheerfully affirming that Churchill had lately been "learning to write." So all was calm and quiet, and far better than those wearing years of journeyings to and from The Hague or Edinburgh to London on errands of delicacy or distress.

John could now live a great deal with his wife. He was even able upon the pay and perquisites of Colonel of the Dragoons and Colonel of a troop of Life Guards—the latter a lucrative appointment—to settle in the country. For the first time they had a home.

The Jennings family owned an old house and a few acres close to St

Albans, on the opposite side of the town to their manor of Sandridge. It was called Holywell House on account of a well in which the nuns of Sopwell had softened their hard bread in bygone times. It stood on the road close to the bridge over the river Ver. About 1681 John seems to have bought out Frances' share in this small property, which, together with the manor of Sandridge, was then owned by the two sisters. Evidently Sarah was attached to her native town and family lands. Some time in 1684 she and her husband pulled down the old house, which was ill situated, and built themselves a modest dwelling in another part of the grounds, surrounded by well-laid-out gardens and furnished with a fine fishpond. Here was Marlborough's home for life. The pomp and magnificence of Blenheim Palace were for his posterity. Indeed, he seems to have been somewhat indifferent to the noble monument which the nation reared in honour of his victories. It was Holywell House that claimed his affections. Within it he gathered the pictures and treasures which he steadily collected, and upon its pediment in later life he portrayed the trophies of his battles. Here it was he lived with Sarah and his children whenever he could escape from Court or service. It was to this scene, as his letters show, with its ripening fruit and maturing trees, that his thoughts returned in the long campaigns, and here the main happiness of his life was enjoyed.

Meanwhile their family grew. Poor "Hariote" was gone, but another daughter, Henrietta, born on July 19, 1681, survived the deadly perils of seventeenth-century infancy. John's third daughter, Anne—note the name—was born on February 27, 1684. She too thrived.

Although to outward appearance King Charles's Court was as brilliant and gay as ever, its inner life was seared by tragedy. The executions of great nobles whom everybody knew, like Stafford on the one side and Russell on the other; the ugly death in the Tower of Essex, so recently a trusted Minister, cast their shadows upon wide circles of relations and friends. Fear and grief lurked beneath the wigs and powder, ceremonies and masquerades.

John Churchill seems at this time to have been most anxious to withdraw his wife altogether from the fevered scene, and to live with her in the country, riding to London only as required by his duties, which were also his livelihood. Sarah dutifully obeyed her husband's wish. But an event occurred which frustrated these modest ambitions.

Hitherto little has been said about the Princess Anne. Henceforward she becomes the fulcrum of our tale. And here and now Sarah begins to play her commanding part. Her first contact with Anne had been in childhood. They had met in children's play at St James's when Sarah was ten and Princess Anne was only six. They were thrown together far more frequently when Sarah came to live in the palace, from 1673 onward. From the outset Anne became deeply attached to the brilliant, vivacious being who blossomed into womanhood before her childish eyes. The Princess was fascinated by Sarah's knowledge, self-confidence, and strength of character. She was charmed by her care and devotion, and by all her resources of fun and comfort which so naturally and spontaneously came to her aid. Very early indeed in these young lives did those ties of love, kindling into passion on one side, and into affection and sincere friendship on the other, grow deep and strong, as yet unheeded by the bustling world. There was a romantic, indeed perfervid, element in Anne's love for Sarah to which the elder girl responded warmly several years before she realised the worldly importance of such a relationship. "The beginning of the Princess's kindness for me," wrote Sarah in after-days,

> had a much earlier date than my entrance into her service. My promotion to this honour was wholly owing to impressions she had before received to my advantage; we had used to play together when she was a child, and she even then expressed a particular fondness for me. This inclination increased with our years. I was often at Court, and the Princess always distinguished me by the pleasure she took to honour me, preferably to others, with her conversation and confidence. In all her parties for amusement I was sure by her choice to be one.
> . . .

The passage of time gradually but swiftly effaced the difference in age, and Sarah as a married woman and mother at twenty-one exercised only a stronger spell upon the Princess of seventeen. "A friend," says Sarah,

> was what she most coveted, and for the sake of friendship which she did not disdain to have with me, she was fond even of that equality which she thought belonged to it. She grew uneasy to be treated by me with the form and ceremony due to her rank, nor could she bear from me the sound of words which implied in them distance and superiority. It was this turn of mind which made her one day propose to me, that whenever I should happen to be absent from her, we

might in all our letters write ourselves by feigned names, such as would import nothing of distinction of rank between us. Morley and Freeman were the names her fancy hit upon, and she left me to choose by which of them I would be called. My frank, open temper naturally led me to pitch upon Freeman, and so the Princess took the other, and from this time Mrs Morley and Mrs Freeman began to converse as equals, made so by affection and friendship.

John Churchill's relations with the Princess, although on a different plane from those of Sarah, were nevertheless lighted by a growing personal attachment. To secure her safety, her well-being, her peace of mind against all assaults, even in the end against Sarah herself, became the rule of his life. Never by word or action in the course of their long association, with all its historic stresses—not to the very end—not even in the bitter hour of dismissal—did he vary in his fidelity to Anne as Princess or Queen, nor in his chivalry to her as a woman.

Anne had but to reach maturity to become a factor of national consequence. Her marriage lay in the cold spheres of State policy. By King Charles's command, and with her father's acquiescence, she, like her elder sister, had been strictly bred a Protestant. The popularity of the union of William of Orange with Princess Mary in 1677 had already helped the King to hold his difficult balances at home and abroad. Here in days still critical was the opportunity for another royal Protestant alliance.

Charles now turned to a Danish prince. Although Prince George of Denmark was, of course, a Lutheran Protestant, he represented only a diminished Continental state, and the whole transaction seemed consigned to a modest plane. Prince George obeyed the command of his brother, the Danish King Christian V; and in July 1683 Colonel Churchill was sent to Denmark to conduct him to England to fall in love with the Princess Anne and marry her forthwith. George of Denmark was a fine-looking man, tall, blond, and good-natured. He had a reputation for personal courage, and by a cavalry charge had rescued his brother during a battle between the Danes and the Dutch in 1677. He was neither clever nor learned—a simple, normal man, without envy or ambition, and disposed by remarkable appetite and thirst for all the pleasures of the table. Charles's well-known verdict, "I have tried him drunk and I have tried him sober, but there is nothing in him," does not do justice to the homely virtues and unfailing good-humour of his staid and trustworthy character. Anne accepted with complacency what fortune brought her. Her uncle the King had so decided; her father acquiesced; Louis XIV was content; and only William of Orange was displeased.

On July 28, 1683, the marriage was solemnized with royal pomp and popular approbation. Prince George derived a revenue of £10,000 a year from some small Danish islands. Parliament voted Anne £20,000 a year, and the King established the royal pair in their suite in a residence called the Cockpit, adjoining the Palace of Whitehall, standing where the Treasury Chambers are to-day.

This marriage of policy in which the feelings of the parties had been only formally consulted stood during twenty-four years every ordinary strain and almost unequalled family sorrows. Anne suffered either a miscarriage or a still-born baby with mechanical regularity year after year. Only one cherished son lived beyond his eleventh birthday. At forty-two she had buried sixteen children; and when so many hopes and grave issues hung upon her progeny, none survived her. Her life was repeatedly stabbed by pain, disappointment, and mourning, which her placid courage, strong, patient spirit, firm faith, and abiding sense of public duty enabled her to sustain. Her life, so largely that of an invalid, attached itself to grand simplicities—her religion, her husband, her country's welfare, her beloved friend and mentor, Sarah. These dominants for many years wrought the harmony of her circle, and their consequences adorned her name and reign with unfading glory. Her love for her husband was richly renewed, and she knew no bounds in her admiration of his capacities. The romantic side of her nature found its satisfactions in her strangely intense affection for Sarah. And behind, ever faithful in her service, lay the pervading genius of Marlborough with his enchanted sword.

Anne lost no time in persuading her father to appoint Sarah one of her Ladies of the Bedchamber. In a manuscript essay by Sarah, called A *Faithful Account of Many Things*, the following suggestive, impersonal, and of course retrospective account is given of their relations:

> * The Dutchess had address and accomplishments, sufficient to engage the affections and confidence of her Mistress without owing anything to the want of them in others. But yet this made room for her the sooner and gave her some advantage; and she now began to employ all Her wit and all Her vivacity and almost all Her time to divert, and entertain, and serve, the Princess; and to fix that favour,

which now one might easily observe to be encreasing towards her every day. This favour quickly became a passion; and a Passion which possessed the Heart of the Princess too much to be hid. They were shut up together for many hours daily. Every moment of Absence was counted a sort of tedious, lifeless, state. To see the Duchess was a constant joy; and to part with her for never so short a time, a constant Uneasiness; As the Princess's own frequent expressions were. This worked even to the jealousy of a Lover. She used to say she desired to possess her wholly: and could hardly bear that she should ever escape, from this confinement, into other Company.

The closing years of Charles II were calm. In the wake of the passions of the Popish Plot and on the tide of Tory reaction the country regathered something of its poise. It seemed after a while as if the executions of the Popish and Rye House Plots had balanced each other, and a fresh start became possible. We observe the formation of a mass of central opinion, which, if it did not mitigate the strife of parties, could at least award the palm of success to the least culpable. This peculiarly English phenomenon could never henceforward be disregarded. Any party which ranged too far upon its own characteristic course was liable to offend a great body of men who, though perhaps marked by party labels, were by no means prepared to associate themselves with party extravagances.

At the end of the reign we see Charles working with several representatives of this moderate Tory view. Among these, opposed to Popery, opposed to France, mildly adverse to Dissent, content with peace, and respecting the government of King *and* Parliament, the famous Halifax was preeminent. His nature led him to turn against excess in any quarter; he swam instinctively against the stream. The taunt of "Trimmer" levelled at him by disappointed partisans has been accepted by history as the proof of his uprightness and sagacity. He compared himself with justice to the temperate zone which lies between "the regions in which men are frozen and the regions in which they are roasted." He was the foremost statesman of these times; a love of moderation and sense of the practical seemed in him to emerge in bold rather than tepid courses. He could strike as hard for compromise as most leaders for victory. Memorable were the services which Halifax had rendered to the Crown and the Duke of York. His reasoned oratory, his biting sarcasm, his personal force and proud independence, had turned the scale against the first Exclusion Bill. His wise counsels had aided the King at crucial moments, and he himself often formed the rallying-point for men of goodwill. His greatest work for the nation and for modern times was yet to be done. Meanwhile he stood, a trusted Minister, at King Charles's side in the evening of a stormy day.

Halifax must have represented Churchill's political views and temperament far more truly than any other statesman. Whether or not John learned war from Turenne, he certainly learned politics from Halifax. As we watch the Great Trimmer turning from side to side, from faction to faction, from Monmouth to William, or back again to James, yet always pursuing his aim of sobriety and appeasement at home and of marshalling all the best in England against Popery, autocracy, and France, we can almost see John's mind keeping pace and threading silently the labyrinths of intrigue in his footsteps. We are sure that when Halifax fought the Whigs against perjured testimony for the life of Stafford, and fought the Crown and the Tories against packed juries for the lives of Russell and Sidney, he carried with him the heartfelt sympathies of the Churchill who had resented the condemnation of Argyll, and whose humane conduct at the head of armies the histories of friend and foe were to proclaim.

Another figure, at that time classed among the moderates, who had sat at the council board was Sir Edward Seymour. He was "the great Commoner" of those days. A fervent Tory of touchy, rancorous temper, of independent and undependable character, with great wealth and position, he marshalled a hundred members from the over-represented West Country. He could upon occasion have produced an army from the same regions for a national cause. He was the first Speaker of the House of Commons who was not a lawyer.

The King himself basked in the mellower light which had followed so much rough weather. He had overcome his enemies; and at whatever cost to his dignity or honour had restored peace at home and kept out of war abroad. He could afford to forgive Monmouth, in temporary exile following an attempt to place him on the throne. He was strong enough to bring back James. He revolved with tolerant mind Halifax's desire to summon Parliament, and might well expect that it would be loyal and serviceable. He still balanced and measured the grievous, insoluble problems with which he was oppressed: the ferocious divisions of his people, his want of money—that damnable thing—his dependence upon France, the odious state of Europe, the dangers of renewed Parliamentary strife, and, above all, the anxieties of the succession. For all his loves and troop of bastards, he had no legitimate heir. Strong and unswerving as he had been for the strict application of the principle of hereditary right, no one knew better than he the awful dangers which James's religion and character would bring upon the land. In spite of his own profound leanings to the old faith of Christendom, he had never lost contact with, and had in the main preserved the confidence of, the Church of England. He had used the laws of England and its Constitution as effective weapons in his warfare with the Whigs. He had never broken these laws in the process, nor trespassed beyond an arguable legality. He knew and loved his brother well, and foresaw how James's virtues and vices alike would embroil him with a nation as stubborn and resolute as he.

Yet where else to turn? How England would have rejoiced could he have but given her his handsome, gifted courageous by-blow—"our beloved Protestant Duke"! But never would he vitiate the lawful succession of the Crown, nor tolerate that picking and choosing between rival claims which would transform an hereditary into an elective monarchy. Had he not for this wrestled with his people and his Parliament? Was not the fate of Russell, of Sidney, of Essex, a proof of his invincible resolve?

Then there was William: the busy—nay, tireless—fiery but calculating, masterful and accepted ruler of Holland, and foremost champion of the Protestant world. The blood royal of England flowed in his veins, and Mary his wife was second heir-presumptive to the Crown. Here was a foreign sovereign, backed by a constitutional government and loyal fleets and armies, whose profound interest in the succession had never been disguised. How shrewd and patient William had been; how skilfully he had steered a course through the English storms! The Prince of Orange was sure that James would never abandon the attempt to compel the English nation to submit to autocratic rule and Catholic conversion, and equally sure that the English nation would never submit to such designs. Hence in his farseeing way he did not wish James's powers to be specially limited by law. It was better for William that James should have a free hand, and if this led him to disaster, then at least his successor would not be a king with a mutilated prerogative.

Charles comprehended this situation with a nice taste; he knew all the moves upon the board. But what more could he do? At any rate, it seemed that time might be allowed to play its part. The King was only fifty-four; his health in general at this time seemed robust. To many intimates his life seemed as good as that of his brother. He could not measure the deep inroads which continuous sexual excitement had wrought upon his vigorous frame. Another ten years, to which he could reasonably look forward, might clarify the whole scene. So he returned with cordial acquiescence to the pleasures and amusements of his Court, toyed with Halifax's proposals for a new Parliament, rejoiced that the ship of State was for the moment on an even keel, and left the baffling problems of the future to solve themselves. They did so.

Churchill was by this time in the middle thirties. He was in a position to judge men and affairs upon excellent information. It is only here and there that some record of his opinion exists. We can judge his politics chiefly by his friends. He was not accustomed to air his views upon grave matters, and such letters as have been preserved concern themselves only with private or family matters. Churchill was definitely ranged and classed with the Tories—and with the high Tories—against all interference with his master's hereditary rights. He had the best opportunities of informing himself about the King's health; he had seen him a few years before smitten with a mysterious and alarming illness. It was now certain that if James were alive at the death of King Charles, he would ascend the throne, and Churchill had every reason but one to hope for the highest favour and advancement at his hands. Yet that one adverse reason was enough to undo all. The wise, observant soldier who had dwelt so long at or near the centre of power had no doubts whatever of the clash that must ensue between his devout, headstrong, bigoted, resolute patron and the whole resisting power of a Protestant nation. Here again his course was determined. In defence of the Protestant religion he would sever all loyalties, extinguish all gratitudes, and take all necessary measures. His wife's intimate, affectionate relations with the Princess Anne, her offer to undertake the office of her Lady of the Bedchamber, must have been in full accord with his wishes and designs. The influence, daily becoming decisive and dominant, which the Churchills exerted in the household of the Prince and Princess of Denmark was steadfastly used to strengthen and fortify its already marked Protestant character, and to link the young Princess with leading statesmen and divines who would confirm her vigorous faith.

The situation had, as we have seen, arisen naturally, by the invisible impulses of friendship and custom. It had now become a definite and primary factor in the Churchills' fortunes, as it was presently to be in those of the nation. From this time forward John and Sarah began to be increasingly detached from the Duke's circle, and noticeably associated —beyond the religious gulf—with his younger daughter. Indeed, during the reign of James II Churchill was regarded by an informed foreign observer as Princess Anne's friend and counsellor rather than the trusted servant of the new King. This in quiet times meant little, but a day was soon to come when it would mean everything. A connexion had been formed around the Protestant royal personage who stood third in the line of succession, cemented by a friendship and sympathy destined to withstand the shocks and trials of more than twenty years. This union of intense convictions, sentiments, habits, and interests was soon to be exposed to the sharpest and most violent tests, and to withstand them with the strength of solid rock.

The King seemed in his usual health at the beginning of 1685. After his dinner on the night of January 26 he sat, as was his custom, with the Duchess of Portsmouth and a small company of friends. Thomas Bruce, the Earl of Ailesbury, with whom Churchill's functions must often have brought him in friendly contact—to whom we owe most delightful, if sometimes untrustworthy, memoirs—was on duty as Gentleman of the Bedchamber. He found the King "in the most charming humour possible." But

> when we came to the district of the bedchamber, I by my office was to light him to the bedchamber door, and giving the candle to the page of the backstairs, it went out, although a very large wax candle and without any wind. The page of the backstairs was more superstitious, for he looked on me, shaking his head.

The King chatted agreeably with his gentlemen as he undressed, and spoke about the repairing of Winchester Castle and the gardens he was making there. He said to Ailesbury, "I will order John" (a familiar word for the Earl of Bath, the Groom of the Stole, who was with the

King when a boy) "to put you in waiting the first time I go thither, and although it be not your turn, to show you the place I delight so in, and shall be so happy this week as to have my house covered with lead." "And God knows," comments Ailesbury, "the Saturday following he was put in his coffin."

That night Ailesbury, lying in the next room, and "sleeping but indifferently, perceived that the King turned himself sometimes, not usual for him." The next morning he was "pale as ashes" and "could not or would not say one word." A violent fit of apoplexy supervened, and after gamely enduring prolonged torture at the hands of his distracted physicians Charles II breathed his last. All untimely, the long-dreaded event had come to pass. The interlude of peace was over, and King James II ruled the land.

CHAPTER TEN

Sedgemoor

ᛒᚢ 1685 ᛞᛉ

FOR two years past James had played an active second part in the government of the kingdom, and once his brother's approaching end became certain, he concerned himself with every precaution necessary to ensure an unopposed succession. Indeed, it was not until after he had posted the Royal Guards at various important points, and had even obtained the dying King's signature to some measures of financial convenience, that, on the promptings of the Duchess of Portsmouth, he secured Charles's spiritual welfare by bringing a priest up the backstairs to receive him into the Church of Rome and give him extreme unction. Within a quarter of an hour of the King's death he met the Privy Council, whose duty it is to recognize the new sovereign. He laboured to contradict the belief that he was revengeful or inclined to arbitrary rule. He declared himself resolved to maintain both in State and Church a system of government established by law,

> for he recognized the members of the English Church as loyal subjects, he knew that the laws of England were sufficient to make the King a great monarch and that he would maintain the rights and prerogatives of the Crown, and would not invade any man's property.

It has even been asserted he went so far at this critical moment as to say that, "as regards his private religious opinions, no one should perceive that he entertained them," but that this sentence was deleted from the official report.

These declarations were received by the dignitaries and magnates of the realm with profound relief and joy, and as the Royal Proclamation spread throughout the land it everywhere evoked expressions of gratitude and loyalty. Charles II had died at the moment when the Tory reaction was at its highest. The sentimental nature of the English people was stirred to its depth by the death of the King, who if he had tricked them often, had not, as they now felt, served them ill, and whose personal charm and human qualities and weaknesses were pervasively endearing. In the wave of grief and hope sweeping the nation the unbridgeable differences of faith, policy, and temper which separated a new prince and an old people were forgotten. James ascended the throne of his ancestors and predecessors with as fair a chance as ever monarch had.

The summoning of a Parliament, after a lapse of more than three years, was now indispensable. More than half the revenues of the State ceased upon the demise of the Crown. The need was otherwise unanswerable, and the hour could not be more propitious. On February 9 the writs were issued, and the general election of 1685 began. On the second Sunday after his accession, near noon, when the Court was thronged, King James and the Queen attended Mass and received the Sacrament in the Queen's chapel, the doors of which were thrown open for all to see. This act of high consequence dispelled the rosy hopes of the Protestant Court and aroused immediately the London clergy. But the Royal Proclamation, striking while the iron was hot, was not overtaken in those days of slow and imperfect news. The nation voted upon its first impulse and returned a Parliament which in quality and character represented all the strongest elements in the national life, and was in temper as loyal to the Crown as the Restoration Parliament of 1660. To this new Parliament James repeated his original declaration as amended. From it he received an enthusiastic response, and the revenues, grudged and meted to his brother, were to him voted in their amplitude for life. He had only to practise his religion for his conscience' sake as a man, to observe the laws of the realm, and to keep the promises he had made respecting them, in order to receive and enjoy the faithful service of his subjects for all his days. He began his reign with that same caution and moderation which had marked his first government in Scotland, and he reaped an immediate reward. Events were, however, at hand which would impel and empower him to cast aside these wise and vital restraints.

Churchill stood in good favour with the new régime. In the list of the nine Lords of the Bedchamber his name was second only to Peterborough's. His colonelcy of the Dragoons was confirmed; and he was immediately despatched on a mission to Versailles, the ostensible object of which was to notify Louis XIV of the accession, and its substantial purpose to obtain an increased subsidy for the English Crown. For this task his negotiations in 1679 and 1681 and his full knowledge of the secret relations of the two Kings had well prepared him. But Louis, taking time by the forelock, had forestalled the request. Before Churchill could reach Paris Barillon had waited upon James with an unsolicited gift of 500,000 livres, and it was thought only becoming to express gratitude for this modest favour before asking for the two or three millions a year which the English King and Court regarded as desirable. Churchill was therefore overtaken by fresh instructions, and his mission was limited to ceremonies and thanks. On this visit Churchill seems to have committed an unusual indiscretion. "The Earl of Galway," says Burnet,

> told me that when he [Churchill] came over [to France] in the first compliment upon the King's coming to the Crown, he said then to him that if the King was ever prevailed upon to alter our religion he would serve him no longer, but would withdraw from him.

He returned to England at the beginning of April in time for the splendours of the coronation. An English peerage was conferred upon him, and he became Baron Churchill of Sandridge. Rougher work was soon at hand.

The news of King Charles's death fell like a thunderbolt on his wellloved, wayward bastard at The Hague. Monmouth by his natural vivacity had lent a fleeting gleam of gaiety to the dull, strait-laced routine of the Dutch Court. Politics apart, he had been received with genuine relish. But in the midst of dancing and ice-carnivals came the news that, instead of a father about to consummate an act of forgiveness, there ruled in England an uncle who had suffered insult and exile through his rivalry, whose last six years had been consumed in struggling against the party he led, and who hated him with all the hatred of intimacy, alike as Protestant and as Pretender.

Monmouth's mood of despair led him to seek in the companionship of his fond mistress, the beautiful Lady Wentworth, a shelter from the mischances of public life. He quitted The Hague at William's request within a few hours, and settled himself with his charming friend at Brussels. But more turbulent and daring spirits were not so agreeably soothed. Argyll—the "hunted partridge"—in his Dutch retreat brooded intently upon the sanctity of synodical as opposed to episcopal Christianity, and burned to be in the Highlands again at the head of his adoring clansmen. The plotter Ferguson, Lord Grey of Wark, Wade, and a dozen or more prominent men who had escaped from England and Scotland after the Rye House exposure, gripped Monmouth and bound him to a fatal design. Lady Wentworth herself, who loved him so well, loved also that he should be a king. She offered her jewels and wealth for his service. All these exiles had in their minds the picture of England in 1682. They could not believe in the reality of a change of mood so swift and utter as had in fact occurred since then. Monmouth yielded against his better judgment to their importunities. It was agreed that Argyll should invade and rouse the Highlands and that Monmouth should land in England. Two tiny expeditions of three ships each, filled with munitions and bitter men of quality, were organized from slender resources, and three weeks after Argyll had set out for Kirkwall Monmouth sailed for the Channel.

Monmouth tossed on the waves for nineteen days, driven hither and thither by the winds. He escaped the numerous English cruisers which watched the Straits of Dover, and on June 11 dropped anchor in the Dorsetshire port of Lyme Regis. The Duke and his confederates, who had beguiled the anxious voyage with Cabinet-making, landed forthwith. Sword in hand, they repaired to the market-place, where they were received with rapture by the townsfolk, who, like themselves, were still living in the England of the Popish Plot, and looked back with reverence to the great days of Blake and Cromwell. Monmouth issued a proclamation, drawn up by Ferguson, accusing the King of having murdered Charles II, and of every other crime; affirming also that he himself was born in wedlock, and claiming to be the champion of the laws, liberty, and religion of the realm. The rush of adherents to enlist baffled the clerks who registered their names. Within twenty-four hours he was joined by fifteen hundred men.

Meanwhile messengers from the Mayor of Lyme, who abandoned the contumacious town, were riding as fast as relays of horses could carry them to London. On the morning of June 13 they broke in upon

Sir Winston with the startling news that his constituency was in rebellion. He took them to the palace, and, summoning his son, was conducted to the King.

This must have been a great day for old Sir Winston, and one in which all the harmonies of his life seemed to merge. Here was the King for whose sacred rights and line he had fought with sword and pen, for whom he had suffered so much, once more assaulted by rebellion. The old cause was once more at stake in the old place; and here stood his son, Colonel of the Dragoons, the rising soldier of the day, high in the favour of the threatened monarch, long linked to his service—he it was who would march forward at the head of the Household troops, the *corps d'élite*, to lay the insolent usurper low. It was Sir Winston's apotheosis. There must have been a strong feeling of the continuity of history in this small group coincidence had brought together.

Instant resolves were taken. All available forces were ordered to Salisbury. That very night Churchill set out with four troops of the Blues and two of his own Dragoons—in all about three hundred horse—followed by Colonel Kirke with five companies of the Queen's Regiment.

Monmouth could scarcely have struck a more unlucky moment: Parliament was in session, the King's popularity was still at coronation height. An Act of Attainder against Monmouth was passed. The price of £5000 was set on his head. The Commons voted large, immediate supplies, and both Houses assured the King of their resolve to die in his defence. Moreover, the troops from Tangier had already landed. A prompt requisition was presented to William of Orange to send back, in accordance with the convention under which they served, the six English and Scottish regiments maintained in Dutch pay. William lost no time in complying. He had been unable to stop Monmouth's expedition from starting—it had got safely away; he could now make sure that it was destroyed. However painful it must have been to him on personal grounds to aid in the ruin of his inconvenient Protestant rival—so lately his attractive guest—he had to do his duty. The troops were dispatched forthwith; and William even offered to come over in person to take command of the royal army. This kindly proposal was declined.

Churchill marched south with great rapidity. He reached Bridport on June 17, having covered 120 miles in four days.

On the 18th he was at Axminster, and on the 19th at Chard, in country which he knew so well (Ashe House was but eight miles away). Here his patrols came into contact with the hostile forces; and here also was a messenger from Monmouth reminding him of their old friendship and begging his aid. Churchill dismissed the messenger and sent the letter to the King.

Monmouth, at the head of some three thousand men and four guns, had entered Taunton on the 18th. Here he was received with royal state and lively affection. He was persuaded to proclaim himself King, thus confirming William in his sense of duty to James. The rebel numbers rose to above seven thousand, and he might have doubled them had he possessed the arms. His handful of cavalry, under Lord Grey of Wark, were mounted upon horses mostly untrained or even unbroken. His infantry were only partly armed with muskets, and for the rest depended upon scythes fastened on broomsticks. They had neither more nor less training than the militia, out of whom, indeed, they were largely composed. Nevertheless, in their zeal, in their comprehension of the quarrel, and in their stubborn courage, they were the ore from which the Ironsides had been forged.

John, appointed to the rank of Brigadier-General, certainly hoped, and probably expected, that he would have the command of all the troops available; but in this he was disappointed. There were second thoughts. On June 19 Sunderland wrote to inform him that the Frenchman Feversham had been appointed Commander-in-Chief. This was a significant event. Here was a campaign begun which he had in his own hands, on which his heart was set, and which he knew himself more capable than anyone to direct. He did not entirely conceal his anger. "I see plainly," he wrote on July 4 to Clarendon, "that I am to have the trouble, and that the honour will be another's." One of the remaining links which bound him to James's personal fortunes may well have broken here: nevertheless, with his customary self-control he subordinated his feelings to his duty and his policy, submitted himself with perfect propriety to Feversham, and directed his wrath solely upon the enemy.

Churchill, once in contact with the rebels, never let go. His well-trained force of regular cavalry, widely spread, enveloped and stabbed the flanks and rear of Monmouth's army. He followed them wherever they moved, changing from one flank to the other as occasion served, and always labouring to impress upon the enemy, and especially upon Monmouth, whose temperament he knew well, that they were aggressively opposed by the loyal regular forces of the Crown. At the same time he endeavoured to keep the militia out of danger, to have them concentrated and as far from the enemy as possible at points where he could, with his professional troops, ensure alike not only their lives but their fidelity.

Meanwhile such parts of the regular forces as could be spared from an agitated capital were approaching. Kirke, newly landed from Tangier, with his companies of the Queen's Regiment, joined Churchill at Chard on June 21. With this reinforcement Churchill revolved the chances of a decisive action. The quality and temper of the militia was, however, prohibitive; they were prone to join the rebels rather than fight them—in fact, they went over by whole companies. Churchill did not in this event feel strong enough to bar the way to Bristol, as was desired at Whitehall. No course was open to him but to await the arrival of the royal army, and meanwhile claw the enemy.

Monmouth's only chance was swiftness and audacity; without a wide, popular uprising he was doomed. The elements existed which might make him a King, but these elements were political rather than military. He must seize towns and cities and gain their arms and supplies before the royal troops arrived in strength. Bristol, the second city in the kingdom, was full of his partisans. Here was his first obvious objective. To gain the mastery of Bristol would be a formidable advantage. It was not until June 25, a fortnight after his landing, that, with forces now swollen to eight thousand foot and a thousand horse, he stood before the decayed ramparts of Bristol. He was too late. Feversham had entered the city on the 23rd with two hundred horse. The Duke of Beaufort held the hill where the castle had formerly stood, and thence intimidated the population. The royal army was already near Bath, and Churchill lay upon Monmouth's other flank. In these circumstances, only some of which were known to him, he abandoned his design; and with his turning back from Bristol his adventure became forlorn.

Churchill followed close at his heels, cutting off stragglers, hunting his patrols, and looking for a chance to strike.

On Friday, the 26th, Churchill joined Feversham at Bath, where his brother, Charles Churchill, had also arrived, having escorted a train of artillery from Portsmouth. The next day Feversham advanced with the bulk of his forces to attack the rebels at Norton St Philip. The affair was ill-conducted. Five hundred of the royal foot, with some cavalry under the Duke of Grafton, involved themselves in a narrow lane, the hedgerows of which were lined by Monmouth's musketeers. These two by-blows of Charles II—bastard versus bastard—were locked in semi-fratricidal strife. Feversham and Churchill both arrived on the scene. The rebels fought stoutly, and the royal forces, drawing off with a loss of eighty men killed, retired to Bradford in some dissatisfaction. In spite of this incident, Monmouth's army began to melt. Two thousand men deserted. A convoy of arms and stores which was sorely needed was captured near Frome. Taunton, lately so ardent, sent a deputation to beseech him not to return to their town. Upon all this came the tidings that Argyll's revolt had been extinguished and that he and Rumbold had already been beheaded. Despondency and fear began to overspread not only Monmouth's troops, but all those friendly districts which had compromised themselves in his cause. Nowhere did they weigh more heavily than in his own heart.

On July 3 Monmouth in the deepest gloom re-entered Bridgwater, which he had left eleven days before. Not one man of note had joined him. His peasant army, officered by tradesmen, was wearied and per-plexed by ceaseless marches and counter-marches in mud and rain, evi-dently to no purpose. But those fires still smouldered in their hearts which success would have fanned into flame and which in many only death could quench. On the 5th Feversham, with Churchill and all the royal forces in one body, came from Somerton and camped at Weston Zoyland. His cavalry billeted themselves in the village of Weston, on the right of his line; his artillery was on the opposite flank, a quarter of a mile farther off. The militia were left out of harm's way a good many miles behind. Not counting these auxiliaries, he mustered seven hundred horse, including the Household Cavalry and six battalions of infantry—in all, nearly three thousand regular troops with sixteen guns.

The two small armies were now scarcely three miles apart, and Mon-mouth must choose his course without delay. Should he assault the royal position? Should he defend himself in Bridgwater? Should he march once again northward on the Bristol road towards Gloucester-shire, Cheshire, and the adherents who were believed to be assembling there? To attack the regulars in the open field was to court destruction.

To be shut up in Bridgwater was only to postpone it. But the roads to the north were still open. He could certainly march past Feversham's right and cross the Avon at Keynsham before him. Though pursued, he would advance into a friendly region and a new scene. He chose the last alternative, and during the 4th and 5th disposed and prepared his forces with that intention. To deceive the enemy he employed the inhabitants of Bridgwater ostentatiously upon the fortification of the town, and also issued orders for a retreat upon Taunton. Churchill, who digested every scrap of information, wrote on the 4th to Clarendon:

> I find by the enemy's warrant to the constables that they have more mind to get horses and saddles than anything else which looks as if he had a mind to break away with his horse to some other place and leave his foot entrenched at Bridgwater.

Monmouth, in fact, meant to march with all his force—at least, at the outset. But when, on the morning of the 5th, he quitted Bridgwater and was crossing the town bridge to join his men in the Castle Field, a local farm labourer met him with intimate news of the royal army. It lay scattered in negligent fashion without entrenchment. The last night at Somerton no proper guards had been set; and it was said that laxity, drunkenness, and roystering prevailed. From the tower of Bridgwater Church the whole camp could be seen. Monmouth returned to the town, climbed the tower, saw for the first time the loosely spread camp, and took alike the most daring and the most prudent decision of his life—a night attack!

He called a council, and his supporters agreed. The plan was less simple than plans of war by night should be. The whole force would make a march of about six miles round Feversham's right. Grey's cavalry would branch off and, avoiding Chedzoy village, cross the Bussex Rhine at one of the plungeons to the east of the royal camp, surprise the Dragoons and Blues in Weston Zoyland, fire the village, and sweep round the rear upon the camp, the artillery, and the baggage at the same time that the infantry broke into the front of the position. It was a desperate cast; but Monmouth had about 3500 brave, determined men. In the night all cats are grey; and the confusion of a hand-to-hand grapple, with all its hopes of surprise and panic, was the best chance left. Indeed, it was a good chance; and but for this, that, and the other, no one knows what might have come of it. Accordingly, a little after eleven o'clock the rebels set forth along the Keynsham road, and after shuffling along for about two miles wheeled to the right into the mist of the moor.

Serious charges have been levelled at Feversham by many historians. Burnet declares that Feversham "had no parties abroad, . . . got no intelligence, . . . and was abed without any care or order." It is certain he was asleep in bed when the musketry fire exploded all around. The royal officers spoke of their commander with contempt, mocking at his broken English and declaring that he only thought of eating and sleeping. However, though he omitted to post a guard on the plungeon beyond his right flank, he had not fallen far short of ordinary military routine. He had camped in a good position; he had posted at least five strong pickets of horse and one of foot on the approaches from the enemy; he had an inlying picket of a hundred men under arms, and he had sent Oglethorpe's troop of the Blues to patrol both of the roads from Bridgwater to the north, whither he, like Churchill, expected Monmouth to attempt escape.

Meanwhile Monmouth and his men plodded onward across the moor, with Grey, guided by Godfrey, in the van. The Black Ditch, one of the great drainage ditches called 'rhines,' had been successfully crossed. Grey, with his scraggy cavalry and part of the rebel foot, were already over the second (the Langmore Rhine), and the clock of Chedzoy Church had struck one, when suddenly a vedette of the Blues fired a pistol in alarm. Frantic excitement broke out. The assailants were now very near their still sleeping foes. Contrary to most accounts, the rebels knew about the Bussex Rhine, and Grey and his horsemen, improvidently leaving Godfrey behind, rode forward, looking for the plungeon. He struck the ditch at an impassable point. Instead of working to the left in harmony with his mission to turn the flank and rear, he swerved to his right with most of his men and rode along the edge across the front of Monmouth's infantry, whose rear was still scrambling across the Langmore Rhine in the darkness behind him. Meanwhile the royal trumpets sounded, the alarm was given, the drums beat, and the threatened camp sprang in an instant into fury and confusion. The startled Grey saw through the mist a small array of gleaming lights and moved towards them. Some say he thought they were the lights of Weston. There was a different explanation. It had not yet been possi-

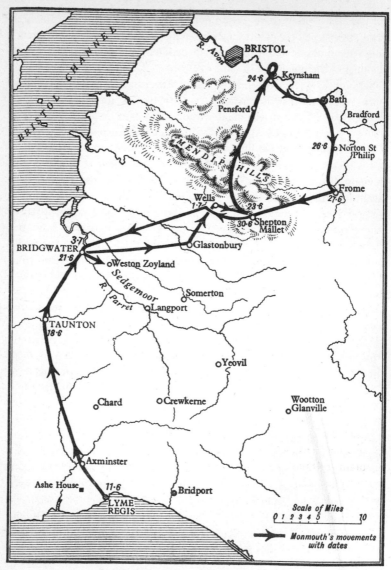

2. The Campaign of Sedgemoor, 1685

ble to rearm Dumbarton's regiment with flintlocks. The lights were their slow matches burning as the troops stood to arms. "Who are you for?" cried a voice from among the matchlocks. "The King." "Which King?" "King Monmouth, God with him!" "Take that with you," was the rejoinder, and a volley, followed at brief intervals by a second and a third as each platoon accomplished its ritual, crashed across the ditch. Grey or his untrained horses, or both, were stampeded, and scurried in complete disorder around the flanks of the infantry whom Monmouth was now leading up at the double, still in column of march. But the rest of the rebel cavalry had found the plungeon, and were only stopped at the last minute by Compton and a handful of the Blues from crossing by it.

Churchill had had a long day, but he was awake, armed, equipped, and on the spot. In the absence of his chief he instantly took command. The rebels, who halted to deploy about eighty yards short of the rhine, began to fire wildly across it, while the royal regiments were rapidly forming. The danger of their bursting into the camp had been averted; but they outflanked the royal right, and when their three cannon, under a competent Dutch gunner, began to fire at a hundred yards into the masses of Dumbarton's regiment and the 1st Guards, men fell fast. Churchill therefore rearranged the infantry. He made the two left-hand battalions march behind the others to prolong his front to the right, and summoned the artillery. These were very slow; but the Bishop of Winchester, 'Old Patch,' who accompanied Feversham as spiritual guide, took the horses out of his coach, and by these six guns were dragged successively to the critical point.

Churchill felt the injury Monmouth's artillery was working at such close quarters upon the infantry. It was probably by his orders that Captain Littleton, of the Blues, who were spread about the front, passed the plungeon, formed up on the other side, and just as the sky was paling with the first light of dawn charged and captured the rebel guns. He did not, as is usually stated, lead the charge of this small body himself. Some foot soldiers from the nearest battalion waddled across and held what the cavalry had gained.

The firing had now lasted nearly three hours without the two sides being able to come to grips, and, according to Wolseley, the rebel ammunition was running short. Certainly their wagons with the reserve of powder and ball, left two miles behind, had been deserted by the teamsters in the panic of Grey's horse. Day was breaking, and the royal artillery had at length arrived. Drear and doom-like was the dawn to Monmouth. He knew, as an officer experienced in Continental warfare, that his chance had failed and nothing could now save his little army. It is amazing he did not resolve to die on the field with all these earnest simples he had drawn to their fate. But had he been capable of that, he would have been capable of so much more that all our tales would be different. Just as the full light grew upon the plain he, with Grey, who had now rejoined him after his excursion, and about fifty horsemen, rode from the field, hoping to reach a port and seize a ship. On the rising ground beyond the moor these fugitives and deserters drew rein. There, still on the edge of the fatal ditch, stood the stubborn remnants of the Nonconformist foot. The royal cavalry enveloped them or pursued their routed comrades. Feversham's infantry, who were able to cross the ditch everywhere without apparent difficulty, advanced upon them at the charge; but the valiant peasantry, miners, and weavers, small, devout folk serving the Lord in humble station, with the butts of their muskets and their scythes met the regulars breast to breast, and closed their ranks with invincible behaviour. At last the cannon came into action upon this lump of men. All the sixteen guns had to fire for a considerable time before it was torn to shreds and the scattered survivors fled, the prey to a merciless pursuit. Of this tragedy Monmouth had but one fleeting glance. He only knew that his followers were still resisting when he quitted the field.

We must not be drawn too far from our particular theme. Enough that the charming, handsome prince was caught—drenched and starving—in a ditch; that, carried to London, he grovelled in vain for life at the knees of his implacable uncle; that he repudiated the cause for which he had fought; that he offered to turn Catholic to save not his soul, but his life; and that finally, when these discordant sounds were ended, he died with perfect composure at the hands of a clumsy and demoralized executioner. The Lady Wentworth followed him a few months later, her heart being broken. Death can be kind.

By noon on the 6th Churchill was in Bridgwater with a thousand soldiers. Unhappy town, with its rank offences, its wounded, its mobs of prisoners or fugitives, its terrified inhabitants! Feversham followed more slowly. He had the Continental view of war. To him these English peasants and common folk were but an unsuccessful jacquerie. He had to festoon the trees with hanged men. With him was Kirke, who had the Tangier outlook, and whose soldiers, newly returned from the crusade against the Moors, bore the emblem of the Paschal Lamb. He and his Lambs showed no mercy except for cash. Worse still was to come.

It is pleasant to find that the foremost man in the fighting had no part in the aftermath of atrocities. Churchill seems to have disentangled himself from the tortured West Country with astonishing deftness. The rout having been accomplished, he returned home.

The royal rewards for the victory went to Feversham; he received the Garter and the command of the first and most lucrative troop of the Life Guards. But nothing could free the public mind from the impression that Churchill had saved and won the battle. The whole Army knew the facts.

We must suppose in our attempt to revive from these fragments of history the personality of John Churchill that his treatment by James during and after the Sedgemoor campaign crystallized their private relations. John's sagacious eye weighed with precision his claims upon the royal favour. He must also have comprehended the King's point of view as fairly as he would have measured the virtues and weaknesses of any other adversary, once classed as such. But, apart from his own course and career, there were some matters which stirred his depths. To the butcheries of the Sedgemoor battlefield succeeded the horrors of the Bloody Assize. The Lord Chief Justice Jeffreys, quick to catch his master's mood and spurred by his own sadistic passions, wreaked vengeance upon Bridgwater, Taunton, and the guilty countryside. Nearly four hundred executions marked his progress. Twelve hundred rebels were sold as slaves for the Trinidad and Barbados plantations. To this day in Trinidad there exists a colony of white men who, though they have not intermarried with the negroes, toil as equals at their side. They are called the 'red-legs.' They have lost all track of their origin or family trees. Their names have perished; and few there are who know that they include the rearguard of Monmouth's army, lagging a couple of centuries behind.

James II. NATIONAL PORTRAIT GALLERY.

Louis XIV. BY PERMISSION OF THE DUKE OF MARLBOROUGH.

CHAPTER ELEVEN

Plot and Counter-Plot

ᛰ 1685-88 ᛰ

In the autumn of 1687 the King made a royal progress in the West of
England. Churchill accompanied him. They traversed many of the districts which two years before had been aflame for Monmouth. But the
resolve of the King to extend liberty of conscience to the Nonconformists, although it was but a help for his Catholic policy, had raised hopes
which for the moment almost effaced the memories of the Bloody Assize. The Catholic King received a passable welcome from the ultra-
Protestants whose relations he had lately slaughtered or sold into slavery. 'Liberty of conscience' and the removal of the penal laws were war-
cries which drowned even the screams and lamentations of the hideous
yesterday. James felt that, with his Army dominated by Irish soldiers
and Catholic officers and allied to the Dissenting masses of the Cromwellian tradition, he could afford to brave the wrath of the old, devoted friends of his house, of his line, of his person. Vain hope! Frightful miscalculation! At the best a desperate enterprise! At the least the
lists were set for a destructive civil war. But was it not his duty, if need
be, to tear his realm to pieces for his soul's salvation and the glory of
God? Thus this melancholy zealot persevered along the road to his own
ruin.

On this same progress in the West the King touched about five
thousand people for the King's Evil, and at Winchester was attended
in the ceremony by Catholic priests.

The provocations of the royal policy constantly increased. The publication of Dryden's *The Hind and the Panther* offers their poetical

justification. In April 1687 the King, dispensing with the law by his prerogative, issued his first Declaration of Indulgence. The spring saw his attempt to force a Catholic President upon Magdalen College, Oxford, and the expulsion of the Fellows for their resistance. In July James planned the public reception of the Papal nuncio, d'Adda. The Duke of Somerset when commanded to conduct the ceremonial objected on the ground that the recognition of Papal officials had been declared illegal at the Reformation. "I am above the law," said James. "Your Majesty is so," was the reply, "but I am not." He was at once dismissed from all his offices.

The King had, in modern parlance and now familiar style, set up his political platform. The second step was to create a party machine, and the third to secure by its agency a Parliament with a mandate for the repeal of the Tests. The narrow franchise could be manipulated to a very large extent by the Lord-Lieutenants of counties, by the magistrates, and in the towns and cities by the corporations. Upon these, therefore, the royal energies were now directed. The Lord-Lieutenants, including many of the greatest territorial magnates, who refused to help pack a favourable Parliament, were dismissed, and Catholics or faithful nominees of the Court installed in their place. The municipal corporations and the benches of magistrates were drastically remodelled so as to secure the fullest representation, or even the preponderance, of Papists and Dissenters. The Government tried to extort from all candidates a pledge to vote for the King's policy.

These measures implied a complete political and social transformation. The nobility and the country gentlemen were outraged by being either turned out of their local dignitaries or made to receive representatives of the hitherto depressed classes as colleagues. The process of setting Papists and Dissenters over, or in place of, Anglicans and Cavaliers must rupture and recast the whole social structure of English life. The purpose, character, and scope of these measures were profoundly comprehended in that incredibly rigid society from the proudest, wealthiest nobles down to the mass of the common people in town and village. The simples, like the gentles, feared the Pope, hated the French, and pitied the Huguenot refugees. They too, though voteless, counted. Their superiors could not be insensible to an atmosphere of ardour and goodwill around them.

The six English and Scots regiments in Dutch pay and service which had been sent over to resist Monmouth had all returned to Holland. James and his Ministers became apprehensive lest this fine body of men should some day pay them another and less friendly visit. For some months in 1687 James and Louis were trying to arrange for the transfer of these regiments from the Dutch service to the French. Churchill seems to have used all his personal influence—such as it then was—with James to prevent their departure from Holland, and to obtain the command of them in Holland for himself.

Churchill's desire for the appointment, the significance of which is apparent, was, as Sunderland foresaw, frustrated. But the troops stayed in Holland. William and the States-General, for reasons becoming increasingly obvious, refused point-blank to let them go. An acute tension arose between the two Governments. Their fundamental differences were exposed, and for the first time war was felt to be in the air.

The defenders of James's conduct are concerned to exaggerate the number of English Catholics. It is even claimed that one-eighth of the population still adhered, in spite of generations of persecutions, to the Old Faith. According to a return of 1689, there were then only 13,856 Catholics in the whole country, or less than one in four hundred of the people. The royal attempt to make a remarkable political spectacle of these few thousands of Papists, advanced to the headship of local and national affairs, even though supported by the Dissenters, was bound to range all the dominant national forces, incomparably stronger, against the Crown. The old Catholic families in England, apart from individuals advanced to high office, were deeply apprehensive of the headlong adventure upon which the King was launching them. They felt this sudden disproportionate favour was far from being in their true interests, and would only bring upon them the wrath and frightful passions which were being raised all about them. Still the King hardened his heart and strengthened his Army.

For many months, however, there was still parley. The parsons preached against Popery. Statesmen and divines exerted themselves by the dispersal of pamphlets throughout the country to offset James's attempt to rally the Nonconformists. Halifax issued his cogent *Letter to a Dissenter.*

Churchill had, as we have seen, entered fully into all the movements of protest against the royal policy. In December 1686 Anne had written to Mary assuring her of the strong Anglicanism of the Churchills. In March 1687 Churchill had conversed with Dykevelt. In May he wrote to William. In November he tried to get the command of the English regiments in the Dutch service, and so escape from the net which was closing round him at home. In December he supported and animated Anne in her endeavour to retain in her service Lord Scarsdale despite his refusal, as Lord-Lieutenant of Derbyshire, to obey James's orders. Finally, in January 1688 Churchill told James directly that he would not himself support the repeal of the penal Tests. A contemporary letter of January 12 states, "Lord Churchill swears he will not do what the King requires of him."

No man in all the stately company that represented the national character in these crucial days had made his opinion more plain, but James continued to rely on the intimacies and fidelities of twenty years of service on one hand and his benefactions on the other. He could not realize the truth that personal gratitude could never weigh in any great mind against the issues now presented to Englishmen. He knew Churchill loathed his policy, but fondly believed he loved his person more. At the crunch he was sure he could count on his influence, his diplomacy, and his sword. Meanwhile master and servant dwelt in all their old familiarity, and Churchill was constantly at the King's side in his bedroom, at his toilet, behind his chair at meals, and on horseback beside his carriage, just as he had been since he was a page.

How did this prolonged situation, with its many delicate, repugnant, and irreconcilable features, affect his inner mind? Was he distressed or was he indifferent about his personal relations with the King? On the surface he showed no trace of embarrassment. He possessed to a degree almost sublime the prosaic gift of common sense. His sure judgment and serene, dispassionate nature enabled him, amid the most baffling problems of interest and duty, to dwell inwardly and secretly at peace with his gravely taken decisions; and, of course, without further self-questionings to take in due season all measures necessary to render them effectual. The personalities which warm our hearts often cast much away from sentiment or compunction. Not so this man. He made up his mind with cold, humane sagacity, and a profound weighing of all the largest and smallest circumstances: and thenceforward he faced obloquy, if it were inevitable, as calmly as the ordinary chances of battle, after all had been done to prepare victory with the least loss of life. From the beginning of 1686 onward he was resolved to resist his master's designs. He saw in the Prince of Orange the agent who alone could bring in the indispensable armed power. He made his choice, if the worst should happen, to quit James and join William. He saw that the importance of his part in such a conflict would be measured by his influence over the Princess Anne and by his authority in the Army. If the hour of action should strike, he meant to use both potent factors to achieve, as smoothly and reasonably as possible, the public purpose and success of the course he had chosen.

In modern times such decisions would not be required. An officer or a courtier could resign his employments, retire to the country, and await events or the process of public reaction to his sacrifices. But for Churchill to leave the Court, to resign his command in the Army, would not merely have meant exclusion from all forms of public service and from all share in the impending crisis. No one who had been so close to the sovereign could, while he was in the full flush of manly activity and acquainted with so many secrets, retire without incurring the gravest suspicions. Instead of dwelling at Holywell with his family, he would probably have found himself in the Tower. He could, no doubt, have attempted to leave the kingdom and follow the long string of refugees and exiles who gathered in the Netherlands. But a simple flight like this would have been only to abandon simultaneously his King and his country; at once to desert the cause of Protestantism and to leave the Princess Anne, who had hitherto followed his guidance and depended so much upon him, in complete isolation.

He had certainly made two definite attempts to quit the Court under conditions which would not have entirely divested him of power, and thus to end a personal connexion with James already become false and painful. If Princess Anne had been allowed to go to The Hague, as he had planned, he and Sarah would certainly have gone with her. If he had obtained command of the British troops in Holland he would have been at William's side and in a position to exert an influence upon events. These courses had been barred: and, apart from reducing himself to a cipher and destroying all his means of service to causes which profoundly stirred him, there was nothing left but to remain and face all the dangers and peculiar reproaches of his station. All he could give the King was the faithful declaration of his opinion, and this on many occasions he made abundantly clear. If James, knowing his mind, employed him, it was at his own risk.

It was remarkable, indeed, that the King still kept Churchill about him. He made it plain to all his intimates that those who sought his favour, or still more his friendship, must embrace his faith. Many of his personal attendants yielded to the glamour of the royal smile or the fear of the royal frown. Salisbury, Melfort, Lorne, and many others thought that office was well worth a Mass. And no one needed official employment more than Churchill. He had no spacious estates in which to dwell, he lived only in the Court, at the head of his regiment, or with the prince he served; but to all attempts upon his faith he remained obdurate. He watched with silent disgust Sunderland, with whom he had many relationships and was to have more, take the plunge. The chief Minister of England, with all his wealth and high birth, bare-headed and barefooted, knelt in his shirt and knocked humbly at the door of the confessional. Churchill had only to imitate him to be the King's right arm, captain of his host, his long-cherished friend.

He never seems to have had the slightest trouble in rejecting such possibilities. Of course, he was a devout and lifelong Anglican Protestant. But we doubt if his choice, as his apologists contend, was made only upon religious grounds. He had a political opinion too. He knew England, and measured with superior accuracy the force of the passions now rising throughout the land. All the great men whose friendship he enjoyed, Halifax, Shrewsbury, Rochester, were moving in the one direction. On that same course he had launched the Princess Anne. Never mind the army at Hounslow! There would—at the worst—be two opposite factions there, and beyond the seas there was the Prince of Orange with trustworthy troops. But suppose it was the French who landed, instead of the Dutch! Still, he had chosen the part he would play.

The phrases 'religious toleration' and 'liberty of conscience' command spontaneous approval in modern times. The penal laws against Catholics and Dissenters were harsh and bitter. To create an England in which all men could seek God as they pleased and dwell in peace with their fellows was indeed a noble aim for a King. But it was not the aim of King James the Second; he sought the conversion of England to the Roman Catholic faith. He admired and applauded the intolerance of Louis XIV; he rejoiced intensely at the revocation of the

Edict of Nantes; he longed to use against the heresy in which his kingdom was sunk the secular terrors and torments which his brother sovereign could so happily apply.

Our ancestors saw, with the uncanny shrewdness which long, slow, increasing peril engenders, an endless vista of oppression and persecution, decked in a tinsel of fair-seeming toleration. They saw daily landing on their shores the miserable victims of Catholic 'toleration' as practised in France by the most powerful sovereign in the world. They knew the close sympathy and co-operation of the French and English Governments: they saw all that they cared for in this world and the next threatened, and if they failed to defend their rights and freedom, there might soon be no refuge open to them in any part of the globe. They therefore entered, not without many scruples and hesitations, but with inexorable resolve, upon the paths of conspiracy and rebellion.

If appeal is made to present-day opinion, the tribunal, while it acclaims 'religious toleration,' will at the same time inquire whether the conspiracy was only upon one side. Must the whole British nation submit, as the French people had been forced to do, to the religious convictions—whatever they might be or might become—of their anointed King? Was that King to be absolved from all reproach if night and day he concerted his plans, marshalled his adherents, trained his armies, in order to change the whole life, laws, and beliefs of his people? Was he entitled to break the solemn promises he had made, to practise every deceit and manœuvre which served his purpose, to use all the pressures of force and favour to compel obedience? Was he not guilty in his turn of conspiring against the people over whom he ruled? Was he not in rebellion against all that was most sacred, most precious, to the hearts of millions? Surely, then, it was a double conspiracy that was afoot, and must now on both sides go forward to an issue.

CHAPTER TWELVE

The Protestant Wind

⟨ 1688, Autumn ⟩

THE lines of battle were now slowly yet remorselessly drawing up in our island. Everything pointed, as in 1642, to the outbreak of civil war; but now the grouping of the forces was far different from the days when Charles I had unfurled his standard at Nottingham. The King had a large, well-equipped regular army, with a powerful artillery. He believed himself master of the best, if not at the moment the largest, navy afloat. He could call for powerful armed aid from Ireland and from France. He held the principal sea-ports and arsenals under trusty Catholic governors. He enjoyed substantial revenues. He had on his side his Catholic co-religionists, all the personal following which the Government and the Court could command, and, strangely assorted with these, a very considerable concourse of Dissenters and traditional Roundheads. He assumed that the Church of England was paralysed by its doctrine of non-resistance, and he had been careful not to allow any Parliament to assemble for collective action.

Ranged against him were not only the Whigs, but almost all the old friends of the Crown. The men who had made the Restoration, the sons of the men who had fought and died for his father at Marston Moor and Naseby, the Church whose bishops and ministers had so long faced persecution for the principle of Divine Right, the universities who had melted their plate for King Charles's coffers and sent their young scholars to his armies, the nobility and landed gentry whose interests had seemed so bound up with the monarchy: all, with bent heads and burning hearts, must now prepare themselves to out-face their King in arms.

It would indeed have been a strange war in which the sons of Puritans, Roundheads, and regicides would have marched for a Catholic and catholicizing King against Churchmen and Cavaliers, while the mass of the people remained helpless, passionate, terrified spectators. It would have been a war of the extremes against the means; a war of a heterogeneous coalition against the central body of English wealth, rank, and grit. Few there were who could truly measure the value of all these various elements and the force of their harmonious combination, should it occur. And above and beyond all lay the incalculable hazards and accidents of the battlefield.

Very fearsome and dubious must the prospect have seemed to the nobility, gentry, and clergy who embodied the life and meaning of the England that we still know. They had no army; they had no lawful means of resistance, expression, or debate. They could not appeal to the unenfranchised millions of peasants and townsmen. They saw in mental eye the King in martial panoply advancing upon them with all that royal power in whose sanctity they themselves were the chief believers, with French troops ready to descend at any moment upon their shores to quell rebellion, with the children of the Ironsides hand in hand with Jesuit priests. Never did the aristocracy or the Established Church face a sterner test or serve the nation better than in 1688. They never flinched; they never doubted. They comprehended and embodied "the genius of the English nation," they faced this hideous, fraudulent, damnable hotch-potch of anti-national designs without a tremor, and they conquered without a blow. Why they conquered and, above all, why they conquered bloodlessly, turned upon the action of no more than as many men and women as can be counted upon one's fingers.

Nearly all the preliminaries of the struggle in England were concerned with public opinion. The King could give his orders to the land and sea forces, and to all his great officers and adherents. He possessed a complete executive machine which, if it worked, was probably irresistible. But the nobility, the parsons, squires, and merchants who formed the conscious entity of England, were divided by the recent feuds of Whig and Tory and by many gradations of unorganized thought and temper. Their salvation depended upon their cohesion, and that cohesion could only be achieved by spontaneous action arising in a hundred loosely connected centres. Here lay the main risk. Unless their leaders could act together, each playing his part in his own station, their chances were precarious. Together they had to wait for indefinite and uncertain periods, together they must strike with the hour. Yet to concert action was treason.

In so wide and secret a confederacy, with scanty means of council and communication, every divergence, personal or local, was pregnant with disaster. Two main divisions of policy persisted almost to the end; each had massive arguments. The moderates, led by Halifax and Nottingham, urged caution and delay. The Ministry, they pleaded, was breaking up. Sunderland, Godolphin, Dartmouth were now striving to restrain the headstrong King. Alternatively, "Let him have rope enough!" Either things would get better or an overwhelming case would be presented upon which all could unite. No case had yet arisen to warrant actual treason. Nothing was more imprudent than a premature resort to arms. Remember Sedgemoor only three years ago, and how a standing army rallies to its duty once fighting has begun, and the soldiers see an enemy before them. "All is going well, if you do not spoil it."

On the other hand stood the party of action, headed by Danby. Danby was the stalwart. He was the first man of great position who definitely set himself to bring William and a foreign army into England. With Danby were the Whig leaders—Shrewsbury, Devonshire, and some others. These men urged that the danger was growing each day; that the King was bringing over Irish troops, that the Catholic grip upon the Army was strengthening, that the House of Lords could be watered and the House of Commons packed, and above all that no reform or mitigation could be trusted from such a bigot. The only hope lay in a disciplined Protestant army. As early as the spring of 1688 they took a most audacious decision. They invited William to invade England; and William replied that if he received at the right moment a formal request from leading English statesmen he would come, and that he would be ready by September. What followed played into the hands of these resolute men.

From April onward the party of action made good preparations. They took others into their confidence in proportion to what they needed to know. Trusty persons were informed, and their duties allotted. Efforts were made to draw in the moderates. The whole design was laid before Nottingham. At first he agreed, and then, upon misgivings in which cowardice played no part, he retracted his promise. How deadly the conspiracy had become can be judged from the story that his fellow-statesmen, leaders of a great party, Shrewsbury at their head, determined to ensure his silence by shooting him. He admitted to them that it was their right. Eventually, and with justice, they trusted to his oath. A nation-wide conspiracy was on foot by the end of May. Detailed plans were made, and a great many personal contacts established. The land was full of whisperings and of mysterious comings and goings. Sunderland, elusive, baffling to his enemies, incomprehensible to posterity, heard and understood much, not all of which was imparted to his master. Barillon knew less, but reported all he knew to both the Kings whose interests he served. Louis took a grave view. James shut his ears, pursued his course, and reviewed his troops.

Upon the troops much, though not all, depended. If the Army obeyed its orders and fought for the King, England would be torn by a civil war the end of which no man could foresee. But if the Army refused to fight or was prevented from fighting by any means, then the great issues at stake would be settled bloodlessly. It seems certain, though there is no actual proof, that the general revolutionary conspiracy had a definite military core; and that this formed itself in the Army, or at least among the high officers of the Army, step by step with the designs of the statesmen. The supreme object of all the conspirators, civil or military, was to coerce the King without using physical force. We cannot doubt that this was Churchill's long-formed intention. It is reasonable to assume that in this resolve he took every measure in his power; and, of course, these measures contemplated, if the need arose, treason and mutiny as known to the law, and personal treachery to his master. With him in secret consultation were the colonels of the two Tangier regiments, Kirke and Trelawny, the Duke of Grafton, commanding the Guards, the Duke of Ormonde, and a number of other officers.

Bishops, generals, Jesuits, and Nonconformist leaders eyed each other in a sinister silence as spring blossomed into summer. And now events struck their hammer-blows. At the end of April James issued a second and more far-reaching Declaration of Indulgence. In a reasoned manifesto he bid for the whole-hearted support of all—and they were many —who suffered—and they suffered grievously—from the penal laws. He ordered that the Declaration should be read in all the churches. On May 18 the Seven Bishops, headed by the Primate, the venerable Sancroft, protested against this use of the dispensing power. The clergy obeyed their ecclesiastical superiors, and from few pulpits throughout the country was the Declaration read. James, furious at disobedience and apparently scandalized at this departure, by the Church he was seeking to undermine, from its doctrine of non-resistance, demanded that the Bishops should be put on trial for seditious libel. Sunderland, now definitely alarmed, endeavoured to dissuade the King from this extreme step. He saw the spark which would fire the mine on which he knew himself to dwell. Even Lord Chancellor Jeffreys told Clarendon that the King was going too far, and had also the impudence to observe, "As to the judges, they are most of them rogues." The King persisted: the trial was ordered, and the Bishops, all of whom refused the proffered bail, were committed to the Tower.

On June 18, while the trial was still pending, the Queen gave birth to a son. This prodigious event produced general consternation. Until then every one might hope that the stresses which racked English society would die with the death of the King. Till then the accession of either Mary, the heir presumptive, or Anne, the next in order, promised an end to the struggle between a Catholic monarch and a Protestant people. Peaceable folk could therefore be patient until the tyranny was past. But here was the succession assured in the male line to an indefinite series of Catholic princes. It was unendurable.

The conveyance of the Bishops to the Tower, their two days' trial, and their acquittal on June 30 by a Middlesex jury, were occasions of passionate outbursts in their favour by all classes in the capital. Enormous crowds thronged the riverbanks to watch the barges carry the prisoners to and fro, or knelt in the streets in the hopes of being blessed by them. The humblest citizens were swayed by the same emotions which convulsed the rank and fashion of London. The troops at Hounslow joined in the rejoicings of the people. "What is that clamour?" asked the King, as he was leaving the camp after a visit. "Sire, it is nothing; the soldiers are glad that the Bishops are acquitted." "Do you call that nothing?" said James. These manifestations were repeated as the news spread throughout the country.

On that same night, while cannon and tumults proclaimed the public joy, the seven leaders of the party of action met at Shrewsbury's town house, and there and then signed and dispatched their famous letter to William. The signatories were Shrewsbury, Danby, Russell, Bishop Compton, Devonshire, Henry Sidney, and Lumley. Of these seven Compton had long been in the closest touch with Churchill at the Cockpit, yet he did not know how far Churchill was engaged, nor exactly what he knew. Shrewsbury and Russell were Churchill's intimate friends. Though not always colleagues in office, all three acted in concert for many years.

The letter, in the sure hands of Admiral Herbert, disguised as a common sailor, sped to The Hague, and its authors dispersed throughout the island for the purpose of levying war upon the King. Shrewsbury, though brought up a Catholic, had become a Protestant in the storms of 1681. He never detached himself from his new faith. Now, after mortgaging his estates to raise £40,000, he crossed the sea to join William and thenceforward stood at his side. Danby undertook to raise Yorkshire; Compton toured the North "to see his sisters." Devonshire, who had been condemned to an enormous fine for assaulting a Court partisan in the royal palace and had lain since 1685 in rebellious obscurity at Chatsworth, raised a regiment of horse from his tenantry. William, stricken in his ambition by the birth of a male heir, exclaimed, "Now or never!" and began the preparation of his expedition.

Churchill was not of sufficient political rank or territorial influence to be a signatory. Whether, if asked, he would have signed is unknown; but there is little doubt he would have deemed it an honour. Though of secondary importance, he lay more in the centre of the web and held more threads than the larger figures. Day by day he waited on the King, and watched the temper of the troops. Night by night he sat in the narrow, devoted cluster at the Cockpit. If he was in touch with Shrewsbury and Russell and their party of action, he was also intimate with Sunderland, the chief Minister, and with Halifax, the outstanding moderate. His countenance was inscrutable, his manner bland, his discretion unfailing.

The birth of the baby Prince who set so many ponderous wheels in motion was received with general incredulity, sincere or studiously affected. From the beginning doubts had been thrown upon the belated pregnancy of the Queen. The prayers and intercessions in which the Catholics had indulged, and their confident predictions that a son would be born as the result, led to a widespread conviction that a trick had been practised. The legend that a supposititious child had been smuggled into St James's Palace in a warming-pan was rife before the ashes of the official bonfires had vanished from the streets. By a strange imprudence of the King's the majority of persons present at the birth were Papists, the wives of Papists, or foreigners. The Archbishop was absent: he had that day been conducted to the Tower. Neither of the Hydes had been summoned, though as Privy Councillors, brothers-in-law of the King, and uncles of the two Princesses whose rights to the Crown were affected, their presence would have been natural. More important perhaps than all, Princess Anne was not there. She was at Bath. The Churchills were with her, and Sarah no doubt received an authentic account from the still beautiful Frances, now Duchess of Tyrconnel, who was on the spot.

It was vital to the nation to establish the doctrine that the child was an impostor. Sincerely attached to the principle of legitimacy, confronted with the appearance of a Papist heir, the English Protestants had no other means of escape from the intolerable admission. With the characteristic instinct and ingenuity of the English people for reconciling facts, law, and propriety with public interests and their own desires, they enshrined the legend of the warming-pan as a fundamental article of political faith. It was not dispensed with until after some eventful years, and when the question had ceased to have any practical importance.

Churchill now, as the days of action drew near, renewed his pledge given fifteen months before, and wrote to William:

> August 4, 1688
>
> Mr Sydney will let you know how I intend to behave myself: I think it is what I owe to God and my country. My honour I take leave to put into your royal highness's hands, in which I think it safe. If you think there is anything else that I ought to do, you have but to command me, and I shall pay an entire obedience to it, being resolved to die in that religion that it has pleased God to give you both the will and power to protect.

Such a letter written by a serving officer, at a time when conspiracy was rife and invasion imminent, was a deadly guarantee. Its capture or betrayal would justly involve the forfeit of his life at the hands of either a civil or a military tribunal. The invitation of the seven notables had been sent in the precautions of cipher. But Churchill's letter, which survives to this day, is in his own handwriting, signed with his name. He seems to have wished to share in a special degree the risks which his friends the signatories had incurred.

All this impending struggle, so ominous for our island people, so decisive upon their destiny, was one factor, but a vital factor, in the world war now about to begin. Across the sea, watching with strained vigilance the assembling armies of France, lay William of Orange with the troops and fleet of Holland. England, in her griefs and rages, was the decisive piece on the Continental board. Profoundly Protestant, vehemently anti-French, was she, with all her resources, to be cast upon the side of Gallican intolerance and French aggrandisement? Was she so to be committed, probably with fatal effect, against the whole instinct and interest of her people by the perverse obstinacy of a single man? Protestant Europe and Protestant England alike looked to William, as the champion of freedom against the many-sided tyrannies of Louis, to break the accursed spell. William accepted the dangerous duty. In the terse words of Halifax, "he took England on the way to France."

Before the Prince of Orange could invade England he had not only to prepare and assemble his troops and ships, but to obtain freedom to use them for such a purpose. At a moment when the whole of the French Army was massed and ready for immediate advance, it was not easy to persuade the threatened princes of Germany or the anxious burghers of Holland that their best chance of safety lay in sending the Dutch Army into England upon an expedition so full of uncertainty. The Great Elector was dead, but Frederick III, who had succeeded him in April, was resolute for war and, like his father, convinced that England must be gained. He even lent William a contingent of Prussian troops under the command of Marshal Schomberg. The other German princes acquiesced in the Prussian view. Most Catholic Spain set political above religious considerations, and made no bones about an expedition to dethrone a Catholic king. The Emperor alone demurred. Although dethronement was not suggested, his religious scruples were aroused. Lulled by communications from the Vatican at William's instance, he eventually agreed to an expedition to restore harmony in England and detach her from France. Only a dominating sense of common danger could have united these diverse interests and creeds upon a strategy so farseeing and broadminded.

William had next to convince the States-General: they had agreed to an enormous expenditure during the last two years upon the Dutch armaments; their land forces were upon a war footing, their fleet decisively stronger than the English. But the decision of the Dutch, and their ruler also, must be governed by the action of France. If the French armies marched against Holland the whole Dutch strength would be needed to meet the invader, and England must perforce be left to her fate. If, on the other hand, Louis struck upon the Rhine at Prussia and Germany, then the enterprise on which the Stadtholder's heart was set could go forward. All therefore hung in suspense. Meanwhile a great fleet of transports, with all the necessary supplies, had gathered in the Texel under the protection of the Dutch Navy, and the expeditionary force lay concentrated close at hand.

Louis XIV, with whom the initiative rested, delayed his choice till the last moment. He was ready to come to James's aid if James would definitely throw England on to the French side in the impending European struggle. All through July and August he offered him money, an army of thirty thousand men, and the French fleet. The French troops would enforce discipline and loyalty upon the English Army, and together they could certainly crush all resistance to the royal will. James, partly from patriotic pride in the independence of his country, partly from fear of the resentment which a French alliance would arouse among his subjects, and under the advice of Sunderland, made light of his own dangers and dallied with the French offers. He was still absorbed in his electioneering plans to produce by hook or by crook a House of Commons favourable to the repeal of the Test Act. All prospect of this would be swept away by an outbreak of war, the announcement of a French alliance or the arrival of French troops. On September 2 Louis, with large armies straining at the leash, and compelled by the military situation, resolved to bring matters to a head. He delivered through his Ambassador at The Hague an ultimatum to the Dutch Republic. It was declared that William's military preparations were a menace to England: that "friendship and alliance" existed between England and France, and that any enterprise undertaken by the Dutch against England would involve an immediate French declaration of war on Holland.

This violent step defeated its own object in both the countries affected. The States-General were enraged by the menace. James, in the utmost embarrassment at the declaration, publicly repudiated all idea of an alliance. The rejection of his aid not only offended Louis; it aroused his suspicions. It was so contrary to James's vital interests that it seemed explicable only by some secret arrangement between James and William, or between Sunderland and the States-General. The irresolute, shifting policy of the English Government lent colour to the belief in Holland that it was tied to France, and in France that it was tied to Holland. At any rate, the die was cast. Louis abandoned the hope of procuring England as an ally; he must be content with seeing her, as he believed and trusted, torn by a savage civil war in which William would be involved, and during which the island kingdom could play no part in Europe. On September 25 all the French armies were set in motion, not against the Dutch frontier, but towards the middle Rhine. From the moment that this movement became certain the States-General eagerly granted William permission for his English descent, and James's hour was come.

As the autumn weeks slipped by, excitement and tension grew throughout the island, and the vast conspiracy which now comprised the main strength of the nation heaved beneath the surface of affairs. The King's attempt to bring in some of the regiments of Irish Roman Catholics which Tyrconnel had raised for him produced symptoms so menacing that the process was abandoned. All turned on the wind. Rumour ran riot. The Irish were coming. The French were coming. The Papists were planning a general massacre of Protestants. The kingdom was sold to Louis. Nothing was safe, and no one could be trusted. The laws, the Constitution, the Church—all were in jeopardy. But a deliverer would appear. He would come clad with power from over the seas to rescue England from Popery and slavery—if only the wind would blow from the east. And here one of Wharton's couplets, which nominally applied to Tyrconnel, gained a new and, indeed, an opposite significance.

> O, why does he stay so long behind?
> Ho! by my shoul, 'tis a Protestant wind.

The Protestant wind was blowing in the hearts of men, rising in fierce gusts to gale fury. Soon it would blow across the North Sea!

> "Lero, lero, lilliburlero!
> Lilliburlero, bullen-a-lah!"

sang the soldiers and peasants of England in endless repetition through those days, "singing," as its author afterwards claimed, "a deluded prince out of three kingdoms."

Sunderland and Jeffreys were at this moment in chief control of the Cabinet. The magnitude of William's preparations and the alarming state of feeling throughout England produced a complete change in their attitude. Confronted by impending invasion from abroad and by imminent revolt at home, these two Ministers, recently so pliable and so reckless, strenuously advised the King to reverse his whole policy. They abandoned at one stroke all the meticulous efforts to pack a Nonconformist House of Commons upon which infinite labour had been spent, and by which widespread irritation had been caused. Parliament must indeed be called without delay, and the King and his Government must face the fact that it would be Episcopalian in character. All further aggressive Catholic measures must be stopped, and a reconciliation made with the Church of England. The fact that this advice came from the two Ministers who had hitherto been the most hardy, and who were both, it seemed, committed beyond forgiveness to the royal policy and all the hatreds it had roused, was staggering. They must indeed have swept the King off his feet by their outburst of warning. He crumpled under their pressure and panic. Within a week he was persuaded that he could not make head against William of Orange without the support of the Church of England. To gain this support he must negotiate with the bishops. He must stoop to conquer—or even to escape.

On October 3, in a conference at which the Primate and most of the bishops were present, he agreed to abolish the Ecclesiastical Commission, to close the Roman Catholic schools, to restore the Protestant Fellows of Magdalen College, to put the Act of Uniformity into force against Catholics and Dissenters. Action was taken accordingly with the utmost speed. The Lord-Lieutenants who had been dismissed were invited to resume their functions. Their charters were restored to the recalcitrant municipalities. The bishops were begged to let bygones be bygones. The Tory squires were urged to take their old places in the magistracy. Too late! The adverse movement had slowly but at length gathered a momentum which was uncontrollable even by those who had started it. It was evident that this sudden, belated repentance was a proof only of the weakness of the Government in the presence of approaching peril.

Now the unhappy King began to realize that by his folly and Sunderland's advice he had lost all. At the end of October he dismissed his Minister for vacillation and lack of firmness in counsel. James had drawn upon himself the evils of all courses and gained the benefit of none. He had alienated his friends; he had united all his enemies. William was about to invade him. Louis had abandoned him. The Pope, for the sake of whose faith he had hazarded all, in aversion to whom his subjects were in revolt, was working with his enemies. Outside France he had not a friend or sympathizer in Europe; and France was marching away from him upon Germany. At home he had centered upon himself the anger of almost all the wealth and power and learning of the nation without winning support from the popular masses. He had wounded Cavaliers without gaining Roundheads. He had estranged the Church without rallying the Chapel. Although Penn and the Nonconformist organizations had naturally supported his attempt to remove the penal laws, the great bulk of their followers remained vehemently hostile to Popery, and would rather endure maltreatment themselves than join in a Catholic crusade. The Catholic gentry whose wrongs had stirred his heart were now panicstricken by the plight into which he had led them. He was not even destined to go down fighting for the cause in which he so fervently believed. In the last few months of his reign he was compelled to desert the standard he had himself set up, and to try in vain to placate the furies he had aroused, by the sacrifice of all the objectives in whose pursuit he had aroused them.

Nor has the passage of generations vindicated his efforts for Catholic toleration. Had he joined the Catholic Hapsburgs and the Protestant princes in their war against the domination of France, he would have established with his own subjects a confidence and comradeship which might well have enabled him, if not to remove, at least gradually to neglect the enforcement of the Tests. Had he allowed the incomparable soldier whose gifts he had himself so long discerned to gain for him Protestant battles upon the Continent, the English people, relieved from their fear, might well have been generous to the co-religionists of the victorious prince who had served them well. So supple a part was beyond him, and, indeed, beneath him. Instead, he set in train a movement of events which made anti-Popery and a warming-pan the foundation of a dynasty, and riveted upon the English Catholics for more than a hundred and fifty years the shackles of the penal laws.

CHAPTER THIRTEEN

The Revolution

⟨ 1688, November ⟩

ON October 19 William set out upon the seas. His small army was a microcosm of Protestant Europe—Dutch, Swedes, Danes, Prussians, English, and Scottish, together with a forlorn, devoted band of French Huguenots who had no longer any country of their own. They were embarked upon about five hundred vessels escorted by sixty warships—almost the entire Dutch fleet. The English Rear-Admiral Herbert led the van, and the Prince of Orange hoisted, together with his own arms, the flag of England, on which was embroidered his motto, "I will maintain," with the addition, "the Protestant religion and the liberties of England"; all of which was made good. Dalrymple has written of the feelings of the Dutch as they watched this impressive concourse of vessels quitting their shores:

> . . . some flattered with the grandeur of their republic, others reflecting with anxiety that their frontier on one side was in the hands of the ancient tyrants, and on the other, exposed to an army of foreign mercenaries, all the artillery of their towns carried off, only a few ships of war left in their harbours, and the whole strength of the republic sent, during the rigours of Winter, to depend upon the hazards of winds and seas, and the fortune of war.

A violent gale scattered the fleet and cast it back upon the ports of Holland. One vessel, upon which no fewer than four companies of infantry were embarked, was driven on to the English coast and captured. The numbers of troops on this single vessel, together with the size of the fleet, gave the idea that William's army was four times as large as it was. But, anyhow, it had been driven back and ruined by the storms. James saw the finger of God. "It is not to be wondered at," he said, when he received the news at dinner, "for the Host has been exposed these several days." Convinced that the divine power and Holy Church had given him his son, he thought that they would also destroy his foes; and he dismissed Sunderland from his office as First Minister for being a faint-heart. But the new Secretary of State, Preston, a Protestant, renewed to him the advice of the fallen Minister. He must call a Parliament without manipulation and without delay.

Now this was a deadly matter for the King. No such Parliament could assemble in such a situation without calling in question not only the whole prerogative of the Crown, but, far graver, the *bona fides* of his son's birth. And here, by the mercy of God, was the hostile fleet scattered. Of course he refused. On this the Lord Chancellor Jeffreys abandoned himself to despair. "It is all naught," he exclaimed, with his customary profanity. "The Virgin Mary is to do all."

It was believed that William would strive to land in the North, and thither considerable bodies of the royal troops were proceeding. But the winds decided otherwise, and William ran south under full sail. On November 3 he anchored, so as to regather his whole fleet, in the Straits of Dover, in full view of the crowded coasts of England and France. The same wind that carried him here prevented Dartmouth from coming out of the Thames in any formation fit for battle, even if the loyalty of his captains and their seamen would have undertaken it. When to doubt, disinclination, and inferior strength are added adverse weather conditions, the inaction of naval forces is to be expected. The English fleet followed tardily behind the invader, and the same Protestant wind which blew him back to Torbay when he had overshot it forced the pursuers, who had got as far as Portland, to take shelter at Spithead. On November 5 William landed at Torbay, on the coast of Devon.

James was not at first unduly alarmed at the news. It was better that the invasion should have fallen on the Western counties than upon Yorkshire. He hoped to pen William in the West, and to hamper his communications by sea. The troops which had been sent to Yorkshire were recalled to the South, and Salisbury was fixed as the point of assembly for the royal army. Meanwhile William established himself at

Exeter and awaited the arrival of adherents. For ten days none came. Danby had expected him in Yorkshire. The West had learned its lesson after Sedgemoor, and no preparations for the rebellion had been made. William was disconcerted by this apparent apathy, and thought at first he was betrayed. However, gradually some notables arrived, and Sir Edward Seymour formed an association in his support. In this lull the King still looked with confidence upon his Army, and it is thither we must turn for the next event.

Some confusion of thought is evident in the searing reproaches with which both parties and successive generations have disfigured Churchill's reputation and have singled him out to bear whatever there was of shame in the wonderful deliverance of which all stood sorely in need. No one has impugned the sincerity of his religious convictions or the wisdom of his political view. No one can dispute the proofs of his long attachment to both, or of the reported declarations by which his position became well known to all whom it concerned. Few will urge that personal indebtedness to a prince requires behaviour contrary to a man's conscience and to the interests of his native land. Every one will repudiate the idea that Churchill—a fervent Protestant, a resolved opponent of French domination in Europe, and an adherent of our laws and Constitution as then known—should have lent his gifts and sword to the bloody task of forcibly converting his fellow-countrymen to Popery, and of setting up in England a despotism on the French model, by French arms and in French interests.

It follows, therefore, that Churchill was right to abandon King James. The only questions open are When? and How? Ought he to have quitted the King when he wrote his first letter of May 1687 to William of Orange? Surely not: the circumstances in question might never have come to pass. The King might yield to the increasing pressure brought upon him from all sides. He might reverse his policy. He did, in fact, reverse it. Was it, then, when he wrote his second letter to William, in August 1688, that he should have deserted James? But by this time he knew from Sunderland of the intended change of policy which even the most hard-bitten, self-seeking Ministers resolved to press upon their master, and of the probable summoning of a new Parliament chosen in the old way. Ought he, then, to have left the King's service, given up his commissions and appointments, and gone to his home or, if need be, to prison, when James dismissed Sunderland at the end of October and withdrew the writs for a free Parliament? But by now William was on the seas. Trusting in the solemn written promises of leading Englishmen—among which Churchill's undertakings were the most explicit—he had launched out upon the hazardous enterprise to which they had called him. Ought Churchill, then, in November 1688 to have extinguished himself as a factor in the momentous events actually impending, and left William to look for his pledged aid in vain? Surely there is more shame in a breach of faith contrary to convictions than in the severance of loyalty in harmony with them. A flight from responsibility was only treachery in another and an abject form.

It was a hideous situation into which he had been drawn by no fault of his own, by no unwise or wrongful action, by no failure of service, by no abandonment of principle. But it was a situation which had to be faced and dealt with calmly and sensibly in the manner most likely to minimize the public dangers and sufferings, and to procure a good result for his country and for himself. Moreover, in conspiracies and rebellions the penalties for failure are rightly so severe that all who are unluckily drawn into them have not only a vital need for themselves, but also a duty to others associated with them and to the cause at stake, to ensure success, and above all bloodless success, by forethought and every well-concerted measure. To lure, like Monmouth, associates and humble followers on fools' errands to their doom can find no defenders. Thus Churchill had to go through with his undertakings, and by such steps as were likely to win.

This was a dangerous time for James to have at the head of the host the Frenchman, Feversham, who had been so harshly lampooned round London and in all the garrisons after Sedgemoor. There was at the King's disposal Feversham's brother, the competent French general Roye. He certainly thought of offering the chief command to him. Roye, who had learned since his arrival of the intense feeling in the Army against France and French patronage, was well enough informed to put the suggestion aside. He could not, he said, command an army not one word of whose language he could speak. So Feversham remained Commander-in-Chief. All the more necessary was it to have Churchill almost on any terms at the royal headquarters. In the opinion of those rather loosely disciplined professional soldiers, with their brave and haughty society officers, he was without equal or rival the leading English general. The habit of soldiers to fix upon a leader who embodies to them a martial ideal and to obey him in a crisis has often been proved. Here was an hour when everything hung upon the temper of the troops. The only hope of inducing the army, and especially its officers, to fight for the King was to give the impression that the best fighting man of English blood would give or be associated with the orders they received. The misgivings which James had owned when he superseded Churchill before Sedgemoor must have recurred to his mind in an aggravated form at this juncture. But what else was there to do? Accordingly on November 7 Churchill was promoted Lieutenant-General with the command of a brigade, or, as we should now call it, a division, of the army concentrating at Salisbury.

Churchill could not consider this advancement as a mark of favour It was, in fact, the hopeful appropriation of his military prestige to the royal cause at a moment when all title deeds were called in question. Acceptance involved no assumption of new obligations on his part. In this important but subordinate position he had a seat at the councils of war and a voice in their decisions. He was not, however, in either nominal command or actual control of the army. His opinion was invited; his influence and authority were invoked. He was saddled before the nation with the responsibility. But the King really leaned upon the two Frenchmen. They were immune from the passions which shook England. He could count on their fidelity however his own subjects might behave. Thus Churchill was at the same moment made to fill the public eye and kept under supervision and control. In the circumstances this was probably the best course open to the King.

During these heart-shaking days many alternative solutions of the nation's problem presented themselves. When the royal headquarters arrived at Salisbury, it might well be found that the mood of the troops was such that no battle could be fought; but that, on the other hand, a negotiation would be entered into, as afterwards happened, with the Prince of Orange and his invading army. At that time none of the English conspirators had contemplated the dethronement of the King, and William had carefully dissembled his ambitions. His small, solid army was only the steel tip of the spear of a British resolve. He could not conquer six million English with fifteen thousand men. The constable had arrived upon the scene of disorder. He was helpless without the support of public opinion and of sturdy, well-disposed citizens. It might well be that a parley between the chiefs on both sides would result in an agreement. James might become a limited monarch, permitted to exercise his personal religion in private, but compelled to govern with Parliamentary institutions, to preserve the Protestant character of England, and, as part of the League of Augsburg, to make war upon France. He might even be compelled to choose between having his son excluded from the succession or brought up a Protestant. Again, there might be a regency, with William as Mayor of the Palace, with James as a powerless but much respected Merovingian king, the succession at his death assured to his daughters, the Protestants Mary and Anne. All these possibilities were still open when James left London.

The King had barely arrived at Windsor when disconcerting news was received. Lord Cornbury, eldest son of Lord Clarendon, an officer of the Life Guards, found himself for a few hours in command of the troops assembling at Salisbury. Cornbury intended to carry the whole three regiments into the Prince's army. William, duly appraised, had set superior forces in motion to surround them, and the troops would certainly have been disarmed or, if possible, incorporated. But the officers were puzzled by the length of the marches and the obvious imprudence of the operation. They demanded the production of the orders. Cornbury, seeing himself detected, rode over to William with about two hundred men, while the rest of the brigade only extricated themselves with difficulty from the trap into which they were being led.

Cornbury's desertion was the first of the successive blows. It was impossible to tell who among the officers of the Army could be trusted. It seemed certain that if they could all be trusted the Army would fight, and if it fought it would probably win.

The fact that Cornbury was intimate with his cousin the Princess Anne and was constantly at the Cockpit; the fact that the military arrangements had been so cast as to leave this young officer in chief command at Salisbury for some critical hours, and that he should have taken such audacious action, all pointed to a plot in which the superior chiefs of the Army, and Churchill above all, were engaged. There is no proof; but it may well be so. Certainly Churchill was trying to bring about the predominance of William without the fighting of a battle, and this would well have served for a preliminary move.

On November 17 the King set out from Windsor to join the army at

Salisbury. It was a strange party that fared with him to the wars. More than half were resolved, and most of these already pledged, to abandon him. Some had been for months actively conspiring with the invader. His own son-in-law, Prince George of Denmark, had actually agreed to the arrangement by which the Princess Anne should at the chosen moment leave London for William's camp. His own Household troops were honeycombed with disloyalty. His nephew, the Duke of Grafton, and nearly all his most capable officers, the leaders of many of his trusted regiments, were merely awaiting an opportunity to transfer their services to the enemy. Every decision, except those of hour and method, had been taken. Apart from his own Catholic communion and the French agents, there was no one upon whom he could depend. Even his fiercest partisans of Sedgemoor three short years before, men like Kirke and Trelawny, were now his foes. On all sides salutes and ceremony, unaffected respect and reverence for his person, and yet on all sides implacable treason, indistinguishable from public duty.

Among these men rode Churchill. None was more sure of himself than the newly promoted Lieutenant-General. His mind had long been made up, his pledge given, and his plans laid. Indeed, these evidences of design are the ground upon which censure has specially fastened. The elaborate, smooth-working preparations which are admired when they produce the march to Blenheim are repellent, though not less necessary, in a conspiracy. In London Sarah had her instructions about the Princess Anne, which she would fulfil with sure punctuality. Afloat, his brother George was working, with an ever-growing crowd of sea officers, to gain the fleet, and was himself about to carry his ship, the *Newcastle*, to William. Churchill himself was united in resolve and confederation with the principal nobles and functionaries. All—each playing his part wherever stationed—were taking day by day the steps which, should their designs miscarry, would cost them hearth and home and life itself. Ruin, exile, the scaffold—these were the stakes to which the compulsory game of politics had risen. They were already cast upon the board; there could be no withdrawal of them. Irrevocable! All grim, cold, doom-laden!

At this crisis in his fortunes King James could marshal as large an army as Oliver Cromwell at his height. Nearly forty thousand regular soldiers were in the royal pay and moving at the royal command towards Salisbury and the Dutch invader. But the Scottish troops, about four thousand strong, had only reached Carlisle, the bulk of the three thousand Irish were still beyond Chester, and at least seven thousand men must be left to hold down London. Still, twenty-five thousand men, or double the number of William's expedition, were around Salisbury when the King arrived on November 19. Here was the largest concentration of trained full-time troops which England had ever seen. What would they do?

This was the question which dominated the thoughts of all the leading figures who composed the King's headquarters or held the commands. There had been several vexatious delays and hitches in the assembly of the troops. The King and Churchill eyed each other, the sovereign in mute appeal, the servant in grave reserve: and both sought to penetrate by every channel open to them the secret of the Army. To the King, with his two French generals and the French Ambassador ever at his side, the aspect was obscure and dubious. To Churchill and the commanders banded with him it was highly disconcerting. Most of the officers were no doubt thoroughly disaffected. The Protestant regimental officers were divided and in evident distress. But the Papist officers and their men were ardent in their loyalty, and no one could be sure that the Protestant rank and file, if strongly gripped, were not capable of being led against the foreign foe or foreign deliverers. The least trustworthy regiments at James's disposal were those upon whom he should have been able to count the most. The Guards, the Dragoons and Cavalry, those officers and men who habitually surrounded the Court, who had felt the mood of London, and were aware of the political issues at stake, were known to use mutinous language. But the main body of the Line at this juncture, though Protestant in sentiment, were still governed by their discipline and their uniforms.

James, warned from many quarters, meditated Churchill's arrest. Feversham on his knees demanded it, declaring his disaffection patent. Churchill's incarceration at Portsmouth was debated. This was not a light matter to decide. His appointment had been advertised to the troops. The news of his arrest would have been not less injurious than his desertion. The shock to the Army would have been as great. So many were involved, so near, so intimate, so long-trusted and proved so faithful, that the unhappy sovereign knew not where to begin, nor, if he began, where to stop. On all sides his narrow circle of Papists, Irish, and Frenchmen encountered whisperings, averted eyes, or even cold shoulders and hostile looks. The King hesitated, delayed, put the matter off until the morrow.

We need not delve into a painful analysis of Churchill's feelings at this juncture. Lord Wolseley has drawn for us a harrowing picture of the moral and sentimental stresses through which his hero is supposed to have passed on the night of November 23, when he is represented as finally making up his mind to desert James, and how he must have balanced his duty and gratitude to his master and patron on the one hand against the Protestant cause upon the other. These well-meant efforts of a friendly biographer have certainly no foundation. All had, as we have shown, been settled long before. There never had been any process of weighing and balancing which side to take. The only difficulty had been to judge a ceaselessly shifting situation. But now all was simple. Policy and plans were settled; the last preparations had been made. The hour of action was always, to him, the least arduous of trials. That hour had now come.

A council of war was held on the evening of November 23. Churchill, supported by Grafton, when asked his opinion, advised an advance towards the enemy, while Feversham and Roye were for retreat. The King accepted Feversham's opinion. Churchill's may well have been the right advice to give on military grounds. There is a curious symmetry about his actions on many occasions which seems to range a correctness and justice of view on the event of the moment with his general designs. But it is equally arguable that he gave the right advice either because he knew the opposite course would be adopted, or because, if he had been taken at his word, that would have been convenient to his resolves. Every forward march would carry him nearer to William, would enable the two women for whose safety he was concerned, his wife and the Princess Anne, to make their escape more easily, and even his own decisive ride would be shorter. Once the Army was dispersed in its retreat, and the loyal were separated from the disloyal regiments, his arrest would be easy. All these matters are covered by the general relationship in which the chief actors stood to one another and by judgment upon the main issues.

We believe that Churchill stayed with the Army till the very last moment that he dared—and he dared much. By the end of the council on the 23rd he had convinced himself that the military plot had failed; that there was no prospect that the English commanders would be able to go to the King and say in the name of the Army, "You must open negotiations with William, and you must call a free Parliament." They had used, so far as it was possible, all their influence upon the troops without decisive results, and brought themselves into extreme peril thereby. Nothing remained but to escape with their immediate retinues and followers.

Therefore, on this same night Churchill, the Duke of Grafton, and Colonel Berkeley, with about four hundred officers and troopers, mounted their horses and rode forth from their camp by Salisbury. Some time during the 24th they arrived at Crewkerne, about twelve miles from William's headquarters at Axminster, after a march of nearly fifty miles. Churchill left the following letter to the King behind him:

Sir,

Since men are seldom suspected of sincerity, when they act contrary to their interests, and though my dutiful behaviour to Your Majesty in the worst of times (for which I acknowledge my poor service is much overpaid) may not be sufficient to incline you to a charitable interpretation of my actions, yet I hope the great advantage I enjoy under Your Majesty, *which I own I can never expect in any other change of government*, may reasonably convince Your Majesty and the world that I am actuated by a higher principle, when I offer that violence to my inclination and interest as to desert Your Majesty at a time when your affairs seem to challenge the strictest obedience from all your subjects, much more from one who lies under the greatest personal obligations to Your Majesty. This, sir, could proceed from nothing but the inviolable dictates of my conscience, and a necessary concern for my religion (which no good man can oppose), and with which I am instructed nothing can come in competition. Heaven knows with what partiality my dutiful opinion of Your Majesty has hitherto represented those unhappy designs which inconsiderate and self-interested men have framed against Your Majesty's true interest and the Protestant religion; but as I can no longer join with such to give a pretence by conquest to bring them to effect, so I will alway with the hazard of my life and fortune (so much Your Majesty's due) endeavour to preserve your royal person and lawful rights, with all the tender concerns and dutiful respect that becomes, sir, Your Majesty's most dutiful and most obliged subject and servant,

Churchill

In the records at Blenheim a copy of this letter was found wrapped in another written by Prince George of Denmark, no doubt at the same time and under Churchill's advice. But the Prince, who, with Ormonde, deserted his father-in-law the next day, takes a view which extends beyond the island that had become his home; and for the first time we see how large a part the Protestant coalition against France played in the councils of the Cockpit.

"Whilst the restless spirits of the enemies of the reformed religion," wrote the Prince,

> backed by the cruel zeal and prevailing power of France justly alarm and unite all the Protestant princes of Christendom and engage them in so vast an expense for the support of it, can I act so degenerate and mean a part as to deny my concurrence to such worthy endeavours for disabusing of your Majesty by the reinforcement of those laws and establishment of that government on which alone depends the well-being of your Majesty and of the Protestant religion in Europe.

We have no doubt that these words expressed the deepest convictions of Churchill as well as those of the honest Prince who wrote them. James's ideal of England redeemed to the true faith, dwelling in definitely established absolute monarchy, advancing independently, but in royal alliance with the great King of France to the extirpation of Protestantism in Europe, shone for him clear and bright. In the mind of his servant there arose perhaps another picture more practical, not less dire, not less majestic. John Churchill saw the rise of Britain to the summit of Europe, curbing and breaking with the aid of William of Orange the overweening power of France. He saw himself, with the Dutchman if need be, or under England's Protestant Princess, advancing at the head of armies to the destruction of that proud dominion. He may even have seen at this early time the building up upon the ruins of the French splendour of a British greatness which should spread far and wide throughout the world and set its stamp upon the future.

To William, Churchill's arrival at Axminster was an enormous relief. Next to defeat his deadliest danger was victory. To avoid bloodshed, to avoid beating with foreign troops a British army in the field, was essential to his aim of securing the throne. He welcomed his new adherent with formal ceremony, and used his services to the best advantage.

It cannot be proved that the defection of so many important officers destroyed the possibility that the Army would fight. If a regular purge had been made, as Feversham proposed, and sergeants promoted to fill all vacancies in the commissioned ranks, if Catholic or French officers had been placed in the key commands, and if the King himself had led his soldiers to battle, it is probable that a most fierce and bloody event would have followed. But Churchill's desertion, followed as it was by that of his own relations and closest servants, broke the King's spirit. When he saw that he could not even keep the Churchill who had been till now his intimate, faithful servant for nearly a quarter of a century, he despaired. He collapsed morally, and from that moment thought only of sending his wife and child to France and following them as soon as possible. It is this fact, and the personal elements that entered into it, that have made Churchill's desertion of James at Salisbury, although compulsory and inevitable, the most poignant and challengeable action of his life.

And now revolt broke out all over the country. Danby was in arms in Yorkshire; Devonshire in Derby; Delamere in Cheshire. Lord Bath delivered Plymouth to William. Byng, a Rear-Admiral representing the captains under Dartmouth's command, arrived at his headquarters to inform him that the fleet and Portsmouth were at his disposal. City after city rose in rebellion. There was an eager rush of notabilities to greet the rising sun. By one universal, spontaneous convulsion the English nation repudiated James.

It was high time for the wives to do their part. Anne and Sarah had no mind to await the return of the indignant King. James sent orders to search both Churchill's houses, and to arrest Sarah. The Princess prevailed upon the Queen to delay the execution of this last order till the morning, and in the night the two women fled from the Cockpit.

In the dead of night they descended the wooden staircase, found the Bishop and Lord Dorset awaiting them, waded through the mud of Pall Mall, in which Anne lost her shoe, to Charing Cross, and thence were carried in a coach to the Bishop of London's residence in Aldersgate.

All search for the fugitives was vain, and when the unhappy King reached Whitehall in the afternoon, he could but exclaim in despair, "God help me! Even my children have forsaken me!"

The King, having assembled such peers and Privy Councillors as were still in London, was advised by them to enter into negotiations with the Prince of Orange and to accord an amnesty to all who had joined him. He nominated Halifax, Nottingham, and Godolphin as his Commissioners to treat with William. He did not know that Halifax and Nottingham had both been privy to William's design. Neither did Halifax know that the King had no intention to treat, and was only using the negotiations as the means of gaining time to send his wife and child abroad and to follow them himself. William, on his part, was in no hurry, and more than a week passed before the necessary safe-conducts were granted to the Commissioners, and they were conducted to his headquarters, which had now reached Hungerford. Meanwhile James had sent his infant heir to Portsmouth with orders to Dartmouth to send him at once to France. Dartmouth, for all his loyalty, refused to obey this fatal command, which he declared would render him "guilty of treason to Your Majesty and the known laws of the kingdom."

But James was not to be deterred. The baby Prince was brought back from Portsmouth, and on the night of December 9 the Queen, escorted only by Count Lauzun and Riva, an Italian gentleman, escaped, with her child, to Gravesend and thence to France. As soon as the King knew that his wife and son were safely off he prepared to follow them. Elaborate arrangements having been made to deceive the Court and the Council, the King stole from the palace an hour or two after midnight on December 11, crossed the river, and rode hard for the coast. He endeavoured to plunge his realm into anarchy. He threw the Great Seal into the Thames; and sent orders to Feversham to disband the Army, and to Dartmouth to sail with what ships he could for Irish ports. Dartmouth, stricken to the heart by his master's desertion of his post, placed the fleet under the orders of William. But Feversham, with reckless wickedness, scattered the soldiers, unpaid but not disarmed, upon the population. General consternation ensued. The King's Commissioners saw they had been befooled. The wildest rumours of impending Irish massacres spread through the land. The London mob sacked the foreign embassies, and every one seized arms in defence of hearth and home. A wild panic and terror, long remembered as "Irish Night," swept the capital. Undoubtedly a complete collapse of civil government would have occurred but for the resolute action of the Council, which was still sitting in London. With difficulty they suppressed the storm, and, acknowledging William's authority, besought him to hasten his marches to London.

But the very next day, while the Council was sitting, a poor countryman arrived at the door with an appealing message from the King. James had actually got on board a ship, but, missing the tide, was caught, mauled, grabbed, and dragged ashore by the Faversham fishermen and townsfolk, who took him for a Jesuit in flight. What followed is briefly and well told by Ailesbury, who gives unconsciously a picture which historians seem to have missed. Ailesbury had striven hard to dissuade James from his flight, and when the news that the fugitive had been intercepted at the coast was brought to the decapitated Council, he broke the prolonged silence by proposing that his Majesty should be invited to return forthwith to his post. Charged with this task, he set out by coach and a-horse to retrieve his master out of the hands of the mob at Sheerness. He was haughtily received by the royal captive. His high jack-boots prevented him from falling on his knees when entering the presence, and he could only bob his knee. Whereat James, unshaven, ill-fed, rounded up and put in the pound like an errant bull by the local townsfolk and seamen, but unshakably sure of his royal rights, remarked, "Ha! It was all Kings when I left London." To this reception at the end of his loyal and difficult journey through the turbulent, panic-stricken towns of Kent and by roadways infested with revolt and disorder Ailesbury—so he tells us—used some extremely plain language, to which his sovereign was graciously pleased to hearken. He then proceeded to collect some victuals, bake the best bread possible in the circumstances, and ask the King whether he would not dine in state. His Majesty signified his pleasure; the local dignitaries and some of the populace were admitted wonder-struck to the miserable dwelling, and the faithful Gentleman of the Bedchamber, jack-boots notwithstanding, managed (by holding on to the table) to serve him on the knee; thus restoring public confidence and decorum. At intervals throughout the day fragments of the disrupted royal household arrived in Romney. The barber, with the valets and clothes, arrived in the afternoon; the cooks a little later. The Board of Green Cloth was on the spot by dusk; the royal saddle-horses came in during the night, and a troop of Life Guards were reported approaching the next morning. Thus the Court was reconstituted, though in a somewhat skeleton state.

Ailesbury stayed by his master thenceforward. He arranged for a hundred troopers of the Life Guards to be drawn up in single file to encourage him with their acclamations. He persuaded James to drive through the City of London, where the people, perplexed and dumbfounded by the awful event of his flight, received him with relief and almost enthusiasm. He accompanied James from Whitehall when, at William's order, he was escorted by the Dutch Guard down the river to Rochester. He shared with him the peril of the "hideous shooting of the bridge" on the swift, outflowing tide. Once this danger was overcome, the royal party picnicked agreeably in the boats, the King passing food and wine to the Dutch captain of the convoying flotilla.

Ailesbury abode with the King at Rochester, and again endeavoured to prevent his leaving the island. William, who had been profoundly inconvenienced by his return and longed for his fresh departure, caused hints to reach him that his life was in danger. James, no physical coward—indeed, as we have seen, a proved veteran by sea and land—was cowed to his marrow by the overwhelming tide of adverse opinion and the wholesale desertion and repudiation of almost all on whom he had counted. After some days of painful suspense the unhappy man escaped to the river by the back door, which the Prince of Orange had taken pains to leave unguarded, and this time succeeded in leaving English soil for ever. We are told in his so-called memoirs that he expected he would be sent to the Tower, "which no King ever quitted except for his grave," and he felt it his sacred duty to preserve his royal person from such outrageous possibilities.

But though the downfall and flight of this impolitic grandson of Henry of Navarre were at the time ignominious, his dignity has been restored to him by history. Heredity, fatalism, the besetting Stuart infatuation of obstinacy, his stern religious faith, his convinced patriotism according to his lights, all combined to lead him to disaster. He was doomed alike by his upbringing, his office, and his nature. His fixed domestic ideas made an effective foreign policy impossible. His Catholic convictions left him a stubborn anomaly upon a Protestant throne. He was at once a capable administrator and a suicidal politician; a man virtuous in principle and gross in practice; a personage equally respectable and obnoxious. Yet he carried with him into lifelong exile an air of royalty and honour which still clings to his memory.

On the afternoon of December 23 William learned that the King had fled, and felt himself in one form or another undisputed master of England. He lost no time in taking the step for the sake of which he had come across the water. The French Ambassador was given twenty-four hours to be gone from the island, and England was committed to the general coalition against France.

CHAPTER FOURTEEN

Marlborough and William

✧ 1688-90 ✧

THE Prince of Orange had now become the effective military ruler of his new country; but there was no lawful Government of any kind. The Convention Parliament—assembled on the authority of the revolutionary junta—dived lustily into academic disputes, and the differences between the Whigs and the Tories, temporarily merged in their common danger, soon reappeared. Was the throne vacant? Could the throne ever be vacant? Was there a contract between the King and the people which James had broken? Had he abdicated by flight, or merely deserted? Could he be deposed by Parliament? Arising from all this, should William become Regent, governing in the name of the absent James? Should Mary become Queen in her own right? Had she not, in view of the virtual demise of the Crown, in fact already become Queen? Or should William be made sole King; or should William and Mary reign jointly; and if Mary died, should Anne forthwith succeed, or should William continue to reign alone as long as he lived? Both Houses, both parties, and the Church applied themselves to these lively topics with zest and without haste.

William's aim from the first was to obtain the Crown of England for himself alone. Until James's flight he would have been content with any solution which brought England into the coalition against France; but thenceforward he saw no obstacle to his full ambition. Years before Burnet had earned William's gratitude by inducing Mary to promise, should she succeed her father, that they should be joint-sovereigns. The Stadtholder now flew higher still. He intimated first that he would not be Regent, governing in the name and against the will of a dethroned sovereign with whom he would certainly be at war. "He had not," he said, "come over to establish a Commonwealth or be a Duke of Venice." Rather than that he would return to Holland. Mary's rights were espoused by Danby, who had been disappointed that William had not landed in Yorkshire, and that his own share in the event had not been larger. He proposed that Mary should be Queen. William disposed of this idea by putting it about that he would not be "his wife's gentleman-usher." Through Bentinck, his Dutch confidant, he bid high for the sole kingship, with his wife but a consort. Burnet was staggered by this ingratitude to Mary. The idea of supplanting her in her lawful and prior rights caused widespread anger. William's appetite found its only prominent supporter in Halifax. It was, in fact, the first shock to his popularity in England.

Churchill steered a middle course, at once independent and judicious, through these controversies. Like most of the Tories, he could not vote directly for the dethronement of James; but neither would he actively support the Tory proposal for a regency to which William objected so strongly. He stayed away from the critical division on January 29, and a regency was voted down by fifty-one to forty-nine. He voted later that James had "deserted" the throne and had not "abdicated"; but when the Lords gave way to the Commons and agreed that the Prince and Princess of Orange should be joint sovereigns, he supported their decision. Sarah, under her husband's advice, persuaded Anne to surrender in favour of William her right to succeed to the throne on Mary's death. Thus William gained without dispute the Crown for life. This was a service of the first order, and probably counted in William's mind even above the desertion at Salisbury which had prevented a battle. From the very beginning, however, and even on this subject, the King showed a definite coolness towards the Churchills. On Halifax suggesting to him that Lord Churchill "might perhaps prevail with the Princess of Denmark to give her consent" he bridled, saying, "Lord Churchill could not govern him nor his wife as they did the Prince and Princess of Denmark." Halifax, who recorded this conversation, noted in William "a great jealousy of being thought to be governed," and added, "That apprehension will give uneasiness to men in great places. His dislikes of this kind have not always an immediate effect as in the instance of Lord Churchill," but "like some slow poisons work at a great distance of time."

William accepted the arrangements made by Parliament with good grace. He confirmed Churchill in his rank of Lieutenant-General. He employed him practically as Commander-in-Chief to reconstitute the English Army. In this important task Churchill's military knowledge and organizing capacity had full scope. At the coronation in April Churchill was created an earl. The title Earl of Marlborough, so honourably borne, had since 1680 been extinct. We can understand why Churchill chose it for his own.

In May war was formally declared against France; and as William was detained in England and later embroiled in Ireland, Marlborough led the English contingent of eight thousand men against the French in Flanders. The world conflict which had now begun only gradually reached its full intensity. The French, who had a magnificent army, found eventually in Luxembourg a commander not unworthy to be named with Condé and Turenne. The allies ranged themselves along a three hundred-mile crescent from the Upper Rhine to the Belgian coast. They were more numerous than the French, and able everywhere to assume the offensive. Four separate armies advanced simultaneously, but in the leisurely fashion of those days, against the French frontiers. In the north the Spaniards and Dutch moved through Belgium towards Courtrai under the Prince of Vaudemont. Next in the line and farther south the Dutch and Swedes, together with the English contingent, sought, under the command of the Prince of Waldeck, to operate between the Sambre and the Meuse. Beyond the Ardennes the Prussians and North Germans under the Elector of Brandenburg aimed at the capture of Bonn, upon the Rhine; and farther south still the forces of the Empire, under the able leadership of the Count of Lorraine, struck at Mainz. A modest but definite measure of success rewarded all these operations.

When Marlborough landed at the end of May he found the British troops in very poor condition, and the three months which elapsed before active operations began were indispensable to their training and discipline. He made a great improvement in both. He drilled his men sedulously, saw to their pay, food, and clothing with that meticulous housekeeping from which his armies always profited, and repressed abuses of all kinds. In a few months the British force, from being the worst, was recognized as the best managed in Waldeck's army of about thirty-five thousand men.

The Prince of Waldeck was one of William's trusted leaders. His prolonged experience had made him a pedant in the art of war. Indeed, it was to him, as to most of the commanders at this time on both sides, very like a game of chess. The gambits and defences of each were well known to all players of a certain professional standing. As long as no obvious mistakes were made nor any serious risks run, no marked change in the situation was likely. Here a fortified town might be taken, there a small area of hostile country might be used as feeding-ground. But if the conventional counter-measures were taken by the opponent, these small prizes were placidly relinquished, and the armies continued to face and manœuvre against each other with the decorum of performers in a minuet. For this sedate warfare Waldeck's age of sixty-nine was no disqualification. He soon saw the improvement in the quality of the British, and took a liking to Marlborough. On August 24, having crossed the Sambre, he stood before the small ancient town of Walcourt, which rises on its hillock from an undulating and wooded landscape. Here he was well satisfied to live upon the enemy's country, sending his foraging parties out to gather supplies.

Marshal d'Humières, who commanded the opposing French army, felt bound to resent this trespass. He marched with becoming haughtiness to expel the intruders, and on the morning of August 25 fell upon the allied foraging parties and outposts about two miles south of Walcourt. It happened that Marlborough was in charge of these petty operations, and that the 16th Regiment of Foot (now the Bedfordshire Regiment), together with some three hundred Dutch horse and dragoons, formed their support. At nine o'clock the approach of large French forces was noticed, and soon after it was realized that these were the vanguard of the whole French army. Cannon were fired to recall the foragers and alarm the camps. Meanwhile the English regiment barred the advance of the French. They were heavily attacked; but under Colonel Hodges offered a stubborn resistance. For nearly two hours these six hundred English infantry prevented the hostile advance. When Marlborough learned that all was in readiness in Waldeck's army, he directed them to withdraw to the higher ground on the east of the hill of Walcourt, where other British troops and several batteries had come into line. The manner in which this single battalion effected its orderly retreat in the closest presence of very powerful French cavalry was a foretaste of the qualities which Europe was taught reluctantly to recognize in the English Army.

Meanwhile the Prince of Waldeck had occupied the town of Walcourt and had posted his army in position mainly on its eastern side. All the foragers had returned to camp, and d'Humières could take his choice whether he wanted a battle or not. It was now noon. The ground was not at all favourable to the French, but d'Humières seems to have been inflamed by the sharp fighting in which his vanguard had been engaged and did not take the trouble to reconnoitre. He ordered a strong column of French infantry, including eight battalions of the French Guard, to carry the town of Walcourt by assault. This was certainly a very difficult task to undertake voluntarily. The defences of the town were antiquated, and the walls had crumbled in several places. Still, it stood upon a hill, was partly covered by a river, and was girt about with a strong field army. Nevertheless, the French made a most determined attack upon the town, and although raked by Marlborough's flanking batteries from the eastern heights as they approached, they very nearly mastered its defenders. These were, however, reinforced by two battalions under the English Colonel Tollemache. Although the French Guard strove to burn the town gates, and everywhere fought with determination, they could make no progress, and the greensward around the ramparts was strewn with the bodies of five hundred of their men. D'Humières saw himself forced to widen the battle. He threw in his whole army in an improvised attack upon the allies' right, which had by now been extended west of Walcourt. This was the moment for Waldeck's counter-stroke. At six o'clock Slangenberg led the Dutch infantry forward from the western side. Simultaneously Marlborough attacked from the eastern side of the town. Placing himself at the head of the Life Guards and Blues, and supported by two English regiments, he charged upon the French right flank, inflicting very grave injuries upon the troops already unduly tried. The French cavalry was not only numerous, but was led by that same Villars of whom we have heard twenty years before at the siege of Maestricht, and whom we shall meet twenty years later at Malplaquet. Villars saved the French infantry from destruction, and d'Humières was able to withdraw his army as the night fell with a loss of six guns and two thousand of the flower of the French foot. As the casualties of the allies were about three hundred, the action wore the aspect of a victory. Feuquières, the French military critic, remarks severely "that this combat should never be cited save as an example to avoid." D'Humières' military reputation received a fatal blow, and in the next campaign he was superseded by Luxembourg.

The Prince of Waldeck rejoiced in his good fortune, nor was he ungenerous to those who had contributed to it. To William he wrote, "Colonel Hodges and the English did marvels and the Earl of Marlborough is assuredly one of the most gallant men I know." "Marlborough *in spite of his youth* had displayed in this one battle greater military capacity than do most generals after a long series of wars." William, being, like Marlborough, only thirty-nine himself, was not perhaps deeply impressed by this reference to the infirmities of youth. He wrote, however, in handsome terms to Marlborough:

> I am happy that my troops behaved so well in the affair of Walcourt. It is to you that this advantage is principally owing. You will please accordingly accept my thanks and rest assured that your conduct will induce me to confer on you still further marks of my esteem and friendship on which you may always rely.

Marlborough was made Colonel of the Royal Fusiliers, a regiment armed with a light musket called a fusil and employed in the special defence of the artillery. Such appointments were lucrative, and the fact that this regiment was under the Master-General of the Ordnance might encourage Marlborough to hope that this financial plum, so necessary for the support of his earldom, would some day fall into his hands. Walcourt was the only recognizable success which greeted the Dutch and English peoples in the year 1689. Thus the new King's reign opened auspiciously for him.

It happened, however, that during the summer a dispute had arisen between the King and Queen Mary on the one hand and Anne and her husband on the other, the brunt of which fell entirely on the Churchills. Up to this point all had been love between the two royal sisters, with the added thrill of conspiracy against their father. Till now Sarah had seemed to be the bond of union between them. But all things change with time, and many in a very short time. Sarah has reason on her side when she contends that her influence upon the succession settlement in the event of Mary's dying before William was used in the general interest rather than from any unworthy eagerness to ingratiate herself or her husband with the new sovereigns. For soon afterwards came the question of the Parliamentary grants to the Royal Family. And here began the rift.

Anne, who had agreed willingly to the sacrifice of inestimable reversionary rights, naturally wished, especially in the event of her sister's death, to have an independent income granted directly to her by Parliament. William resented this desire, and his wife championed his view. Both thought, moreover, that £30,000 a year was ample for the Princess's household; indeed, William expressed his wonder to Lord Godolphin how the Princess could spend so much, "though," adds Sarah, "it appeared afterwards that some of his favourites had more." Considering that Anne already had £20,000 a year settled upon her for life by Parliament, this was not generous treatment of a Princess who had voluntarily resigned an important contingent claim upon the Crown. The Cockpit household took care that Parliament was informed of the dispute, and, by way of having something to concede, suggested £70,000 as an appropriate figure. It was soon apparent that they had strong support. Mary sent for Anne and advised her to trust herself entirely to the King's gracious bounty. Anne replied sedately that "she understood her friends had a mind to make her some settlement." "Pray what friends have you," rejoined the Queen, "but the King and me?" A nasty family dispute about money matters; and not only upon money matters, but status!

Anne was found to have the House of Commons on her side. The Marlboroughs steadfastly espoused her interest. While John was fighting at Walcourt Sarah had actively canvassed the Tory Party. An independent position for the Princess Anne was held in Parliament to be essential to the Revolution settlement. Tempers rose high on both sides. Every form of pressure from ugly threats to dazzling bribes was put upon Sarah to persuade her mistress to a compromise. The figure was no longer in dispute. Shrewsbury himself undertook to win through Sarah Anne's acceptance of £50,000 from the King. Sarah was impervious. After what the Cockpit had seen of the royal generosity, they insisted upon a Parliamentary title. Sarah stood by her mistress and her friend. She cast away for ever the Queen's favour; and this at a time when there was no reason to suppose that Anne would outlive

Mary. There is no doubt that Marlborough guided the helm and faced the blizzard. But this was no Quixotism. It was his private interest that the matter should be settled so; it was his duty to the Princess; it was also the public interest, with a foreign king on the throne, and an ex-king claimant, that an English princess, heir designate, should be independently established. Again we see in Marlborough's story that strange coincidence of personal and national duties at crucial times. The new sovereigns had to accept a definite, public defeat, and the House of Commons voted the Princess Anne a life grant of £50,000 a year.

Marlborough had his own position in the country and with the King. But the Queen henceforward pursued Sarah with keen hostility, and this she soon extended to Sarah's husband. She blamed Sarah for the estrangement which had sprung up between herself and her once dearly loved sister. Repeatedly she urged Anne to remove this obstacle to their natural affection. Anne, forced to choose between the Queen and Sarah, made it plain with all the obstinate patience of her nature that she would stand by her friend, as her friend had stood by her. This choice, so deliberate and unshakable, was deeply wounding to her sister. Perhaps all this had as much to do in the future with Marlborough not getting the commands to which by rank and capacity he was entitled as had the exigencies of William's political system or his proclivities for Dutchmen. At any rate, it lay and lurked behind the daily routine of war and government.

King William was neither the first nor the last statesman to underrate the Irish danger. By May, when the European campaign was beginning on all the fronts of France, he found a serious war on his hands in Ireland. James had arrived in Ireland, was welcomed as a deliverer, and now reigned in Dublin, aided by an Irish Parliament and defended by a Catholic army of a hundred thousand men, of whom half were organized by French officers and furnished with French munitions. The Irish army was further sustained by a disciplined French contingent. Soon the whole island except the Protestant settlements in the North was under Jacobite control. William in 1690 found himself compelled to go in person with his main force to Ireland, and by the summer took the field at the head of thirty-six thousand men. Thus the French Government, at the cost only of five thousand troops, a few hundred extra officers, and moderate supplies, diverted the whole power of England from the main theatres of the war. Had Louis backed the Irish enterprise with more force, he would have gained even larger rewards.

William left the government in the hands of Queen Mary, assisted by a council of nine, four Whigs and five Tories, of whom Marlborough was one, besides being at the same time Commander-in-Chief. A most critical situation now developed. The Prince of Waldeck was encouraged by the memory of Walcourt to lay a trap for the French. But Luxembourg was no d'Humières, and at the battle of Fleurus in June he inflicted a crushing defeat upon the allies. At the same time the French fleet was stronger in the Channel than the combined fleets of England and Holland. Admiral Herbert was none the less ordered to bring them to battle. On June 30/July 10 he was defeated in a sea-fight off Beachy Head, the brunt of the action falling upon the Dutch. This was, according to Mahan, "the most conspicuous success the French have ever gained at sea over the English." It was said in London, "The Dutch had the honour, the French the advantage, and the English the shame." The French, under the energetic Tourville, now enjoyed the command of the sea. They could land an invading army in England; they could prevent the return of William from Ireland. The council of nine over which Queen Mary presided had to face an alarming crisis.

They were sustained by the loyalty and spirit of the nation. The whole country took up what arms could be found and feverishly organized the home defence. With a nucleus of about six thousand regular troops and the hastily improvised forces of the nation, Marlborough stood ready to resist an invasion for which an excellent French army of over twenty thousand men was available. William's decisive victory at the Boyne on July 1/11 threw James out of Ireland and back to France; but the English peril continued at its height. The anxious weeks of July and August slipped away, with no more injury or insult to England than the burning of Teignmouth by French troops. The French fleet was dismantled and laid up for the winter, and the English and Dutch fleets were refitted and again at sea. Thus the French opportunity was lost.

When the news of the naval defeat had been received at Queen Mary's council board, Marlborough and Admiral Russell were among the few Cabinet officers who did not volunteer to take command of the fleet. We must admire the spirit of these elderly nobles, none of whom knew one end of a ship from the other, and most of whom were devoid of military instruction or experience. They said they would sit on board the flagship and make the sea captains fight. Fortunately such desperate remedies were not required.

In the middle of August the Council was astonished to receive from the Commander-in-Chief a proposal of which he guaranteed the success, and on which he declared to the Queen that he would stake his reputation. This was to send the bulk of the regular troops out of the country upon an expedition to Ireland. Their minds, so lately exposed to the apprehensions of invasion, did not respond to his view that the danger had passed, and that the initiative should be regained.

Marlborough's plan was to seize the ports of Cork and Kinsale, which were the principal contact bases of the French in Ireland, and thus cut Ireland from French reinforcements. A double attack on the Jacobite forces in Ireland from the south as well as from the north would, he declared, be decisive. William, who was besieging Limerick, debated the matter with his Dutch generals. They, like the English Council of State, were adverse. But the King saw at once the strategic merits and timeliness of the plan. He discarded his generals' advice, overruled the Council, and placed Marlborough in charge of the expedition.

This was Marlborough's first independent command. He had not sought to go to Ireland before, and it is presumed that he did not wish to fight against an army led by King James in person. But now James was gone. The season was far advanced, and all preparations were made with the utmost speed. The expedition and its shipping were concentrated at Portsmouth, whither Marlborough repaired by August 26, and embarked on the 30th. He spread false rumours that it was intended to raid the coast of Normandy as a reprisal for Teignmouth; but the French were not deceived. Marlborough's sailing was delayed for a fortnight by contrary winds while every day was precious. The health of the troops on board suffered, and their supplies were partly consumed. But the mere rumour of the thrust produced a strategic effect. Leaving their Irish allies to their fate, Lauzun and Tyrconnel, who were tired of Ireland, and had no intention of being cut off there, retreated to France with the remainder of the French contingent.

Marlborough, very seasick, sailed on September 17, "bound (by God's assistance)," as the cautious master of the flagship wrote, "for ye coast of Ireland, Being of all Sorts about 82 Sayle." After silencing the batteries at the mouth of Cork Harbour he ran in upon the tide to Passage West and disembarked his army of about six thousand men seven miles inland during Tuesday, September 22. William meanwhile had abandoned the siege of Limerick, and returned to London. He had left orders with Ginkel to send five thousand men to join Marlborough in accordance with the plan. Marlborough had particularly asked that this detachment should consist of English troops, of whom there was no lack in the main army, and for Kirke, who was available, to command them. The Dutch general had no intention of allowing any purely English force or English commander to gain an independent success. It was with all the Dutchmen from William downward a maxim that the English were ignorant of war and must be strongly led by trained foreign officers and upheld by disciplined foreign troops. Ginkel had therefore, with many profuse apologies, selected five thousand Danes, Dutch, and Huguenots, who had now arrived on the north side of Cork under the Duke of Würtemberg.

This magnifico was junior in military rank to Marlborough, but far above him in birth. He claimed, as a prince of a royal house, to command the whole operation. A vexatious dispute, which Ginkel had foreseen with relish, arose. Marlborough displayed his commission from the Queen, and the Duke referred to his lineage and lost his temper. Meanwhile their two forces occupied the outlying works of Cork by separate action. There was no time to appeal for a decision about the command to William, and no certainty how he would have settled it. To secure unity, therefore, Marlborough was forced, not for the last time in his life, to propose the vicious expedient of antiquity that the rival generals should exercise command on alternate days. Würtemberg was with difficulty persuaded to accept this compromise. When the first day fell by lot to Marlborough he chose "Würtemberg" as the password for the troops. The Duke, surprised and mollified by this courtesy, selected "Marlborough" as the word for the second day, and thereafter made no further difficulties. Indeed, he seems to have yielded himself naturally and easily to Marlborough's guidance, once he felt it.

The governor of Cork, Colonel McElligott, returned a disdainful answer to the summons to surrender, and the attack upon the city was at once begun. Its defences were in a neglected condition, and its garrison of about five thousand men was too small to hold all the necessary works. Powerful batteries were landed from the fleet, and a breach made in the eastern wall. Marlborough was ready to assault on the evening of the 26th; but the governor beat a parley, which, though it came to nothing, allowed the tide to rise and gained him another day. At dawn on Sunday, the 27th, all was again in readiness. The batteries, supported by a frigate, which came up the river on the flood, bombarded the breach in the town. A Danish column a thousand strong forded the northern arm of the river, and at one o'clock Charles Churchill, Marlborough's brother, whom he had made a Brigadier, with fifteen hundred English infantry, headed by many noblemen and gentlemen volunteers, plunged into the estuary. The water, though ebbing, was breast-high, the current strong, and the fire from the ramparts heavy. But both Danes and English advanced undaunted and occupied the counterscarp. As they re-formed here for the final storm McElligott hoisted the white flag. In view of his trick of the day before, no terms were offered. What was left of the garrison, about four thousand men, became prisoners of war. Marlborough entered the city the next day, and sternly suppressed the looting which had begun.

From Cork Marlborough, without an hour's delay, turned to Kinsale, and the very next day his cavalry summoned the two forts which guarded the harbour to surrender. The town, which was undefended, was seized before it could be burned, thus affording the necessary shelter for the troops. Marlborough arrived himself on the Thursday, October 1, by which time considerable infantry forces had entered the town. He saw at once that the "New Fort" was much stronger than had been reported and if defended would require a regular siege. The governor, Sir Edward Scott, rejected the very favourable conditions that were offered, and, treating with contempt the threat that he would be hanged if he put the assailants to the trouble of a formal siege, addressed himself to a stubborn defence.

Trenches were opened forthwith, and by October 7 the English and Danes had sapped almost to the counterscarp. On the 11th the heavy batteries, transported with the utmost difficulty over the appalling roads from Cork, began their bombardment, and by the 15th a breach was pronounced ready for assault. The intrepid governor felt that enough was done for honour. He therefore opened negotiations, and Marlborough, whose trenches were knee-deep in water and who was worried by the approach of winter and fearful for the health of his troops, was glad to give him generous terms. Scott was allowed to march off to Limerick with his twelve hundred survivors under the customary compliments of war. But "as the enemy marched out, the Earl took a note of all their names, telling them that if ever they were hereafter in arms against King William, they should have no quarter." The siege had cost Marlborough 250 men, and the hospitals were already crowded with sick. A hundred pieces of cannon and much military supplies fell to the victors. But this was the least part of the success. The capture of these southern harbours deprived Irish resistance of all hope of French succour, and rendered the entire reduction of the country possible as soon as the winter was over. Charles Churchill was appointed governor of Kinsale, and Marlborough's army went into winter quarters. He himself landed at Deal on October 28, having accomplished what he had planned and guaranteed with complete success.

He was extremely well received in London. "In twenty-three days," says Lord Wolseley, "Marlborough had achieved more than all William's Dutch commanders had done both in Ireland and abroad during the whole of the previous year." William was most gracious: but the patronizing compliment he paid was characteristic of the Dutch attitude towards British generals. "No officer living," he said, "*who has seen so little service as my Lord Marlborough,* is so fit for great commands."

Marlborough did not return to Ireland, as some writers aver. We find him dining in January with Lord Lucas, Constable of the Tower, and ordering £100 to be distributed among "the poor Irish taken at Cork and Kinsale." He certainly desired to have the chief command in Ireland in the campaign of 1691, and public opinion expected it. But it was no part of William's policy to let English soldiers gather laurels. The closing scenes in Ireland were reserved for Ginkel, while Marlborough, at the head of the British contingent in Flanders, was to make the campaign as one of the generals of the large army William had determined to command in person. He no doubt appreciated the kindness of the King in thus repairing the deficiencies of his military education; and his experiences in this campaign must at least have had the value of showing him some methods of war to be avoided.

CHAPTER FIFTEEN

The Personal Cleavage

⟨⟨ 1690-91 ⟩⟩

WE have seen our England, maddened by the Popish Plot into Test Acts and Exclusion Bills, placing after a few years a Popish sovereign on the throne with general acclamation. We have seen her also, angered by his offences, unseat him by an almost universal shrug of the shoulders and set the island Crown upon the brow of a foreign prince. And now we shall see a very strong reaction which arose against that Prince or Parliamentary King and cast gleams of public favour upon the true King over the water. The possibility of the return of James could never be absent from the minds of those who had been witnesses of the miracle of the restoration of Charles. Moreover, many of the reasons which had led to the expulsion of James had disappeared. A new Constitution had established the power of Parliament and limited effectually the prerogative and authority of the Crown. No one could doubt that if James returned it would be as the result of a bargain which consolidated the principles of a limited monarchy and upheld beyond the chance of challenge the Protestant character of the English people. Those who write with crude censure of the shame of deserting James for William or William for James seem to forget that James and William were not ends in themselves. They were the instruments by which the power and happiness of England might be gained or marred. The loyalties due to their kingly office or hereditary titles were not the only loyalties to which English statesmen had a right and duty to respond. There was, for instance, the interest of the country, to which an increasingly conscious loyalty was due. In those days, as in these, men were by character true or false; but unswerving fidelity to a particular king was no test of their virtue or baseness.

The events of the Revolution had created conditions in England to which no parallel exists in later times. Many of the magnates who had dethroned and expelled James still revered him in their hearts, in spite of all the Acts of Parliament they had passed, as their real, natural sovereign. Every one regarded the imperious and disagreeable Dutchman who had had to be brought in and set up for the sake of Protestantism and civil liberty as a necessary evil. They saw his dislike and contempt for Englishmen. They understood that he regarded England mainly as a powerful tool for his Continental schemes, conceived primarily in the interest of Holland. With anxious eyes they watched his unpopularity increasing with the growth of taxes and distress through long years of war rarely lighted by success. The danger of his death from natural causes, from assassination or upon the battlefield, where he so often bravely exposed himself, and the grave constitutional issues which would renew themselves upon such an event, were ever present to their minds. Devoted to the Protestant faith, and determined that the English Constitution should not sink to a despotism upon the French model, they none the less had to take into account the possible pursuance of their objects under violently and suddenly changed conditions. It was not wonderful that they should have acted upon the ancient Greek maxim, "Love as though you shall hereafter hate, and hate as though you shall hereafter love." It was an epoch of divided loyalties, of conflicting interests, of criss-cross ties, of secret reserves and much dissembling. When kings forswear their oaths of duty and conspire against their peoples, when rival kings or their heirs crowd the scene, statesmen have to pick and choose between sovereigns of fluctuating values, as kings are wont to pick and choose between politicians according to their temporary serviceableness. The conditions and standards of this period, like its tests and stresses, were different from our own. Nevertheless, as we contend, the main feature which emerges is that of steadfastness and not deceit, of patriotism above self-interest, and of courage and earnestness, rather than of craft and opportunism.

Through all these baffling changes, of which only the barest outline can be realized by posterity, Halifax seems to have threaded his way with truer hold upon the essential interest of England than any other figure of whom we have record. We have seen him a Protestant opponent of the Exclusion Bill and a Minister of James II. We have seen him an opponent of James II. We have seen him harshly conducting that fallen sovereign to Rochester. We have seen him the trusted counsellor of William III. He was soon to reopen his relations with the exiled James. No one but a blind partisan of the Whig or Tory factions of those vanished days would find it impossible to vindicate all these successive and superficially inconsistent actions of Halifax as being both sincere and in the public interest. On the whole throughout this long, tempestuous period Marlborough, as we have seen, moved politically with Halifax. His broad outlook upon affairs, his sane and reasonable temperament, his indifference towards the two parties, his hatred of excess or revenge, his antagonism to France, his adherence to the Protestant cause, all conform to the Halifax type, and step by step his actions harmonize with those of the illustrious 'Trimmer.'

We must now look more closely upon the extraordinary Prince who for good reasons and in the general interest had robbed his father-in-law of his throne. From his earliest years William's circumstances had been harsh and sombre. His life was loveless. He was always fatherless and childless. His marriage was dictated by reasons of State. He was brought up by his termagant grandmother, Amalia of Solms, and in his youth was passed for regulation from one Dutch committee to another. His childhood was unhappy and his health bad. He had a tubercular lung, was asthmatic and partly crippled. But within this emaciated and defective frame there burned a remorseless fire, fanned by the storms of Europe, and intensified by the stern compression of his surroundings. His great actions began before he was twenty-one. From that age he had fought constantly in the field and toiled through every intrigue of Dutch domestic politics and of the European scene. For the last four years he had been the head of the English conspiracy against James.

His public hatred of France and his personal quarrel with Louis XIV constituted the main theme of his life. All his exertions were directed against the tyrant who had not only compassed the ruin of the Dutch Republics, but had actually seized and dragooned the small principality of Orange from which he had sprung, and with which his native pride and affections were interwoven.

It was the natural characteristic of such an upbringing and of such a mission that William should be ruthless. Although he did not conspire in the murder of the de Witts, he rejoiced at it, profited by it, and protected and pensioned the murderers. His conduct in the Massacre of Glencoe was entirely unfeeling. Neither the treachery nor the butchery of that crime disturbed his cynical serenity. He was vexed and worried only about the outcry that arose afterwards. He would break a political opponent without pity, but he was never needlessly cruel, and was glad to treat foes no longer dangerous with contempt or indifference. He wasted no time on minor revenges. His sole vendetta was with Louis. For all his experience from his youth at the head of armies and for all his dauntless heart, he was never a great commander. He had not a trace of that second-sight of the battlefield which is the mark of military genius. He was no more than a resolute man of good common sense whom the accident of birth had carried to the conduct of war. It was in the sphere of politics that his inspiration lay. Perhaps he has never been surpassed in the sagacity, patience, and discretion of his statecraft. The combinations he made, the difficulties he surmounted, the adroitness with which he used the time factor, or played upon the weakness of others, the unerring sense of proportion and power of assigning to objectives their true priorities, all mark him for the highest fame.

William watched with ill-concealed disfavour the protracted wranglings of the English chiefs and parties. He was never fond of England, nor interested in her domestic affairs. Her seamy side was all he knew. He repeatedly urged Parliament to address itself to the Continental situation. He required the wealth and power of England by land and sea for the European war. It was for this he had come in person to enlist her. Although he had himself darkly and deviously conspired the undoing of his foolish kinsman, he thought little of the English public men who had been his confederates. A prince himself, he could not but distrust men who, albeit at his instigation, had been guilty of treason to their royal master. He knew too much about their jealousies and intrigues to cherish for them sentiments of liking or respect. He had used them for his own ends, and would reward them for their services; but as a race he regarded them as inferior in fibre and fidelity to his Dutchmen. English statesmen to him were perjured, and what was even worse, local-minded. English soldiers seemed to him uncouth and ill-trained by Continental standards. English generals lacked the professional knowledge which, he believed, long experience of war alone could give. The English Navy was no doubt brave and hardy, but his own sentiments naturally rested upon the traditions of Tromp and de Ruyter. The Dutch were his children; the English could never be more than his step-children, to whom, indeed, he owed a parental duty and from whose estate he was entitled during his guardianship to draw substantial advantages.

Once securely seated on the throne he scarcely troubled to disguise these sentiments.

His unsociable disposition, his greediness at table, his silence and surliness in company, his dislike of women, his neglect of London, all prejudiced him with polite society. The ladies voted him "a low Dutch bear." The English Army too was troubled in its soul. Neither officers nor men could dwell without a sense of humiliation upon the military aspects of the Revolution. They did not like to see all the most important commands entrusted to Dutchmen. They eyed sourly the Dutch infantry who paced incessantly the sentry-beats of Whitehall and St James's, and contrasted their shabby blue uniforms and small stature with the scarlet pomp of the 1st Guards and Coldstreamers now banished from London. It was a pity, thought they, that the public interest had not allowed them to give these fellows a drubbing.

Cracks had speedily appeared in the fabric of the original National Government. The Whigs considered that the Revolution belonged to them. All they had suffered since their far-seeing Exclusion Bills, all that they had risked in the great conspiracy, should now be rewarded. Their judgment, their conduct, their principles, had been vindicated. Ought they not, then, to have all the offices? Was it just they should be thrust aside in many cases for the "evil counsellors of the late king"? But William knew that he could never have gained the Crown of England but by the help of the Cavaliers and Anglicans who formed the staple of the Tory Party. Moreover at this time, as a king he liked the Tory mood. Here was a party who exalted the authority of the Crown. Here was a Church devoted to hereditary monarchy and profoundly grieved to have been driven by the crisis from the doctrine of non-resistance. William felt that Whig principles would ultimately lead to a republic. Under the name of Stadtholder he was really the King of Holland; he had no desire under the name of King to be only Stadtholder of England. He was therefore ready to break up the Convention

Parliament which had given him the Crown while, as the Whigs said, "its work was all unfinished." At the election of February 1690 "the buried names of Whig and Tory revived"; and the Tories won. Henceforward the party cleavage and party system became rigid, formal, and —down to our own days—permanent.

Shrewsbury, Godolphin, Marlborough, and Sunderland, and from a somewhat different angle Halifax, now ageing, held a middle position apart from party, and, as they no doubt thought, above it. Each of these men drew in others. "Shrewsbury was usually hand in glove with Wharton. Godolphin and Marlborough shared confidences with Russell." It was upon this central body of men, pre-eminent for their gifts, unrivalled in experience of affairs and knowledge of the Court and Parliament, that William was naturally inclined to rely either as counsellors or Ministers, and he added thorough paced Whigs or Tories in different proportions to either flank to suit the changing needs of the years.

But the King's affairs moved inevitably in a vicious circle. He could not trust high military authority to Englishmen, nor allow English soldiers to win fame in the field, without, as he thought, placing himself in their power. In all the key posts of the Army he must have Dutchmen or foreigners. Thus he angered the English officers and the English Army, and found new justification for his distrust in their resentment. Most of all this cycle prejudiced the relations between him and Marlborough. Marlborough's desire was above everything to command armies in the great war now raging. He felt within himself qualities which, if they had their chance, would produce remarkable results for himself, for England, and for Europe. But though William desired the same political ends, he feared their being gained by Marlborough. He remembered General Monk; he remembered what had happened at Salisbury. Therefore it became with him a necessary principle of his existence to bar Marlborough's natural and legitimate professional career. The abler general Marlborough showed himself, the more he must be kept in a subordinate station; the greater his talents the more imperative their repression.

Marlborough was made to realize all this, and perhaps its inevitability, at the beginning of 1691. He had rendered immense and even decisive services to the new régime both in the crisis of the Revolution and during the Revolution settlement. His had been almost the only military achievements of 1690. The charge at Walcourt, the swift seizure of

Cork and Kinsale, were outstanding episodes. It was variously rumoured in London that he would be created a Duke and Knight of the Garter, would be appointed Master-General of the Ordnance, and would be commander-in-chief in Ireland for the coming campaign. A dukedom he considered beyond his means, and he was to refuse one ten years later on the same grounds; but we know from letters which Anne and her husband wrote to the King that he desired the Garter. He wanted the Ordnance to support his title; and above all he sought an independent command in one of the theatres of war. He found himself denied on all points. The Ordnance went to Henry Sidney, a civilian who was destitute of any qualifications of which history can take notice. Ginkel had the command in Ireland, and Waldeck, in spite of Fleurus, had, under the King, the command in Flanders. Of course Marlborough ought not to have minded such treatment. He ought to have been indifferent, like our modern generals, statesmen, and financiers, to personal ambitions or material interests. However, he took it all very much amiss. He seems to have come to the conclusion that William meant to keep him down. Under James he saw his path blocked by Papists: under William by Dutchmen.

The campaign of 1691 opened in imposing style with a conference at The Hague. A league of nations assembled to concert measures against the common enemy, France. England, Holland, Prussia, the German states, the Empire, Spain, and a dozen smaller powers—all sent their representatives. Such a gathering of princes and statesmen had scarcely been seen before in Christendom. At the summit stood William in all his glory, the architect of this immense confederation of rival states and conflicting faiths, the sovereign of its two most vigorous nations, the chief commander of its armies, lacking nothing but the military art. This splendid ceremonial was rudely interrupted by the cannon. It was scarcely etiquette to begin operations before April or May; but early in March Louis XIV, with Luxembourg as his general and Vauban as his engineer, suddenly appeared with a hundred thousand men before the valuable barrier fortress of Mons. William was forced to descend from his pedestal and mount his horse. He could muster an army of barely fifty thousand, and these could only be spectators of the fall of Mons. So much for the Hague conference.

Marlborough had been left in England charged with the task of recruitment for the Army. In May the allied forces took the field with the object at least of recovering Mons. William gave Marlborough the command of the British contingent, and to make the necessary vacancy moved Tollemache to Ireland, to serve under Ginkel. Marlborough and Count Solms were sent forward to organize the assembly of the main army in the neighbourhood of Brussels. Waldeck commanded while William rested awhile in his home palace at Loo. Luxembourg, with a solid French army, barred the way to Mons. At the end of June William arrived at headquarters, and the campaign began in earnest. It was the first time since the reign of Henry VIII that a King of England had commanded in person on the Continent, and all the young bloods of quality and fashion had hurried from London to let off their pistols. But nothing happened. Luxembourg stood on the defensive in positions too well chosen for William to attack. The great armies marched and counter-marched according to the orthodox rules of war, and the precious summer months slipped away. By the end of August all was over. William, baffled and a trifle humiliated, led his armies back to their cantonments. They passed on their way the field of Fleurus, where the grisly spectacle of Waldeck's unburied corpses struck a chill through a disappointed host. William handed over the command to Waldeck and returned to Loo.

But the adversities of the campaign were not yet ended. In the middle of September, when custom should have enforced upon Luxembourg the propriety of retiring into winter quarters, he organized an outrageous cavalry attack upon the rearguard of the allied army while it was moving from Leuze to Grammont. The rising French officer Villars routed the Dutch cavalry and sabred them from the field. The confusion spread to the infantry. The sudden heavy firing rang through the autumn air. There was a tumult of scampering horses and men. Marlborough, marching in his station with the British contingent, had already passed the Catoise stream. He turned sharply back and marched towards the bridges at the utmost speed, apparently in the mood for battle. A broad flush of red and steel spread menacingly across the landscape. But Luxembourg, cool and composed in the cavalry action and content with the day, disengaged his excited army before the British brigades could deploy; and the fighting of the year ended for the allies upon this somewhat ridiculous incident, in which there were, however, above seven hundred casualties. The Prince of Waldeck led the discomfited Dutch and angry English into their winter quarters;

and in all their camps and garrisons the word ran round that King William had "entered the field too late, and quitted it too soon."

It was a heavy exertion for the states of those days, with their narrow finances, to keep such large armies in contact with an equal enemy for a whole season. The loss of a year weighed heavily on the fragile structure of the Grand Alliance. All William's skill in diplomacy had come to nothing at the point of action. John Churchill was then forty-three, in his prime. He possessed all the military knowledge and experience upon which he afterwards acted. As he watched those infirm yet stilted manœuvres, as he brooded on these wasted opportunities, as he no doubt felt how surely and how swiftly he could reshape the scene, and yet how carefully and tightly trammelled he was, can we wonder at the anger that possessed his soul? There was no prophetic spirit at his side to whisper, "Patience! The opportunity will yet be yours." His patience is almost proverbial. He had need for it all. Ten years, half of them years of war—ten years when the chances of a lifetime seemed finally to die—were to pass before he was again to exercise a military command.

CHAPTER SIXTEEN

The Jacobite Illusion

WE now approach the most unhappy and questionable period in Marlborough's life. The peccadilloes of youth, the work he had to do as confidential servant of the Duke of York, his treasonable letter to the Prince of Orange, his desertion of James at Salisbury, are all capable of either excuse or vindication. Indeed, his conduct towards James was justified not only by his religious and political convictions, but even more by the broad and long interest of England. But it entailed consequences.

Now we must record that opposition to King William, those intrigues with King James, which seem to stultify his former action, to rob it of its basis of conscientious scruple, and to arm his innumerable assailants with every weapon that indignant rectitude or implacable malice could desire. Moreover, the picture is not one to be painted in bold blacks and whites. We gaze upon a scene of greys shading indefinably, mysteriously, in and out of one another. A mere recital of facts and outlines would give no true description without a comprehension of the atmosphere.

In judging the character of Marlborough the question arises whether his actions were dictated by undue self-interest. Reasonable care for a man's own interest is neither a public nor a private vice. That Marlborough, like most Englishmen, together with all the Revolution statesmen, should become estranged from the new Government; that he should quarrel personally with King William; that he should seek to safeguard himself in the increasingly probable event of a Jacobite restoration, are not in themselves, and under the conditions of the period, wrongful or odious behaviour. The test is whether he was false in intention or in fact to the cause of Protestantism and constitutional freedom, and above all whether the safety of England or the lives of her soldiers and sailors were jeopardized by his actions; and it is to these aspects that the attention of the reader will be directed.

King James and his family dwelt, refugees, by the throne of Louis XIV. They and their shadow Court, with its handful of Irish troops and Guards, its functionaries and its Ministers, were all dependent for their daily bread upon the bounty or policy of their protector. The vanity of Louis was gratified by the presence in his orbit of a suppliant monarch. He indulged to the full the easy chivalry of affluent pity. Sometimes, indeed, his sentiments for a brother monarch, in whose person not only the Catholic faith but even the Divine Right of Kings had been assaulted, carried him beyond purely French interests. But, in the main, a cool statecraft ruled. The exiled family at Saint-Germains depended for their treatment upon their usefulness in the Continental schemes of France. That usefulness for this purpose was measured by the strength and reality of their English connexions. They had, thus, the strongest inducements—and, indeed, compulsions—to magnify the importance and the intimacy of their British ties and the general vitality of the Jacobite cause. Their supreme object was to obtain from Louis a French fleet to carry them to England, and a French army to reestablish King James upon his throne. They therefore, in their unhappy plight, continually represented themselves to the French Government as being in the most confidential relations with the leading men in England, especially with the members of King William's Council.

They developed every possible contact with English Jacobites and friends, real or pretended, across the Channel. They put their own gloss upon whatever news they could get, and served the result up— more often, perhaps, than was tactful—to the French Ministers. Always they laboured to paint a picture of an England longing for their return and ready to rise the moment a chance presented itself. Let the French supply the army and the ships, and they would make the attempt. Once they landed, all would be well. But the French Ministers were sceptical; they had many independent sources of information, and they had a different point of view.

As early as 1689 Marlborough was reported to James as being dissatisfied with the new régime and anxious to make his peace with the old. But nothing definite was asserted until the beginning of 1691, about which Dicconson's *Life of James* sets forth at length a series of reports by three Jacobite agents, Mr. Bulkeley, Colonel Sackville, and Mr. Floyd, or Lloyd, of conversations which they declared they had had with Admiral Russell, Godolphin, Halifax, and Churchill. That all these servants of King William allowed or invited Jacobite agents to visit them, and that conversations took place, may well be true. But Dicconson's version of what passed is at once malicious and absurd.

Dicconson has qualities of his own. We may note the ecclesiastical flavour.

> Churchill was in appearance the greatest penitent imaginable. He begged of him [Sackville] to go to the King and acquaint him with his sincere repentance and to intercede for mercy, that he was ready to redeem his apostasy with the hazard of his utter ruine, his crimes apeareing so horrid to him that he could neither sleep, nor eat but in continual anguish, and a great deal to that purpose.

No one knows, of course, what Marlborough said or did not say. Dicconson—the sole authority—can only tell us what he thought fit to record of the Jacobite agents' reports of fifteen years before. All this is one-sided assertion. Marlborough never volunteered explanations or justification. He appeared unconscious that there was anything to explain.

To what extent he deceived the Jacobite agents with the fair words and pious assurances; to what extent they boasted the value of the fish they thought they had caught; to what extent Melfort, a receiver of customs, and Nairne, under-secretary to James II during his exile, exaggerated the secret service information, the collection of which was their main duty, are mysteries; but in this case (as also with Godolphin, Russell, Shrewsbury, and others,) we certainly have at one end of the chain an important personage anxious not to be too much hated or too much overlooked at Saint-Germains, and at the other an unhappy exile in no position to be vindictive or particular in receiving friendly overtures.

Marlborough's communications with the Jacobite Court, or with his sister's son, the Duke of Berwick, or with James's son, the Old Pretender,* were no passing intrigue. They were a system. They were a life-long policy—just so much and no more—pursued continually for a quarter of a century. Under King William there was no written correspondence. There are accounts of messages and conversations, of promises and assurances without number, many of which may be fabrications, but others which could not have been wholly invented and bear in part the stamp of truth.

In the first phase Marlborough's object, like that of the other Revolution leaders, was to obtain a formal pardon from the Exile, in the unpleasant but by no means improbable event of his restoration. This was a phase in the communications of which William was generally aware, which even had his acquiescence.

At the least William viewed all these intrigues with Saint-Germains with a tolerant eye. "With respect to the riots in Northamptonshire," he wrote on July 15, 1694,

> I recollect that not long ago I was informed that Lord Monmouth had made his peace at St Germain's. Not knowing what to believe, you must try to discover, if possible, whether he, who is lord lieutenant of the county, has fomented or interfered in those riots; and you will please to give me your opinion, whether that employment should not be given to another person.

Here we see the King, the person most affected and best informed, drawing a clear distinction between "making peace with St Germains" and overt unlawful action.

The mere "making peace with St Germains," even by one of his Lord-Lieutenants, was not regarded either by the King or the high circles around him upon the footing of treason; and since almost every prominent leader had safeguarded himself in this way it did not seem to them to be a dishonourable action. It is not our purpose to defend

---

* James Francis Edward Stuart, only son of James II and Mary of Modena, was born in 1688, taken to France with his mother, and on his father's death in 1701 proclaimed (and recognized by Louis XIV) King of England. His persistence, through a long life, in claiming to be the legitimate King of England earned him the title the "Old Pretender . . ." His son, Charles Edward (1720–1788), was the "Young Pretender."

such conduct, but only to reduce it to its proper place in the perilous, tragical politics of those days.

Under Anne we enter a region of purely military camouflage, as in 1702, when Marlborough, actively frustrating the French in the field and seeking eagerly to fight a decisive battle, received Jacobite envoys in his camp, sending them away with who shall say what cryptic or encouraging words; or as in 1708, when he is besieging Lille in circumstances of extraordinary military difficulty, and keeps up at the same time a lengthy and active correspondence with the Duke of Berwick about peace negotiations. We shall return to this later.

There is, lastly, in the long story of Marlborough's relations with Saint-Germains a phase, possibly the least insincere of all, when he endeavoured to establish some kind of amicable relationship with the Old Pretender, "James III." And there are always great civilities and protestations of devotion to the exiled Queen. All baffling; all mystifying; truth and falsehood, pity and deception, intermingled; dual loyalties deliberately exploited. Was it not important for Saint-Germains to be able to tell Louis XIV that they were in close, secret, constant relationship with the Commander in Chief of the enemy's army? They would be grateful for that. It was a real service. It cost nothing. It did not hamper business. It all tended to create uncertainty. The French Government, keenly interested in Berwick's peace negotiations, might have their mind diverted from the defence of Lille and its citadel. This was all part of Marlborough's war-making; and also part of his system. And so, a month or perhaps a week later—a swift march, a sudden assault, thrusting out of a cloud of honeyed words and equivocation, changed fortunes in the field. Webs of intrigue, crossings, double-crossings, stratagems, contrivances, deceit; with smiles, compliments, nods, bows, and whispers—then *crash!* sudden reversion to a violent and decisive military event. The cannon intervene.

There is no disputing the validity of the Jacobite complaint, that they never got anything out of Marlborough except promises which were not made good, and information which arrived only when it was stale. Yet there was no moment at which they could say, "He is only fooling us. He is only feeding us with trifles and smooth words." For there never was a moment when they could not nurse the hope that, if the Exile returned, the Captain-General would put him on the throne;

or when they could dismiss the fear that in the teeth of his resistance all hope of return was ended. In the upshot they were disappointed. As things turned out, they got less than nothing at all. They were mocked with false hopes; placated with counterfeit coin; smothered with empty salutations. A vast system of genuine shams, a prolonged relationship of deceits that were effective because they never excluded the possibility of being real: the whole of this prevailing over twenty-five years and expressed in terms of perfervid loyalty, with promises made, as they declare, of the highest service and of the darkest treachery. But nothing to show for it! Not a corporal's guard turned over! Not a picket conceded in the field; not a scrap of information that they did not know, or that was not public property already; but always hope and always delay, always disappointment—and then more hope. Marlborough betrayed nothing, but to the end no Jacobite agent, courtier, or Minister could ever feel sure he would not some day betray *everything* into their hands. Nor can we at this stage pursue the hypothesis of what he would have done if this or that had happened.

We must confine ourselves to what actually happened. Every account, every record, summed up, shows that the Jacobite Court were for a quarter of a century flattered, duped, baffled, and in the event ruined by an inscrutable and profound personality. They certainly had every reason to blacken the memory of the calm, deep, patient man who threaded his way almost unerringly through the labyrinth of dynastic, political, and military intrigues in five reigns, and who emerged at every decisive moment the successful champion of British interests, of Protestant interests, and of his own interests.

The long succession of historians who follow each other like sheep through the gates of error are all agreed about Marlborough's profound sagacity and that self-interest was his motive power. Let us, then, try the case by these standards. What conceivable interest could he have had in bringing back James? At the best a contemptuous pardon and a justly ineradicable distrust. Of all the notables of England he had the least to hope and the most to fear from such a restoration. How eagerly would triumphant Jacobites, proud Tories, and infuriated Whigs have combined in such an event to drive into obscurity the double-dyed archtraitor who had presumed to be the maker and un-maker of kings! What succour from his old master could he look for against such a storm? Exile, disgrace, or at best some pittance, some sinecure, was the most that magnanimity or indifference could bestow; and James was not the most magnanimous or forgiving of men. What chance had Marlborough but the Princess Anne? There, in the narrow circle of the Cockpit, where long friendship and companionship reigned, where the bonds of union were only forged more tensely by external persecution or danger, lay the only hope. And that a great one! Why should he bring back James and his lusty son, in his own right or under a regency—under a jealous Council of State as a Catholic, or still more as a Protestant—and exclude for ever Anne from the succession? Why should he "abandon wife, children and country" for that? Never for one moment could he have entertained such inanities. We can hear him make his customary comment, "Silly! Silly!" The more sagacious, the more self-seeking he, the less harbourage such devastating contingencies could have found. From the closing years of Charles II, through the unceasing convulsions and confusions of this time, John and Sarah held on to Anne and staked their public existence upon her fortunes and her favour.

CHAPTER SEVENTEEN

The Family Quarrel

ᛄᚨ 1691-92 ᛞᚨ

AT the end of October 1691 William landed at Margate from the wars, and all the way to London he was warmly welcomed by the people. They did not realize the failure of the Continental campaign, and the good news from Ireland roused their enthusiasm. Ginkel had defeated the Irish with an immense slaughter at Aughrim. Limerick had surrendered. The Irish hero Sarsfield had made terms which allowed him to carry eighteen thousand of the best Irish troops out of the country into the French service. It seemed that the Irish troubles were at an end; at least, all resistance was crushed. But the national rejoicing at the local victory was inspired by the hope of an early general peace. Of this there was no prospect. The most costly years of the first part of the world war still lay ahead.

The King brought with him in his coach Bentinck and Marlborough; apparently all were on cordial terms. At Shooter's Hill the coach overturned. Bentinck and Marlborough were hurt. Marlborough, indeed, seems to have been dazed, for he declared that his neck was broken. William, who was only shaken, reassured him that this could not be so, "since he could still speak." The party, somewhat battered, were able to make their entry into London amid cheering crowds.

Nevertheless the realities of the situation might well cause the King anxiety. The injustice done to English officers and the implied insult to the Army aroused strong feelings throughout English society. These vexations were shared by the English Ministers, through whom and with whom William was forced to govern, and especially by that central group to which he naturally inclined.

Marlborough, already offended by what he regarded as ill-usage, convinced that it was William's policy to keep him in the shade, and more excusably vexed by the futile conduct of the campaign in Flanders, did not hesitate to show his hostility. To all this movement which flared up in Parliament and the higher circles of London that winter he lent an influence which was soon found to be potent. He criticized the King openly. He welcomed the tale-bearing which carried his caustic comments to the royal ear. He said at Lord Wharton's before a company that in the previous reign James had been so eager to fill the army with Irishmen that the only question asked was, "Do you speak English?" Now all that had happened was that the word "Dutchman" was changed for "Irishman." He spoke of Bentinck as "a wooden fellow." He remonstrated with William to his face upon his gifts of Crown property to Bentinck and Zulestein. "With great grief of heart many of his faithful servants," he said,

> among whom he requested the honour to be included, saw the royal munificence confined to one or two lords and these foreigners. . . . As far as he was concerned he had no cause to complain; he was amply provided for in the post he held under his Majesty; but in duty bound he felt obliged to lay before him what he ought to know, because he could not otherwise be apprized of means to remedy the disasters that might be the result of such unpopular conduct.

Perhaps he did not express himself so elegantly; but this was the gist of it. He may, indeed, have said more. The King indignantly turned his back upon him.

William's relations with Marlborough, though strained, were not broken by mere words. When the commands for the next year's campaign were being decided, he designed to take him to Flanders as Lieutenant-General attached to his own person. Marlborough demurred to this undefined position. He did not wish to be carried round Flanders as a mere adviser, offering counsel that was not taken, and bearing responsibility for the failures that ensued. He craved leave to remain at home, unless he was required at least to command the British troops, as in the past year. But the King had offered them to Ginkel, and afterwards bestowed them, with lamentable results, upon Count Solms.

Meanwhile Marlborough began indirectly to stir the House of Commons for an address to the Crown on the subject of the Employment of Foreigners, and he proposed himself to move a similar motion in the House of Lords. Widespread support was forthcoming. It even appeared likely that the motion would be carried by majorities in both Houses. The King saw himself about to be requested to dismiss his Dutch followers and favourites from all English offices, and to send back to Holland the five thousand Dutch Guards upon whom he relied as his ultimate security. This was unmistakably a hostile proceeding. Moreover, Marlborough's activities did not end with Parliament. He was the leading British general. "His courage, his abilities, his noble and winning manner, the splendid success which had attended him on every occasion on which he had been in command, had made him," says Macaulay, "in spite of his sordid vices, a favourite with his brethren in arms." Undoubtedly many officers of various ranks resorted to him and loudly expressed their resentment at the favour shown to the Dutch. The "sordid vices" showed themselves, we are told, in the fact that he never entertained them with meat or drink. His influence was exerted on their minds, and not, as was expected in those days, upon their stomachs. In spite of this characteristic omission, he had a great public and personal following in both Parliament and the Army at the beginning of 1692.

The general unrest among the high personnel of the Court and Government could not remain secret from the King. He certainly became aware that during 1691 most of those who surrounded him, to whom he owed much and without whom he could not govern England, were in some sort of communication with the rival he had ousted, and who sought in turn to dethrone him. But he had a far better comprehension of the forces at work than any of his posthumous literary champions. He knew that he was driving England very hard, and forcing upon its Parliamentary system and society treatment to which his own Dutch oligarchy would never have submitted. He could imagine the attitude of "Their High Mightinesses" if purely Dutch offices, Dutch estates, and Dutch commands had been lavished upon Englishmen. He did not therefore resent as strongly as his later admirers have done the doubledealing by which he was encompassed. He accepted it as a necessary element in a situation of unexampled perplexity. He tolerated perforce the fact that all his principal English counsellors were reinsuring themselves against a break-up of his Government or his death on the battle-field. He continued to employ all these men in great offices of State and confidence about his person. He calculated with shrewd wisdom that, though they might turn against him as they had turned against James, yet they would not compromise the two main issues which had made them all his reluctant bedfellows; and he saw almost insuperable difficulties in their being able to dissociate the cause of James from the causes of Popery and France.

He did not, therefore, unduly trouble himself. He knew, or at least suspected, that Shrewsbury was in touch with Saint-Germains through his notorious mother; yet, as we shall see, again and again he implored Shrewsbury to take or retain the highest offices. He knew that Russell had made his peace with James; yet he kept him in command of the fleet, and was to find his confidence vindicated at the battle of Cape La Hogue. He knew that Marlborough preserved the family contacts with his nephew the Duke of Berwick, and that his wife corresponded with her sister, the Duchess of Tyrconnel. He probably knew that Marlborough had obtained his pardon from James by persuading the Princess Anne to send a dutiful message to her father. None the less he thought that the magnet of the Protestant cause and resistance to France would hold these men and others in the essentials to their duty, and that in the end it would be James, and not himself, who would be deceived. He proved right; and it may well be that his wise tolerance and prudent blind eye were the perfection of his statecraft. Meanwhile he relied on his Dutch Guards, and saw to it that no Englishman gained the control of the Army. After all, he was getting a lot out of England for his Continental schemes, of which these ignorant islanders, as he deemed them, only dimly saw the importance.

Up to this point, according to their own accounts, the Jacobites had been extremely well pleased to see all this discontent gathering against the Government. It was already whispered in their secret circles that Marlborough also had made his peace with James. They nursed the hope that this powerful man was working for a restoration. Then they suddenly remembered the Princess Anne and the small, devoted group at the Cockpit. So, then, all this movement and focus of discontent from which they had expected so much, to which they had contributed what weight their party had, was not to be for their benefit! On the contrary, if it succeeded it would exclude James for ever from the throne and would ensure the Protestant succession under Anne, with Marlborough, whose stature and force were already beginning to be understood, as her Captain-General. Their fury knew no bounds. Without consulting King James, who was dreaming that his former skilful servant of so many years would regain him his Crown, they went to Bentinck with tales of a vast and imminent conspiracy.

There is no evidence worthy of the name that Marlborough ever plotted the substitution of Anne for William and Mary. The obstacles were enormous. The risks, if not beyond his daring, were condemned by his practical good sense. It is probable that he had in view nothing more than the placing of the Princess Anne at the head of a combination of all parties, and the consequent assertion of his own power in the State for its great advantage. But though nothing so definite as a *coup d'état* had emerged in Marlborough's mind, he certainly sought to assemble and combine all forces hostile to the Government of the day, which in those days was indistinguishable from the King himself. It was for this reason above all others that he wished at this time to stand well with the Jacobites, and carry them with him as far as they would go. He thought and felt about politics as he did about war, in terms of combinations, and of forces moving up to this point or that, and then a trial of strength and skill, and a new view of the situation thereafter.

A movement in favour of the Princess Anne seemed to William far more dangerous than any that concerned James. He saw the blunt facts to which so many eminent writers have been purblind. He was never afraid of Marlborough trying to bring back James. He understood only too well where Marlborough's interests lay. He was content that James should be fooled. Of all his perils the Jacobite invasion, the most paraded in the history books, gave him the least anxiety. Quite a different mood stole over him when he saw or imagined Parliament, the Army, and the Princess Anne—a fatal trident—in the hand of Marlborough, pointed at his heart. He knew that his own policy obliged him to deny his great subject fair scope for his genius. He expected reprisals. There is a double-edged significance in the remark which the King made in the presence of a group of nobles at Court, that "he had been treated so infamously by Marlborough that had he not been a king, he would have felt it necessary to demand personal satisfaction." There are mutual injuries which efface differences of rank and station, and arouse in generous spirits the desire for an equal combat. We are to find a happier sequel for William's cause and Marlborough's fame.

These griefs on both sides—in all conscience serious enough—between the men were now to receive feminine aggravation. King William was profoundly disturbed at the suggestions of intrigue, or even plot, to transfer the Crown to Princess Anne. But his indignation was surpassed by that of the Queen. That her own sister should be made the instrument to thrust her from the throne and usurp it herself was indeed intolerable, and what step was more urgent than to preserve that sister from the influence—nay, possession—that dominated her and made her the battering-ram of such fell designs? Upon Sarah, therefore, fell the anger of the Queen.

Anne was a very real person. She was by no means the cat's-paw she has so often been depicted. She moved on broad, homely lines. She was devoted to her religion, to her husband, and to friends whose fidelity she had proved. It cannot be doubted at all that she would have faced poverty, exile, imprisonment, or even death with placid, unconquerable resolution for the sake of any of them. Once she got set, it took years to alter her. She was not very wise nor clever, but she was very like England. Now she was, as she conceived it, assailed by her sister and by her sister's husband, whose title to the throne she had willingly completed. She saw clearly what the Marlboroughs had risked and sacrificed for her. Her heart flowed out in love for Sarah and in admiration for John. All those slow, simple qualities which afterwards made her reign as glorious in the history of the British Empire as those of Queen Elizabeth and Queen Victoria now displayed themselves.

Therefore when, early in January 1692, the Queen, hot upon the news of the alleged conspiracy and the wicked intrigues of Lord Marlborough in Parliament and the Army—nay, and with Saint-Germains too, if the truth were known—summoned Anne to her presence and ordered her to dismiss Sarah, she found herself confronted with inexpugnable resistance. The Queen opened upon the enormity of Anne's giving Sarah—that mischief-maker, that breeder of dissension in the royal family, the wife of a dangerous man harassing or betraying the King—an annuity of £1000 a year from her Parliamentary grant. It was the crowning abuse. Was it for this that Parliamentary grants were made? Now we can see why the King should have been trusted to provide what was right for his relations. Sarah must be dismissed forthwith. Anne, who was expecting another baby, met the assault with silent fortitude. From time to time she uttered a few words of phlegmatic negation. In the presence of invincible refusal Mary lost her temper, raised her voice, threatened to deprive her of half her Parliamentary grant—which was certainly not in her power. The talk became an altercation, both sides having a self-convincing case. The courtiers drew back in shocked agitation. The two sisters parted in the anger of what proved to be a mortal estrangement.

The next morning at nine o'clock Marlborough, discharging his functions as Gentleman of the Bedchamber, handed the King his shirt, and William preserved his usual impassivity. Two hours later Nottingham delivered to Marlborough a written order to sell at once all the offices he held, civil and military, and consider himself as from that date dismissed from the Army and all public employment, and forbidden the Court. No reasons were given officially for this important stroke. The Court and Parliament were left to speculate whether it had been impelled by the dispute observed between the two Princesses on the night before, or whether it arose out of Marlborough's House of Commons activities, or whether some graver cause lay behind. The topic for some weeks excited all minds, and, as may be imagined, there was no lack of explanations.

Marlborough took his dismissal, and the abuse, deserved and undeserved, let loose upon him in the highest circles, with unconcern. He had deliberately courted a breach with the King. He may have been surprised that his influence, connexions, services, and ability had not counted for more: evidently he had overrated their value. But he was not the man to take a course of action without counting the cost: there is no record of any complaints, or even comments, uttered by him. His political position was not immediately affected. Parliamentary and public opinion as a whole considered that he had been ill-used, and that he had suffered for standing up for the rights of Englishmen against the Dutch and foreign favourites. His chief associates—the greatest men of the day—were offended. Shrewsbury let his disapproval be known; Godolphin threatened to retire from the Government. Admiral Russell, now Commander-in-Chief of the Navy, went so far as to reproach King William to his face with having shown ingratitude to the man who had "set the crown upon his head." William, who with some reason only trusted Russell more than Marlborough because he feared him less, preserved an obdurate silence.

Anne's distress was acute. She was convinced that the husband of her friend and guide had suffered on her account. She did not attend the Court at Kensington for three weeks, and when at length she did so, she went accompanied by Sarah. This was indeed a step of hardihood on the part of both women. The courtiers were aghast. The Queen, not unreasonably, saw herself affronted. She wrote her sister a long and vehement letter of remonstrance, appeal, and command.

> . . . Never anybody was suffered to live at Court in my Lord Marlborough's circumstances. I need not repeat the cause he has given the King to do what he has done, nor his [the King's] unwillingness at all times to come to such extremities, though people do deserve it. . . .
>
> . . . It is very unfit that Lady Marlborough should stay with you, since that gives her husband so just a pretence of being where he ought not. . . .
>
> Nor could all my kindness for you, which is ever ready to turn all you do the best way at any other time, have hindered my showing you so that moment, but I considered your condition, and that made me master myself so far as not to take notice of it then.
>
> But now I must tell you plainly Lady Marlborough must not continue with you in the circumstances [in which] her Lord is.

Anne replied firmly the next day, saying among other things:

> Your care of my present condition is extremely obliging. And if you would be pleased to add to it so far as on my account to recall your severe comment [about Sarah] (as I must beg leave to call it in a matter so tender to me and so little reasonable as I think to be imposed upon me that you would scarce require it from the meanest of your subjects), I should ever regard it as a very agreeable mark of your kindness to me. And I must as freely own that as I think that this proceeding can be for no other intent than to give me a very sensible mortification, so there is no misery that I cannot readily resolve to suffer rather than the thoughts of parting with her.

The Princess had hoped that her uncle Rochester would take this letter, but he had no intention of prejudicing his future by mingling in this dispute loaded with danger for all but the principals. By way of answer the Lord Chamberlain was directed to forbid Sarah to continue at the Cockpit. This was decisive, but in a manner different from that in which Queen Mary had expected. Anne resolved to share the banishment of her friend. Although she was every day expecting her confinement, she borrowed Sion House from the Duke of Somerset and transported herself and her household there with the utmost expedition.

The King and Queen now vented their disapproval in a series of very small actions. They endeavoured to persuade the Duke of Somerset to reclaim his house; he regretted that as a gentleman he was unable to do so. They withdrew her guards from the Princess, and deprived her of all salutes and ceremonies. Later on, when she went to Bath, they even went so far as to make the Secretary of State write to the local mayor —a tallow-chandler, Sarah calls him—that he was not to accompany her officially to church. These puerilities humiliated only their authors. Anne gained a wide measure of public sympathy, and the Queen was wounded to learn that it was commonly said that she had no natural feeling for her own kin, neither for her father nor for her only sister.

We cannot wonder that Anne, pursued in so many petty ways and seeing her cherished friends ruined, as she thought, for her sake by the malice of her sister and the King, should have used in her intimate letters to Sarah bitter expressions about William. Macaulay says that she "called her brother-in-law sometimes the abortion, sometimes the monster, sometimes Caliban," and describes this as "the style of a fishwoman." The remark is mainly interesting as contemporary evidence of the high standard of erudition among the early Victorian fishwomen. The two sisters met only once again. After Anne had been delivered of a child which almost immediately died, the Queen visited her at Sion House; but this was only to renew her command that Sarah should be dismissed. Anne, who was still weak and quivering from her labour and grieving for her dead baby, refused as resolutely as ever. These, except for some cold and formal letters, were the last words which passed between them.

Did some protecting genius of England inspire Anne's generous, faithful heart? For surely it was in these fires of adversity, and almost persecution, that the links were forged by which the smallest and the strongest executive our country has ever known in the modern age was one day to be gripped together. The Cockpit friendships were the crucible from which the power and glory of England were soon to rise gleaming among the nations.

CHAPTER EIGHTEEN

The Tower

ᚠᚲ 1692-93 ᛞᚷ

MEANWHILE the march of events was unfavourable both to the national and personal interests of Marlborough and to the vast Continental combinations of William. No sooner had the King set out upon the wars than the imminent menace of invasion fell upon the island he had left denuded of troops. Louvois had always been sceptical, and even scornful of a Jacobite restoration; but Louvois was dead, and Louis was freed from the trammels of his famous War Minister. Although his best opportunities had passed with the end of the Irish war and the Scottish revolts, he now planned a descent upon England. The French Channel and Mediterranean fleets, together with a multitude of transports and store-ships, were concentrated in the Norman and Breton ports. An expeditionary army of ten thousand desperate Irishmen from Limerick and ten thousand French regulars was assembled around Cherbourg. James was to be given his chance. Saint-Germains had for two years oppressed the French War Office with their assertions that England was ripe and ready for a restoration. Russell would betray or divert the English fleet; Marlborough would answer for such parts of the Army as remained at home; the Princess Anne would reassure the Church of England. The Jacobites of the northern counties were under arms; the merchants of the City were favourable; the temper of the English people was rancorously hostile to the Dutch. William was now in Flanders, and once the true King landed—with an adequate force—he would drive in his coach to Whitehall. Now was the time when all these assertions so confidently reiterated by the unhappy exiles, so buoyed up by fond hopes, so backed by distortion, fabrication, and forgery, would be put to the test. James's opportunity had come.

It was not until the middle of April, from important papers captured on a small vessel, that the French designs became known to the English Government. Feverish but vigorous preparations were made for defence by land and sea. Some regiments were brought from Ireland, others recalled from Flanders, and the English dockyards resounded with the preparation of the fleets. Despite stubborn adverse Jacobite currents, the nation had but one idea—to repel the French Papist invaders and above all the despised and hated Irish. James's declaration, framed by Melfort, "the evil genius of the house of Stuart," as he has been well called, apprised the nation of its peril. All the old arrogance, religious and political, and a new vindictiveness to pay off recent scores, were reflected in this wanton document. Large numbers of persons, ranging from the greatest nobles to the rough, ignorant fishermen who had manhandled their sovereign upon his flight to Faversham, were specifically excluded from the amnesty. Marlborough's name figured among the proscribed; but this, we are assured by the Jacobites, was only from a desire not to compromise the delicacy of his position. As upon the approach of the Spanish Armada, all England was alert. But everything turned upon the Admiral Russell. He, like Marlborough, had talked with the Jacobite agents: William and Mary feared, and James fervently believed, that he would play the traitor to his country and his profession. James was sure that the fleet was on his side, and had furnished Versailles with lists of the admirals and captains on whom he counted. Now would be proved what substance there was in all these tales. Would that every Jacobite pretension could be brought to an equally conclusive trial!

According to the Jacobites, Russell bluntly told their agent, Floyd, that, much as he loved James and loathed William's Government, if he met the French fleet at sea he would do his best to destroy it, "even though King James himself were on board." He kept his word. "If your officers play you false," he said to the fleetmen on the day of battle, "overboard with them, and myself the first." We have no doubt that Marlborough, his friend and fellow-intriguer, would have done the same with the soldiers had he had them in command. But his lot was hard. An age of revolutions and conspiracies, when all foundations quaked, had produced a tribe of professional plot-denouncers. Titus Oates, living in retirement upon his Government pension, held a veritable school for the making of bogus plots from the exposure of which much wealth and celebrity might be gained. Moreover, there was no lack of material. A rascal named Fuller had already this year from his debtors' prison offered blood-curdling revelations to Parliament, and had been exposed and convicted only by the exceptional diligence of the House of Commons. Now, at this grievous moment, came forth a disciple of Oates and Fuller named Young, also a rogue and a criminal, also in gaol, who devised a scheme to win himself riches and consideration by accusing well-known and likely men of murderous conspiracy.

Young was by his own confession an expert forger. He had obtained a specimen of Marlborough's signature by writing to him about the character of a servant. He drew up a document purporting to be a bond of association between certain persons to take the Prince of Orange, dead or alive, and to restore King James. He forged the names of Marlborough, Cornbury, Archbishop Sancroft, and the harmless Bishop of Rochester, Sprat, with some others, as signatories. His confederate, Blackhead, hid this poisonous evidence in a flowerpot in the house of the unwitting Bishop of Rochester. Young then warned the Cabinet of their peril and where the proof could be found. Above all things, he said, they must search the Bishop's flowerpots. Under the threat of invasion, on the eve of fateful battle with the fleet commanded by a suspected admiral, a panic-fierce mood ruled at the council-board. Marlborough and one or two leading Jacobites were arrested out of hand and sent to the Tower.

Three members of the Council, Lords Devonshire, Bradford, and Montagu, kept their heads; they declined to sign the warrant upon the evidence of a single witness of whose credibility the most that could be said was that "he had not yet had his ears cropped." But Marlborough slept the night of May 4 a prisoner of State upon a charge of high treason.

Stringent search was now made of the Bishop's palace, and almost every flowerpot was examined. But there was one which, because it stood near the servants' quarters, was overlooked. In this lay the paper which, if discovered at that moment, might have cost not only the Bishop but our hero his life. The officers of the Crown returned to

Whitehall with the Bishop in custody, but no evidence. Young then procured from his prison cell the recovery of the document, and sent it with another legend to the Council.

But meanwhile a fortnight had passed and great events had happened. On May 19/29 the English and Dutch fleets, which had effected their junction before the French were ready, encountered Tourville with the main French naval power off Cape La Hogue. The forces were impressive in their number, but Russell's armada, which carried forty thousand men and seven thousand guns, was the stronger by ninety-nine ships to forty-four. Both sides fought hard, and Tourville was beaten. His flagship, *Le Soleil Royal*, named in honour of Louis XIV, was first battered and then burned to the water's edge. The French fleet was scattered and driven into its ports. But this was not the end. Russell and his admirals, three of the most daring of whom were counted on the Jacobite lists as pledged and faithful adherents of King James, followed the beaten navy into its harbours. For five successive days the fighting continued. The fugitive warships were cut out under the shore batteries by flotillas of hardy English row-boats; the store ships and many of the transports were burned; and the whole apparatus of invasion was destroyed under the very eyes of the King it was to have borne to his native shore.

The battle of Cape La Hogue, with its consequential actions, effaced the memories of Beachy Head. More than that, it broke decisively for the whole of the wars of William and Anne all French pretensions to supremacy at sea. It was the Trafalgar of the seventeenth century. We invite the reader to judge whether fact is not stronger than fiction; whether substance is not more solid than shadow. Because Russell had flirted with the Jacobite agents; because these agents had vapourized to the Court at Saint-Germains; because James had wanted to believe all his agents told him, and made the most of it to Louis; and because the Jacobite writers have invented and written whatever they pleased about him, Russell stands convicted before history as a "villain" and a "traitor." This shattering victory and noble feat of arms counts for nothing in his favour. Macpherson, Dalrymple, Macaulay, and the docile flock of scrap-nibblers who have browsed upon their pastures, have managed hitherto to twist history and reality to his condemnation. We submit to modern judgment two propositions about him: that he was wrong and foolish to have trafficked with the Jacobite agents, but that he was quite right to beat the French and ruin King James's cause, which was on the whole rather more important.

The fears of the Council and the excitement of the public were calmed by the victory. Lords Huntingdon and Scarsdale, who had been arrested on other grounds at the same time as Marlborough, were set at liberty. William, who had been perturbed by the irregularity of these arrests, wrote to the Council expressing his doubts about such serious steps. Nevertheless, so strong were the feelings of the Queen that Marlborough was still kept a close prisoner in the Tower. Sarah came from Brentford to London in order to be near him, to help in his defence, and to agitate for his release. No one was allowed to visit him except upon the authority of the Secretary of State, and we have consequently a series of orders signed by Nottingham giving Sarah and some others access to him. Among the few who faced the displeasure of the Queen, Lord Bradford was conspicuous. As is usual with people in such a position, the Marlboroughs found few friends. Other nearer trouble fell upon them. On May 22 their younger son Charles died.

There is little doubt that the King and Queen, heating each other in their anger, explored the question of curtailing Anne's Parliamentary grant. They encountered a steady resistance from Godolphin at the Treasury. Moreover, the House of Commons would have resented any such proposal. Rumours, however, of the project reached Sarah through a sure channel. She continued to suggest that she should relieve the tension by departing—at any rate, for a time. The Princess's attitude was magnificent:

> I really long to know how my dear Mrs Freeman got home; and now I have this opportunity of writing, she must give me leave to tell her, if she should ever be so cruel to leave her faithful Mrs Morley, she will rob her of all the joy and quiet of her life; for if that day should come, I could never enjoy a happy minute, and I swear to you I would shut myself up and never see a creature. You may easily see all this would have come upon me, if you had not been. If you do but remember what the Q. said to me the night before your Lord was turned out of all; then she begun to pick quarrels; and if they should take off twenty or thirty thousand pound, have I not lived upon as little before? When I was first married we had but twenty (it is true indeed the King [Charles] was so kind to pay my debts), and if it

should come to that again, what retrenchment is there in my family I would not willingly make and be glad of that pretence to do it? Never fancy, dear Mrs Freeman, if what you fear should happen, that you are the occasion . . . ; therefore rest satisfied you are no ways the cause; and let me beg once more, for God's sake, that you would never mention parting more, no nor so much as think of it; and if you should ever leave me, be assured it would break your faithful Mrs Morley's heart.

Meanwhile Marlborough had recourse to the Council. To Danby, the Lord President, he wrote:

Having been informed that it is now publicly discoursed in Westminster Hall to-day that a letter under my hand was to be produced to the grand jury, to induce them to find a bail against me, I beg leave to assure your Lordship, upon my honour and credit, that if any such letter be pretended, it must and will, upon examination, appear so plainly to have been forged, that as it can be of no credit or advantage to the Government, so I doubt not but your Lordship's justice will be ready to protect me from so injurious a proceeding, who am, etc.

He also used his rights under the law, invoked the Habeas Corpus Act, and demanded admission to bail. To Halifax he wrote:

My Counsel being to move the Court of King's Bench for my Habeas Corpus the beginning of next term, and [I] being very certain of my own innocence, and that no instance can be shewn why I should not be bailed, I desire the favour of your Lordship to be there and be one of my Sureties for my appearance, not knowing yet how many they may require to be found for me; I shall be unwilling to give your Lordship this trouble without a necessity, and in that case I shall always own it as the greatest obligation to your Lordship's most obedient

Marlborough

On June 11 Young and his accomplice, Blackhead, were brought before the Privy Council. The event was dramatic. Confronted with Bishop Sprat and under the stern eyes of the Council, Blackhead, who had already weakened, broke down completely, and confessed his crime.

The forged document was produced. As we have to deal in Marlborough's life with other charges equally elaborately presented, we give it here as Sprat recollected it.

> That we, whose names were subscribed, should solemnly promise, in the presence of God, to contribute our utmost assistance towards King James's recovery of his kingdoms; that to this end, we would have ready to meet him, at his landing, thirty thousand men well armed; that we would seize upon the person of the Princess of Orange, dead or alive; and take care, that some strong garrison should be forthwith delivered into his hands; and furnish him with a considerable sum of money, for the support of his army.

March 20, 1691

Marleborough	*Salisbury*	*W. Cant.*
		*Tho. Roffen.**
		Cornbury
Basil Firebrace		*John Wilcoxe*

The Bishop was startled at the perfection of the forgery. "I am very much amazed," he said, "to see my hand so well counterfeited; all the difference is they have done me the favour to write it finer than I can: otherwise I acknowledge it is so like that I verily believe I myself, had I seen it in another place, should have been apt to doubt whether it were of my writing or no. I am confident it might, upon the first blush, deceive the best friends I have."

Here Godolphin intervened, and his friendly purpose is easily discernible. "My Lords," he said, "I am very well acquainted with Archbishop Sancroft's hand, and here it is almost exactly counterfeited." He added that the Earl of Marlborough's hand had been so well feigned in a letter that had been written by Young himself that it was very difficult for his most intimate friends to observe any distinction.

Young was now brought before the Council.

> EARL OF NOTTINGHAM (*taking up the association and showing it to Young*): Did you not give this paper to Blackhead and order him to put it in a chimney in the Bishop of Rochester's house, and into a flowerpot, if there were any?
>
> YOUNG: No, I never desired him to carry it thither, or to put it into a flowerpot.
>
> EARL OF NOTTINGHAM: What say you, Blackhead?

* This is Sprat's signature, as Bishop of Rochester.

BLACKHEAD: Mr Young did give me that paper, and directed me to leave it in the Bishop's house; and if I could, to put it in a flowerpot in some room; which I did, in the parlour.

YOUNG: There is no such matter. I absolutely deny it.

EARL OF NOTTINGHAM, LORD SYDNEY, AND OTHERS OF THE COUNCILLORS: Why, then, did you give us such express directions to send and search the flowerpots among other places in the Bishop's house?

YOUNG: I said nothing of flowerpots. I bid you take care that the Bishop's person should be exactly searched; because when he went abroad he carried the association about him; when he was at home, he put it in some private place, for fear of surprise. Perhaps I might say, in the chimney.

THE COUNCILLORS: Nay, we all well remember, you particularly mentioned the flowerpots.

There was now no case of any kind against Marlborough. Not even one of the two witnesses necessary to sustain a charge of treason was available; and the document which incriminated him was a proved and exposed forgery. On June 15, after an imprisonment of six weeks, he succeeded in bringing him once before the Court of the King's Bench on a writ of Habeas Corpus. The Government demanded sureties and bail for £6000. Halifax did not fail him, neither did Shrewsbury. Both these lords, with two other persons, became his sureties. Their action was resented by the Queen. These two famous builders of our constitutional history were forthwith struck off the Privy Council. Marlborough's name was found still, apparently by oversight, upon the roll. The oversight was repaired.

Marlborough was now free, and the Cockpit group reunited at Berkeley House in a companionship of wrath and misfortune. The ordeal had been severe, and escape narrow. The forgeries of Young had been so perfect that Marlborough admitted himself when shown the document that he could have hardly believed that it was not his own autograph. Such a plot, had it not miscarried, might well have sent him during the invasion panic to the scaffold. Moreover, he might expect that at any moment some one or other of the Jacobite agents with whom he had consorted and through whom he had communicated with Saint-Germains might come forward with confirmatory revelations. However, his nerves were steel, and neither imminent peril nor prolonged strain affected his poise and serenity. Nor did he in any respect alter his course. He continued through various secret channels to preserve exactly the same shadowy relations with King James—neither less nor more—as before his disgrace. He persisted in his opposition to the King by every means open to him.

And now from the war came news which must have gnawed his soul. As in 1691, the campaign had opened with a brilliant French success. Louis XIV had laid siege to the hitherto inviolate fortress of Namur before William, through the tardiness of his allies, could be ready. Vauban, under Louis, conducted the siege, while Luxembourg with an army of eighty thousand men stood between William and its relief. Once again the unlucky head of the Grand Alliance and his army watched impotently the fall of one of their most important fortresses. But worse was to come. In August William marched by night with his whole army to attack Luxembourg, whose forces were somewhat divided. The French were surprised near Steinkirk in the early morning. Their advanced troops were overwhelmed and routed, and for an hour confusion reigned in their camp. But Luxembourg was equal to the emergency, and managed to draw out an ordered line of battle. The British infantry formed the forefront of the allied attack. Eight splendid regiments under General Mackay charged and broke the Swiss in fighting as fierce as had been seen in Europe in living memory. Luxembourg launched the Household troops of France upon the British division, already strained by its exertions, and after a furious struggle fought mostly with sword and bayonet beat them back.

Meanwhile from all sides the French advanced, and their reinforcements began to reach the field. Count Solms refused to send Mackay the help for which he begged. A Dutch general on the opposite flank, the valiant Overkirk, brought two battalions to their aid with remarkable effect. But for this, that British force of which Marlborough had been so proud the year before would have been cut to pieces. As it was they escaped with a loss of their two best generals, Mackay and Lanier, and of half their number, more than three thousand being killed or wounded. William seemed unable to control the battle. Witness of this cruel disaster, we are assured that he shed bitter tears as he watched the slaughter and exclaimed, "Oh, my poor English!" But what was the good of that? By noon the whole of the allied army was in retreat, and although the losses of seven or eight thousand men on either side were equal, the French proclaimed their victory throughout Europe.

The wheel of fortune spins with infinite caprice, and no one can tell whether it was Marlborough's good luck or bad that tied him in England unemployed and a prisoner of State while Count Solms cast the English away at Steinkirk. He had sunk now to the minor and unpleasant position of being a critic of mishandled affairs with whose main intention he agreed. This condition was to rule him for a long time, as our short lives go. The Court guerrilla against Anne continued, and she was subjected to many petty impertinences and something very like what we should now call a society boycott. Marlborough presented his general case to Parliament when it met in November. He found support which in modern times might be decisive. The House of Lords ignored the Royal Speech and proceeded to examine the causes why certain of their members had been unlawfully imprisoned. It was argued that once the charges were dropped the retention of bail and the refusal to discharge recognizances were infringements of privilege. Acrimonious debates ensued. The Constable of the Tower, the Treasury Solicitor, even the judges of the High Court, were summoned. William found himself in the presence of one of those tensely wrought, sternly measured constitutional movements towards which he had been taught in the days of Charles II that English kings should not be unbending. He used the royal prerogative to discharge Marlborough from his recognizances. This grievance removed, both Houses turned to the war.

The Lords carried an address praying that no English general should be subordinated to a Dutchman, whatever his rank. In the Commons the Court, or, as we should now say, Ministerial, orators inculcated precepts of humility. In the end the Commons pressed less strongly upon the King than the Lords. The conspiracy of Grandval, a Jacobite enthusiast set on by Saint-Germains to murder the King, had rallied strong English sympathies in his behalf; and the power of the Crown proved overwhelming. If William's government could bear the odium of Solms at Steinkirk, it could bear anything. The King returned brief answers to the addresses, and supplies were voted for another mismanaged and disastrous year of war.

In July 1693 was fought the great battle of Landen, unmatched in its slaughter except by Malplaquet and Borodino for two hundred years. The French were in greatly superior strength, having 96 battalions and 210 squadrons to William's 65 battalions and 150 squadrons. Nevertheless the King determined to withstand their attack, and constructed almost overnight a system of strong entrenchments and palisades in the enclosed country along the Landen stream, within the windings of the Geet. After an heroic resistance the allies were driven from their position by the French with a loss of nearly twenty thousand men, the attackers losing less than half this total. Nevertheless William rallied the remnants of his army, gathered reinforcements, and, since Luxembourg neglected to pursue his victory, was able surprisingly to maintain himself in the field.

Of all these stirring events, which at so many points touched him intimately, Marlborough continued to be a mere spectator.

CHAPTER NINETEEN

The Fenwick Trial

ᘒ 1694-1697 ᘖ

We now reach one of the turning points of this story. At the end of 1694 the Queen was stricken with smallpox. Anne wrote a sisterly letter and asked to be allowed to come to her bedside. A civil answer was returned by Lady Derby, then Lady-in-Waiting, declining the visit for the moment on the very natural ground that it was "so necessary to keep the Queen as quiet as possible." The Postscript was added, "Pray madam present my humble duty to the Princess." Sarah's shrewd eye read into this "that the disease was mortal," and so in a few days it proved to be. On December 28 Queen Mary died, beloved and mourned by her subjects and bitterly missed by her husband.

This unforeseen event produced profound changes in the prospects and relations of those with whom this story is concerned. Hitherto the natural expectation had been that Mary would long survive her husband, upon whose frail, fiery life so many assaults of disease, war, and conspiracy converged. An English Protestant Queen would then reign in her own right. Instead of this, the Crown, thanks in part to the surrender which Anne had made of her rights, devolved on William alone for life. Thereafter it must come to Anne. Any day, any month, certainly as it seemed in a few years, the Princess to whom the sentinels had been ordered to deny their salutes, whom the Mayor of Bath had been forbidden to attend to church, who dwelt quietly with her family and intimate friends in the unfashionable chambers of Berkeley House, would be Queen of the three kingdoms. And at her side, linked by ties which the whole power of the dual reign had been unable to break, would stand the redoubtable couple without whom even in their darkest fortunes it had been impossible to reckon. No wonder Berkeley House, lately so deserted, was thronged with "people of all sorts flocking," in spite of Sarah's ironical smiles, "to pay their respects to the Prince and Princess."

It was no longer Marlborough's part to raise an opposition to the King. From the moment that the Queen had breathed her last his interests were the same as William's. He shared William's resolve to break the power of France. He agreed with the whole character and purpose of his foreign policy. His patience enabled him to wait with contentment for that "sunshine day" of which Anne had written. By the mediation of Sunderland and Somers a formal reconciliation was effected between William and Anne. She was received with her proper ceremony when she waited upon the King at Kensington, and St James's Palace was prepared for her use. Thither in due course she carried Sarah. But the wounds of the quarrel still rankled. The relations between the sovereign and the heiress-presumptive, if correct, were also frigid, and Marlborough remained excluded for four more years from all employment, military or civil, at the front or at home. This, however, did not sway his course of action. Although William treated him with such prolonged and marked personal hostility, he became his steady supporter, and used his graceful arts to prevent anything like a rivalry or open breach between St James's and Whitehall. He continued from time to time to receive the Jacobite agents and preserve his connexion with King James. This was an easy task, since his imprisonment and continuing disgrace at the hands of William pleaded 'for themselves at Saint-Germains.

Europe believed that the death of Queen Mary would greatly weaken William, and the Jacobites at home and in France looked forward to his speedy downfall. But in fact, owing largely to the concord reestablished in the royal circle, he appeared at first even to be strengthened by his loss. His principal Ministers and advisers had long been Marlborough's friends, and were united with him by many open and some secret ties. The death of the Queen only consolidated the general accord of this strong and powerful group. Well was it so, for a new danger was already approaching.

The campaign of 1695 brought William his one success in the European war. He besieged and retook Namur in the teeth of the French armies, which now that Luxembourg was dead could find no better leader than a certain Marshal de Villeroy, destined afterwards to a more serious reverse.

The year 1695 was filled with activities of the Jacobites. The connexions of their party spread throughout the country. In their political clubs, in elegant society, in lonely halls and manor-houses, in the taverns and on the village greens, they held their heads high and exchanged confident salutations. They could not believe that William, deprived of his English Queen, could stand alone. Beneath all their froth upon the surface there grew at a hundred points preparation for armed rebellion, if and when the hour should strike; and beneath this again, as so often happens in movements of this character, at the root of all, there festered a murder plot. King James was privy to both designs, though it cannot be said he directly or specifically commissioned the assassins. In the autumn he sent Berwick into England to concert the insurrection. For several months this daring young man moved about the country in disguise or lay hidden in London. He saw all the leading Jacobites, and endeavoured to bring their plans coherently to a head and fix the occasion.

If Berwick had seen Marlborough he would certainly have recorded it in his *Memoirs*, not written until the events of his mission possessed only historical interest. No such idea ever seems to have occurred to him. Yet his father would surely not have sent him on so mortally perilous a mission without letting him know the full extent of his English connexions. The truth is that James in his inmost heart only placed limited reliance upon the friendly assurances that reached him from the Revolution leaders. They might serve to impress Louis XIV with the strength of the Jacobite movement, or as a basis for history; but James would not risk the life of a well-loved son, nor Berwick his own life upon them.

Berwick found the resources of the conspiracy were by no means inconsiderable. As many as two thousand horse, "well appointed and even regimented," were ready to take the field on the first notice, and "several people of the highest distinction were also engaged in the business." But here came the deadlock. The English Jacobites were "unanimously agreed not to throw off the mask before a body of troops was actually landed in the island." Louis XIV was willing to supply these troops, but only on one condition. After his experiences in 1692 he was determined not to launch an expedition until after a rising had actually begun. Thus on both sides of the channel the potential rebels and the contingent invaders were in suspense, and waited each on the other.

Meanwhile, independently of Berwick, James had sent over a Sir George Barclay with instructions, written throughout in his own hand, authorizing him in comprehensive terms to commit such acts of hostility against William as he might think right and practicable. At the same time by various routes about twenty resolute members of James's bodyguard at Saint-Germains made their way into England, and by secret signals got into touch with Barclay in London. The most deadly and resolute plot since the Gunpowder Treason was now hatched. Every Saturday King William was wont to go a-hunting, and it was designed on his return from one of these excursions to fall upon him, overpower his guards, and kill him. Turnham Green, where on his homeward journey he recrossed the river by boat and was taken up by a new coach with a new escort, was chosen for the ambuscade. For this desperate deed forty men were needed. Twenty had come from Saint-Germains. Twenty more must be found in England. In this delicate recruitment Barclay and his confederates next engaged themselves.

The conspirators had fixed the afternoon of Saturday, February 15, 1696, as the moment for their onslaught, and forty determined men, mounted and armed to the teeth, were gathered hard by the landing-stage at Turnham Green. The Rye House Plot of the Whigs had got no farther than tavern talk: the Jacobite desperadoes had come to the very verge of well-concerted action. A fire was even prepared on the Dover cliffs to carry the news to the anxious party at Calais. But two of the forty, one from fear, the other from scruple, had given warning to Bentinck, and at the last moment William was with difficulty persuaded not to hunt that day.

The Government, having got some threads in their hands, speedily drew out the rest. Many of the conspirators were seized, the alarm was given, and the plot in all its gruesome reality and imminence was exposed. The nation was roused to fury. All classes rallied round the King. Parliament suspended the Habeas Corpus Act, and the vast majority of its Members swore themselves into an association to defend the King's person and revenge his death. It was also resolved that Parliament should not be automatically dissolved upon a demise of the

Crown from any cause, and that the succession should be instantly ensured in accordance with the Declaration of Right. Thus the confusion following the death of the King, on which James's party counted, would be effectually prevented. The trials and executions of the conspirators were speedy and not too numerous. Never had William enjoyed such popularity since the first days of his reign.

Even if the plot had not miscarried, James had no chance of regaining his lost Crown across the murdered corpse of William. The leading Ministers were in the closest contact with Marlborough, and long forethought had taught them to link their future with Anne. No panic or disorder would have followed the bloody deed. Within the compass of a single day, swept upward by a wave of national indignation, Anne would have mounted the throne and Marlborough would have gripped the Army. Not a shot would have been fired. Not a dog would have barked. The new organism of government would have presented itself far stronger than the former combination.

The murder plot brought in its trail a great Parliamentary drama. Sir John Fenwick was no assassin, but he was deeply involved in the preparations for rebellion. Warrants were issued for his arrest, and after some time by chance he was caught. Well born himself, he was through his wife Lady Mary, daughter of the Earl of Carlisle, connected with several of the greatest families. To save himself from swift condemnation and to gain time for powerful influences to come to his aid, he wrote a confession in which he charged Marlborough, Russell, Godolphin, and Shrewsbury with treasonable correspondence with Saint-Germains. The accusation against Marlborough was that he had sent a message by Floyd to King James asking for his pardon. "The answer to my Lord Marlborough," wrote Fenwick, "was, that he was the greatest of criminals where he had the greatest obligations, but if he did him extraordinary service, he might hope for pardon; and a little after he did a considerable piece of service, of which we had an account by one sent on purpose by King James." It was also alleged that King James relied on Marlborough to bring over the Army to his cause. Fenwick betrayed none of his confederates, the real Jacobites who had been waiting with arms and horses for the signal of revolt. He selected only those "false Jacobites" who were or had been employed in the greatest stations round King William, and who had mocked the royal exile with vain promises and deceitful homage. William was in Holland. His action when he received his confession casts a revealing light upon the politics of his reign. The King saw through Fenwick's manœuvre at a glance. He learned from it nothing that he had not known for years and discounted at its proper value. He had no intention of destroying the system upon which he ruled or of deranging the structure of his Government by tearing the heads off both great parties. He therefore sent the paper home to his Council with assurances to its incriminated members that his confidence in them was utterly unaffected by such nonsense. This for the moment sufficed.

But when Parliament was apprised of the confession a graver situation supervened. Nobody would have been surprised at the intrigues of Tories with the Jacobites. It was in their blood. But here were the immaculate Whigs aspersed. The House of Commons was determined to test the truth of Fenwick's accusations. Brought to the bar, he refused to amplify or prove what he had written. One Member, Colonel Godfrey, the husband of Arabella, no doubt at Marlborough's desire, specifically invited him across the chamber to state fully all he alleged against Marlborough. But Fenwick excused himself. Brought at the request of Parliament before the King, he persisted in his refusal. We must presume that, like the historians, he had no proofs, and, like them, was merely repeating the secret talk of the inner Jacobite circles. He was sent back to prison. The charge under which he lay was in any case grievous. Still, since it was not concerned with the actual murder plot, it might not have entailed the forfeit of life. But now he had drawn upon himself the wrath of both great parties, and particularly of the Whigs, who saw two of their most famous leaders impugned without proof or reason. He had also aroused the enmity alike of the powerful men he had accused, and of others whom he might have accused. He had deeply angered the King by what to William was an obvious attempt to rupture his Government. Meanwhile one of the two witnesses indispensable to the treason charge had been bribed or terrorized out of the country, and it seemed that the law stood dumb before him. It was at this stage that the Commons fell back upon the last reserve weapon of the State—an Act of Attainder.

There is no need here to describe the many vehement debates, narrow and exciting divisions, and Parliamentary situations which marked the two months' passage of the Bill through both Houses. They have been so often brilliantly told. We are not concerned with the fate of Sir John Fenwick, but only with the effects of his charges upon Marlborough and the other aspersed statesmen. None of them had been in any way concerned either in the assassination plot or in the projected rebellion. All of them had at some time or other conversed or trafficked with Jacobite agents and thus easily, in King William's phrase, "made their peace with Saint-Germains." Their prolonged ordeal was most severe. When, in a moment of intense public feeling and widespread suspicion, men have to defend themselves from terrible charges, the fact that they have been guilty of comparatively venial conduct of the same kind, compromising in essence and still more in appearance, may shake the strongest nerve and wear down the boldest spirit.

"Every one of the accused persons," says Macaulay,

> behaved himself in a manner singularly characteristic. Marlborough, the most culpable of all, preserved a serenity, mild, majestic, and slightly contemptuous. Russell, scarcely less criminal than Marlborough, went into a towering passion, and breathed nothing but vengeance against the villainous informer. Godolphin, uneasy, but wary, reserved, and self-possessed, prepared himself to stand on the defensive. But Shrewsbury, who of all the four was the least to blame, was utterly overwhelmed.

This fell short of the facts. William knew more from the Jacobite talk of the day. But the King set himself to comfort Shrewsbury. "In sending you Sir John Fenwick's paper," he wrote,

> I assured you, that I was persuaded his accusation was false, of which I am now fully convinced, by your answer, and perfectly satisfied with the ingenuous confession of what passed between you and Lord Middleton, which can by no means be imputed to you as a crime. And indeed you may be assured, that this business, so far from making on me any unfavourable impression, will, on the contrary, if possible, in future, strengthen my confidence in you, and my friendship can admit of no increase.

But Shrewsbury was inconsolable. He buried himself in the country. He declared that a fall out hunting had rendered him unfit for public business. Certainly his health broke down completely. He repeatedly but in vain besought William to allow him to resign. Meanwhile he seems to have left Marlborough to watch over his interests, for we have one of Marlborough's very rare letters in this period to him:

December 2, 1696

Wednesday night—
Although I have not troubled your Grace with my letters I have not been wanting in inquiring constantly how you did. I did about a fortnight ago write a letter to acquaint you with what I had observed of some people, in hopes Mr Arden would have called upon me as he promised, but I did not care to send it by post, and so it was burnt. We had yesterday 'Sir Jo. Fenwick at the House, and I think all went as well as you could wish. I do not send you the particulars, knowing you must have it more exactly from others; but on this occasion I should be wanting if I did not let you know that Lord Rochester has behaved himself on all this occasion like a friend; and in a conversation he had with me he expressed himself as a real servant of yours, and I think it would not be amiss if you took notice of it to him. . . .

Wharton also wrote to Shrewsbury describing what happened when Fenwick came before the Lords:

. . . after the reading of the paper, my lord Marlborough first stood up and spoke to this purpose: "that he did not wonder to find a man in danger, willing to throw his guilt upon any other body; that he had some satisfaction to be owned in such good company; but that he assured their lordships that he had [had] no sort of conversation with him, upon any account whatsoever, since this Government, which he said upon his word and honour." . . . After which my lord Godolphin said, "that he found himself named in two places, first, as having been looked upon as being in King James's interest, from the beginning, and afterwards, as having entered into a negotiation, as was expressed in the paper. As to the first, he confessed he was one of those that had, to the last, continued in King James's service, and he did not know, but from that, King James and his friends might imagine him to continue in that interest, but as to the latter part, there was nothing in the world so false."

In the course of these proceedings a peculiar complication had arisen. Mordaunt, already mentioned as Monmouth, and afterwards Earl of Peterborough, although himself an alleged Jacobite, impelled by his mischievous instincts and the hope of throwing the Government into disorder, endeavoured secretly to persuade Fenwick through his wife to point and elaborate his charges, especially against Marlborough, assuring him that this was the path to safety. Fenwick pondered anxiously upon this suggestion. Ailesbury was a fellow-prisoner in the Tower. Though never a serious rebel, he was an avowed Jacobite and had been drawn unwitting into dangerous company on more than one occasion. Fenwick endeavoured to persuade Ailesbury to join with him in pressing his charges. Ailesbury probably knew as much as Fenwick of all that had been whispered for some time past in the ranks of the English Jacobites. His appearance beside Fenwick at the bar with corroborative allegations would, in the then temper of both Houses, and still more of the public, have created an ugly situation for Marlborough and the impugned Ministers. Ailesbury, however, was, as we have noted, a friend of Marlborough's. They had been thrown together at Court in the days of Charles II. He therefore sought Marlborough's advice through channels which were open. The counsel he received was to have nothing to do with Fenwick and to remain quiet till after the execution, when he would soon be released and all would be well. He had the wisdom to act accordingly, and ever afterwards believed that he had rendered Marlborough an important personal service. Fenwick, unsupported by Ailesbury, rejected Monmouth's suggestions. Monmouth, angered at this, turned against him with extreme bitterness. Lady Mary Fenwick then in revenge exposed Monmouth's conduct to the Lords. There was general indignation at this mischief-mongering. He was stripped of his offices and sent to the Tower, from which he was released only upon abject apologies. But this was not the end of him.

The process of attainder crawled remorselessly forward stage by stage. Marlborough, entirely unaffected by the strain which had broken Shrewsbury and intimidated Godolphin, comported himself with the confidence and vigour of a man conscious of his own innocence. He actively pressed forward the Bill, and voted for it in the important divisions. Calmly and inexorably he threw his whole influence against Fenwick, and it was publicly remarked that he was zealous for his condemnation. His brother George Churchill, who had commanded a ship at the battle of La Hogue with credit and was a member of the House of Commons, observed less decorum. "Damn him!" he exclaimed, with brutal frankness, in the Lobby; "thrust a billet down his throat. Dead men tell no tales." But in truth Fenwick had no tales to tell. He had founded his charges on nothing but hearsay; he had no proof of any kind.

Marlborough sternly pursued his course as if his conscience were clear of any shameful or deadly deed. Perhaps it was. Sir John Fenwick was beheaded on Tower Hill on January 28, 1697.

CHAPTER TWENTY

Avarice and Charm

THERE is no virtue so universally unpopular as frugality. Every one likes the handsome spender who offers lavish hospitality and eases his path through life by a shower of money. In the days of which we are writing all who held high public appointments were accustomed and expected to live in fine style and at a profuse expense. Public opinion was more critical about how important people spent their money than about how they acquired it. Graft, pilfering, and corruption, unless too flagrant, were leniently judged in the governing circle; stinting and saving were resented as peculiar. It does not, however, follow that those who are the most extravagant and easy with their money are the most unselfish, nor that those who are the most niggardly are the most mean. There is a happy medium which can only be defined for each individual by the general opinion of the society in which he lives.

Judged by this standard, Marlborough lay under reproach. He was at once highly acquisitive in the gaining of money and extremely careful in the spending of it. In those days, when almost the only other form of wealth was landed property, public appointments all had a recognized money value. An officer without means could not take his promotion. An officer who had reached high rank was a substantial proprietor, carrying with him in his own person and his appointments the cumulative and reinvested savings of his career. In all but extreme cases these vested interests were respected. There was nothing secret or corrupt about them. They were the system and the custom, and it is only within living memory that the principle of purchase was abolished in the British Army. In the seventeenth and eighteenth centuries those who had no money had no standing. Instances there were to the contrary; but in the main it was not until the French Revolution that the glorious principle of *la carrière ouverte aux talents* was proclaimed or even comprehended.

Marlborough's childhood had been lived in penury. But to Marlborough's early years there was an added sting. He learned almost as soon as he could walk and speak that he and his father and mother were dependants upon the charity and goodwill of his grandmother. As he grew older he saw the straits to which the impoverishments of a Cavalier had reduced his father. He heard the talk of the exactions of the Roundheads and of the frequent litigation for quite small sums in which all the grown-ups of the household were engaged with the Government or with the other members of their family. When, for his father's services and his own good looks, he was taken as a page at Court, he was penniless. He might be finely dressed and well fed, but he was penniless among those who monopolized a large proportion of the entire wealth of the kingdom. On every side his seeming equals were youths of noble fortune, heirs to vast estates and splendid titles. He was the earthenware pot among the iron ones. This was his second strong impression of life.

Before he was eighteen he realized that, unless he could make and save money, he could neither have a career, nor a bride nor a home, nor even a modest independence. It is therefore not at all surprising, however unromantic, that his first preoccupation was the gathering of money. In his twenties and thirties his temper was very similar to that which we have attributed to the French nation—always more generous of life than treasure, ready to encounter every personal hazard, prodigal of blood, but deeply concerned about money. His thrift was not without a certain grandeur, a habit of self-denial differing altogether from a miser's sordidness. We have seen how when, after heartbreaking postponements, he married a girl almost as poor as himself he could offer her no home. We have seen him at twenty-eight marrying for love, and at the same time helping his father out of debt by resigning his own reversionary interest in the small family estate. In all supreme matters his actions were those of a generous spirit. His need and desire to possess a competence and not to be crippled in his career did not outweigh— nay, were cast aside by—true love and family duty.

But these great decisions only made thrift and circumspection more imperative. He could not afford to gamble and carouse with his equals. He could not indulge in the slightest personal extravagance. He ate sparingly, drank little, always more readily at the expense of others than his own, and eschewed all kind of display in dress. He was always strict and punctilious in money matters. He paid his bills with the utmost promptitude. He condescended to keep careful accounts in his own handwriting about quite small household affairs, and generally behaved more like a tradesman whose livelihood depends upon his honesty and solvency than like a gay and gallant courtier and fine gentleman. Even now, fifteen years later, after having held several lucrative posts, he was by far the poorest man in the high circle in which he had taken his natural place. He was an Earl, but the most impecunious in England. He was the first Lieutenant-General, but unemployed. He had braved the displeasure of the Crown. It might well be that his career was closed for many years. The slightest financial imprudence would be fatal to his future. Thus he continued those habits of strict and austere personal economy which had been ingrained in childhood and youth, and without which he would certainly have been submerged.

All this was very deplorable, and no doubt the historians are right to mock and sneer at him. But their taunts are only an echo of the gibes and jokes of his contemporaries. Probably many stories of meanness were fastened on him, once he had that reputation, which are not true. But, true or false or merely exaggerated, they must be accepted by his biographer as representing the impression of the society in which he lived. He had, we are told, in 1692 but three coats ("depuis trois ans il n'a fait que trois habits modestes"), one of which he wore only on the greatest State occasions. "He was," wrote Sarah, "naturally genteel, without the least affectation, and handsome as an angel, tho' ever so carelessly drest." He would walk home from the Palace through the muddy streets to save the hire of a sedan chair. He entertained very few. Even when he wished to gain officers of the Army to his faction, he spent nothing on their meat and drink. Macaulay is no doubt right in stating gleefully that when he was robbed of five hundred guineas by a highwayman it was a bitter blow. There is the story on which Swift founded the scathing insult "that he had risked his life for a pair of stockings." When as Commander-in-Chief the gaiters he wore were so drenched that they had to be cut off him, he gave meticulous instructions to his orderly, before a number of officers, apparently without any proper sense of shame, to rip them up the seams, so that they could be resewn.

It seems undeniable that when he planned the celebrated march to the Danube he also scheduled which brigades and divisions of his army he would dine with at the different dates, without, of course, disclosing the places where the camps would lie. The splendid silver wine-flasks, or pilgrim bottles—as big as small barrels—which have been so much admired travelled with him in his campaigns; but they and other luxurious trappings were used only on State occasions when it was his duty to entertain the princes and generals of the Grand Alliance, or for some special rejoicing.

Ordinarily, instead of keeping, as was the custom of generals in the field of those days, a sumptuous open table to which a fine company sat down every night when war permitted, Marlborough lived very simply with his immediate personal staff. This, again, was a grievous fault in a General at the beginning of the eighteenth century. Brigadiers and even Colonels were attended by sumpter-horses and wagons suitable to their dignity. Although hard fare was recognized to be the lot of the private men and subordinate officers, and such as their station required, it was most inappropriate that the Commander-in-Chief of the main army of a European coalition with princely revenues at his disposal should not travel and dine in the luxury of his august position.

Marlborough seems to have regarded war merely as a serious business in which he was interested to the exclusion of pleasures and personal indulgences. All this puts his admirers to shame. One feels that virtues, valour, and victories alike are tarnished by such traits. We blush; but we must not conceal these shocking facts or legends. The truth is that from his upbringing and the pressures of his life he had acquired a hatred of waste of money in all its forms, and especially of frittering away comparatively small sums. He resembled a certain type of modern millionaires, who accumulate wealth unceasingly, spend hardly anything upon themselves, and use their fortunes for the well-being of their families and the endowment of their children, or apply them to great buildings or public objects.

He was like them in other ways. He had that curious mixture of business capacity and Imperial vision which in our own day excited the admirers and the critics of Cecil Rhodes. In 1666 two French-Canadian Protestants who had opened up the fur trade around Hudson Bay, but

had found no support from their own Government either in Quebec or
Paris, came to England and obtained an audience of King Charles II.
After a successful voyage a permanent company was formed. In 1670
the King granted a charter "to the Governor and Company of adventurers of England trading into Hudson Bay." Prince Rupert, twelve
times re-elected till his death, was the first Governor. In 1683 James,
Duke of York, was elected to succeed him. On James's accession John
Churchill was chosen. He thus became the third Governor of the Hudson's Bay Company. "The new governor," we are told, "threw himself
heartily into the work of the Company." In 1688 it declared a dividend
of 50 per cent; in 1689 a dividend of 25 per cent was paid; in 1690 of
75 per cent; and in that year it was decided to triple by a share-splitting
operation the value of its original stock. Nor was the expansion of
the original £10,500 capital unjustified. The stocks in the warehouse
were alone worth that sum; the trapping of the year was expected to
bring in £20,000 worth of beaver; and a claim for damages against the
French for £100,000 was to be made. The Company then decided to
increase its trade and widen the scale of its operations. The river run
ning into the west side of the bay far to the north was named, in honour of the new Governor, Churchill River, and at its mouth in 1686 a
new port and trading centre for the north and west of Canada was
founded. This project is alive to-day. Many instances are given by the
historians of the Hudson's Bay Company of the energy and helpful-
ness of Lord Churchill.

Churchill's part in the Revolution gave the company a good position
in the new reign. In June 1689 he sent out instructions for William
and Mary to be proclaimed in the posts on the shores of the bay. "He
was able shortly after to report to his Company that a hundred marines
had been detailed to protect the Company's ships." The enthusiasm of
the directors and shareholders at this mark of consideration obtained
through the influence of Lord Churchill was very great, and we learn
from the minutes that profuse thanks were given to the governor, and
a piece of plate of solid gold worth a hundred guineas was presented to
him for his distinguished services. His arrest and imprisonment in 1692
cut through these happy proceedings. It was indispensable to the Company that its monopoly and its charter should have a governor with
great influence at Court. Churchill's dismissal from the Army and all
official employments, which we have already described, carried with it

this private loss as well. In November 1692 Sir Stephen Evance was elected governor in his place.

His habit of personal economy extended to the whole control of Marlborough's armies. He was always worrying about the cost of things in a manner that seemed most petty and unbecoming. It was remarkable, indeed, that he was so popular with the troops; but, then, of course, he always took care that they got their rations and pay punctually, and the country people were always paid promptly for their supplies, so that the rank and file did not feel his cheeseparing at all, and only saw the victories. This naturally prevented their making a true judgment of his meanness. These simple common soldiers only noticed that they were well looked after and never once led to failure of any kind. Little did they know about the gaiters story. Little would they have cared if they had—so defective was their sense of proportion. Indeed, they might only have made jokes about it, and loved him all the more. But history cannot be thus easily satisfied; and we must record the truth. Both Frederick the Great and Napoleon were remarkable for the economy with which they managed their armies. But Marlborough made money go farther in the field than either, or, indeed, than any commander then or since, except perhaps Sir Herbert Kitchener, who kept the accounts of his reconquest of the Sudan as if he had been the manager of an emporium.

We have tried, however painful it may be, to set this out with naked candour. There are, on the other hand, a few mitigating features which may also be mentioned. Paget says:

> His declining, when in poverty and disgrace, to accept the generosity of the Princess Anne; his repeated refusal of the government of the Netherlands, with its princely income of £60,000 a year; his generosity to young and deserving officers; his application of all the money at his private disposal amongst the wounded officers of the enemy after the battle of Malplaquet; his liberal provision during his own lifetime for his children. . . .

are all to be counted in his favour. When to these are added his early imprudences of marrying for love and paying his father's debts at the expense of his inheritance, it may perhaps be recognized that he was not wholly base and sordid. We do not venture to press the point too far.

It is said that, though Marlborough was stingy in small matters—tips and the like—which may well be taken as proved against him, he was uncommonly courteous and considerate to his subordinates and inferiors in the social scale, and a most kind-hearted man. "For his natural good temper," says Ailesbury, "he never had his equal. He could not chide a servant and was the worst served possible, and in command he could not give a harsh word, no not to the meanest Sergeant, Corporal, or soldier." We have found a new confirmation of Ailesbury's testimony that Marlborough, for all his sagacity in large matters, and ridiculous small personal economies, was gentle to the point of laxity with his servants.

These qualities also played their part in European history. "Of all the men I ever knew," wrote Lord Chesterfield,

> the late Duke of Marlborough possessed the graces in the highest degree, not to say engrossed them. Indeed, he got the most by them; and contrary to the custom of profound historians who always assign deep causes for great events, I ascribe the better half of the Duke of Marlborough's greatness to those graces. He had no brightness—nothing shining in his genius. . . . His figure was beautiful; but his manner was irresistible either by man or woman. It was by this engaging graceful manner that he was enabled, during all the war, to connect the various and jarring Powers of the Grand Alliance, and to carry them on to the main object of the war, notwithstanding their private and separate views, jealousies and wrongheadedness. Whatever Court he went to (and he was often obliged to go to restive and refractory ones) he brought them into his measures. The Pensionary Heinsius, who had governed the United Provinces for forty years, was absolutely governed by him. He was always cool, and nobody ever observed the least variation in his countenance; he could refuse more easily than others could grant; and those who went from him the most dissatisfied as to the substance of their business, were yet charmed by his manner, and, as it were, comforted by it.

The Dutch Deputy Sicco van Goslinga, whose hostile opinions we shall encounter later on, has left on record what is on the whole the best word-picture of him as he was a few years later.[1]

> Here is his Portrait, drawn to the best of my insight. He is a man of birth: about the middle height, and the best figure in the world: his features without fault, fine, sparkling eyes, good teeth, and his

[1] Sicco van Goslinga, *Mémoires*, pp. 42–44, *sub* 1707.

complexion such a mixture of white and red as the fairer sex might envy: in brief, except for his legs, which are too thin, one of the handsomest men ever seen. His mind is keen and subtle [*il a beau-coup d'esprit, et délicate*], his judgment very clear and sound, his insight both quick and deep, with a consummate knowledge of men which no false show of merit can deceive. He expresses himself well, and even his very bad French is agreeable: his voice is harmonious, and as a speaker in his own language he is reckoned among the best. His address is most courteous, and while his handsome and well-graced countenance engages every one in his favour at first sight, his perfect manners and his gentleness win over even those who start with a prejudice or grudge against him. He has courage, as he has shown in more than one conjuncture: he is an experienced soldier, and plans a campaign to admiration. So far his good qualities. Now for the weak points which if I am not mistaken I have found in him. The Duke is a profound dissembler, all the more dangerous that his manner and his words give the impression of frankness itself. His ambition knows no bounds, and an avarice which I can only call sordid, guides his entire conduct. If he has courage—and of this there is no question, whatever may be said by those who envy or hate him—he certainly wants that firmness of soul which makes the true Hero. Sometimes, on the eve of an action, he is irresolute, or worse; he will not face difficulties, and occasionally lets reverses cast him down: of this I could adduce more than one instance as an eye-witness. Yet I saw nothing of the kind either at Ramillies or Malplaquet, so it may be that some constitutional weakness, unfitting him to support fatigue, has something to do with it. He does not know much of discipline, and gives too much rein to his men, who have now and then indulged in frightful excesses. Moreover he lacks the precise knowledge of military detail which a Commander-in-Chief should possess. But these defects are light in the scale against the rare gifts of this truly great man.

There is no doubt that Marlborough took from the various offices which he held everything to which he was entitled either by warrant or recognized custom. But no one has ever been able to prove that he took more. The House of Commons was vigilant in those days, and charges of corruption and peculation were constant features of its debates. Danby's second and final disgrace in 1695 is a remarkable instance of the zeal and fearlessness with which Parliament discharged its duties. Both Churchill's brothers, George and Charles, were in a single year sent for a while to the Tower for financial irregularities and abuses, and there are numerous other cases on record. No one was more jealously watched than Marlborough. He had numerous enemies. As he was never a strong party man, he had not the protection which others enjoyed. Yet, although allegations, gossip, and slander pursued him, as they did most prominent people, no charge was ever brought against him till the famous charges of 1712, and these were, as will be seen in due course, completely exploded. It might be supposed that a man who was known to be poor and fond of money, and who was for a long period viewed with extreme hostility by the King and by powerful people at Court, would, if his misconduct was flagrant, as is alleged, have certainly been called to account. In that ruthless age he was the last man to receive exceptional licence.

It is probably a just conclusion that Marlborough's conduct was above and not below the standards of his time; that though he took all the emoluments, perquisites, and commissions which belonged to his offices and appointments, he never took bribes or any money that was not his by usage or law. Although he always recognized the claims of natural love and affection, as in choosing his wife, in helping his father, or providing for his children, and set these far above riches, his own deep-rooted habits of personal thrift and self-denial were carried to a point which drew upon him the mockery of his envious contemporaries and of malicious historians. Yet these habits, unpleasing though they may seem, were an essential part of his character as a gatherer, as a builder and a founder. They were mitigated or often baffled by the pervasive kindness of his nature. They arose from the same methodical, patient, matter-of-fact spade-work which characterizes all his conduct of war, and formed the only basis upon which the great actions for which he is renowned could have sprung. His handling of his private affairs was as grave, as strongly marked by common sense, and as free from indulgence or unwisdom as his conduct of politics and war. His private fortune was amassed upon the same principles as marked the staff-work of his campaigns, and was a part of the same design. It was only in love or on the battlefield that he took all risks. In these supreme exaltations he was swept from his system and rule of living, and blazed resplendent with the heroic virtues. In his marriage and in his victories the worldly prudence, the calculation, the reinsurance, which regulated his ordinary life and sustained his strategy, fell from him like a too heavily embroidered cloak, and the genius within sprang forth in sure and triumphant command.

CHAPTER TWENTY-ONE

Peace and Reconciliation

ᕄᑯ 1696-98 ᕑᕄ

IN its eighth year the so-called War of the League of Augsburg came to an inconclusive end. The Maritime Powers and Germany had defended themselves successfully, but were weary of the barren struggle. Spain was bellicose, but useless. After the withdrawal of the English fleet from the Mediterranean the Duke of Savoy made peace with France, and the Emperor and the King of Spain were constrained to accept the neutralization of Italy. Only the Emperor, with his eyes fixed on the ever-impending vacancy of the Spanish throne, was earnest to keep the anti-French confederacy in being. But this same reason dictated an opposite policy to France. Louis had no mind to see the Spanish empires in the Old and New World become the prize which should inspire all the banded enemies of France with renewed comradeship and ardour. He understood the numerous strains which were rending the Grand Alliance. He saw that it was falling to pieces under the pressure of so many fruitless campaigns. Once resolved into its component parts, the reconstitution of so ponderous and complicated an engine might well be impossible. He believed that no hand but William's could reassemble it; and how long would William last? Peace would dissolve the hostile coalition. Many of its members would lay aside their panoply and go their several ways disarmed. But the great central Power which had hitherto withstood them all, albeit narrowly, would under his absolute sovereignty refit her armies, revive her strength, and pursue her aims better at the moment by peace than by war. Moreover, the long struggle against all Europe had seriously affected the strength of the

French nation. Louis therefore at the end of 1696 made overtures of peace to William. It gradually became clear that France would restore all her conquests in the Low Countries and on the Rhine made since the Peace of Nimwegen except only Strasburg; and for Strasburg she would give an ample substitute.

William, with his lifelong knowledge of Europe, comprehended perfectly the meaning of these proposals. But the pressure for peace, especially in England, convinced him that he had not the power to reject them. The negotiations, opened under Swedish mediation at Ryswick, were protracted. The French, who had been able to draw fifty thousand of their troops from the Italian theatre for the northern front, were in no hurry to close the campaign. The differences between the allies, an elaborate ceremonial, and the necessary adjustments of points of dignity and honour occupied the rest of 1697. The Emperor, who wanted Strasburg, protested strongly. Considering, however, that he had himself made a separate agreement neutralizing the Italian front and liberating the French army operating there, his position was not morally strong. The Spaniards were tamed by disasters at Barcelona and at Cartagena, in the Indies. The English Parliament clamoured for a settlement.

It was not till October 1697 that the group of treaties bringing back peace to the whole world was completed. Apart from the territorial arrangements, Louis agreed tacitly and under curious reserves to recognize William as King of the three kingdoms. He refused to abandon James II by name, but he contracted not to support any enemies of England, adding the words "without any exception," which, since they covered the Prince of Wales as well as the exiled King, were by no means unacceptable. He also withdrew his demand that the mass of the Jacobite refugees apart from the Royal Family should return under an amnesty to their native land. He restored the principality of Orange to its redoubtable owner, stipulating only that no French Huguenots should reside there. William on his part abated his claim that James and his Court should leave French soil, and by a provision which casts a revealing light upon the cool mood of the times undertook to pay to Mary of Modena a jointure ultimately fixed at £50,000 a year. Thus all the polite society of Europe bowed and scraped amicably to one another, and all its harassed peoples rested from their painful strife.

The five-year interlude between the first nine and the last ten years of this world war is commonly viewed as a mere truce. In fact, however, the situation after the Treaty of Ryswick contained many elements of peace. Certainly all its signatories sincerely hoped to accomplish their aims without further resort to arms. All were weary of costly and desultory strife. The great antagonisms of Europe remained; the perils of the Spanish succession impended; but there was an earnest resolve, shared in various degrees by sovereigns, Governments, and peoples, to exhaust every method of diplomacy and bargaining before again drawing the sword. The Peace of Ryswick left in Europe two great figures instead of one. Louis XIV recognized in William III almost an equal. Nicely chosen terms of honour were interchanged between them. William expressed his "veneration and admiration" for Louis, and Louis his "high respect" for William. Both potentates yielded themselves for a space to the sensation that together with goodwill they could settle the problems of Europe and give repose to Christendom.

William was now at the height of his glory. He seemed about to outshine even the Sun King himself. In the east, in the north, and now in the south and west of Europe he seemed about to lay, after generations of religious, dynastic, and territorial wars, the foundations of a lasting peace for the whole world. But at this very moment when all that the hearts of men desired was coming within their reach through his exertions, he was woefully and even fatally weakened by the action of the House of Commons. To deal with Louis XIV as an equal—the only key to safety—it was imperative that he should be strong. Not only must he marshal all his influence in Europe, not only must he wield the overwhelming sea-power of England and Holland, but he must have at his back a considerable British Army.

Very different were the mood and outlook of the Tory country gentlemen and Whig doctrinaires who assembled at Westminster. The wars were over; their repressions were at an end. They rejoiced in peace and clamoured for freedom. The dangers were past; why should they ever return? Groaning under taxation, impatient of every restraint, the Commons plunged into a career of economy, disarmament, and constitutional assertiveness which was speedily followed by the greatest of the wars England had ever waged and the heaviest expenditures she had ever borne.

PEACE AND RECONCILIATION

England came out of the war with an army of eighty-seven thousand regular soldiers. The King considered that thirty thousand men and a large additional number of officers was the least that would guarantee the public safety and interest. His Ministers, in contact with Parliament, did not dare propose more than ten thousand, and the House of Commons would only vote seven thousand. The Navy underwent a less severe compression. The picture is complicated by a considerable garrison which all admitted must be kept in Ireland, by two thousand men in the West Indies, and by three thousand marines borne as sailors, though actually infantry. A new Parliament only reiterated more stridently the demands of its predecessor. Its Members had vowed on the hustings that they would cut the expenses to the bone and break up the standing army. They ingeminated economy. The reductions were carried out in the most brutal manner, the war-bitten veterans and the Huguenot refugees who had fought so well being summarily flung on the streets and treated as rogues and vagabonds on the first provocation. The process was only tempered by the half-pay granted to the officers as a retaining fee, and delayed by the inability of Parliament to pay the arrears due to the men before discharge. An orgy of insult and abuse in which all classes of the civil population heartily joined began around all uniformed men, the half-pay officers, and especially those who had already been disarmed and turned adrift and had no means of support. The roads and countryside became infested with desperate, starving footpads who had lately grappled with the French Guard and shed their blood for King and country. The days of Robin Hood returned, and what was left of the English cavalry was largely occupied in hunting down their old comrades-in-arms now driven into outlawry. The gibbet and the lash were meted out with ruthless vigour on all who fell into the clutches of the law. Such was the process of demobilization in the seventeenth century.

A new and in many ways a singularly modern figure whom every one nowadays can understand had appeared in the House of Commons. Robert Harley was born and bred in a Puritan family and atmosphere a Whig and a Dissenter. In the process of opposing the Court he gradually transformed himself from Whig to Tory and from Dissenter to High Churchman, so that eventually he became the chief of the Tories both in Church and State. Already in 1698 he had become virtually their leader in the House of Commons. He it was who conducted the reckless movement for the reduction of the armed forces. He it was who sought to rival the Bank of England with the Land Bank. He appealed to moderate opinion even when heading the attack. He kept in touch with the Whigs, while delighting the Tories. He made the Court feel that, though he was their most serious enemy, he might also some day, perhaps, become their best friend.

Behind Harley, Seymour, the pre-eminent 'sham goodfellow' of the age, cheered on his West Country pack with all the zest of a huntsman on a good scenting day. The Tory squires roared about the expense of useless and insolent popinjays; and the Whigs joined them in descanting upon the menace to freedom inherent in a standing army. The King was aghast at these furious manifestations. His heart bled for the officers and men with whom he had marched and fought during the long, sombre campaigns. Every fibre in his nature revolted at the baseness, cruelty, and ingratitude with which his faithful troops were treated, and at the same time he felt his whole European position undermined by the blotting out of England as a military factor. But he was powerless. Moreover, it was resolved that such troops as must perforce be retained should not comprise a single foreigner. The Dutch Guards must forthwith quit the island. Accordingly this well-trained, devoted brigade began its march to the coast.

Can we wonder that the unhappy prince, insulted in the hour of his greatest triumph, hamstrung in the full stride of his most beneficent activity, outraged in his honour and comradeship as a soldier, wished to quit the insensate and ungrateful people whose religion, whose institutions he had preserved, and whose fame he had lifted so high? He would abandon the odious and intractable race. He would retort their hatred of foreigners with a gesture of inexpressible scorn. Europe might clatter again into confusion so that insular ignorance should reap its harvest. That he mastered these emotions is a measure of his quality. It was the hardest of his victories, and without it his life's work must have perished. Yet if we reflect on his many faults in tact, in conduct, and in fairness in the earlier days of his reign, the unwarrantable favours he had lavished on his Dutchmen, the injustices done to English commanders, Count Solms' maltreatment of the English troops at Steinkirk, his uncomprehending distaste for the people of his new realm, their relegation to be mere pawns on his Continental chess-board—anyone can feel that all the blame was not on one side. His present anguish paid his debts of former years. As for the English, they were only too soon to redeem their follies in blood and toil.

Few features in Marlborough's long life are more remarkable than the manner in which he steadily grew in weight and influence through the whole of the six years when he was banished from favour and office. The Whigs were jealous of Shrewsbury's honour, and the Tories felt a strong interest in Godolphin. But Marlborough had no party to take care of him, and he alone bore the weight of the royal displeasure. He took a regular share in the business of the House of Lords. Apart from the attainting of Fenwick, he preserved a conciliatory attitude towards the Jacobites. He remained the trusted friend of the Princess Anne. For the rest he lived in tranquil retirement, seeming not to fret at the great war-opportunities which were slipping away, or at the years of his prime which were being consumed. He was happy with Sarah and his children, and his equanimity was perfect. He rarely wrote letters, except to Sarah when he was parted from her, or on public business when he was employed. We have, therefore, only the scantiest records of his daily life during these years or of his public actions. Still he grew, and at the end of this lengthy period of eclipse was felt by every one around the summit of affairs to be one of the greatest Englishmen of the day.

William was very slow resuming relations with him. After the death of Queen Mary in 1694 he had been readmitted to the Court, but to no employment. At last, however, the barrier fell to pieces. Anne's eldest son, the Duke of Gloucester, was now nine years old. It was thought fitting to provide the future heir-apparent to the Crown with a governor of high consequence and an establishment of his own. Parliament in voting the King a Civil List of £700,000 a year had foreseen such an arrangement. William's first thoughts turned to Shrewsbury, who was still brooding in the country and constantly asking to be relieved of his office. He had, as we have seen, more than once pressed Marlborough's claims upon the King. He now declined the appointment for which his friend seemed the obvious choice. Nothing could be more agreeable to the young Prince's parents. Still the King hesitated, and a current of Tory opinion brought Rochester's name forward. Sunderland seems to have exerted his still potent influence in Marlborough's favour.

It may well have been, however, that a new associate of Marlborough's carried the greatest weight. William had become deeply attached to the young Dutch courtier Keppel. He had advanced him in a few years from being a page to a commanding position in the State. He had newly created him Earl of Albemarle. There was an affinity between them—honourable, but subtle and unusual. The lonely, childless monarch treated Keppel as if he were a well-beloved adopted son. The King's old faithful intimate, Portland, had long been Marlborough's enemy. He had not perhaps forgotten a description of him as "a wooden fellow." But Portland was now on his embassy in Paris, and Keppel had supplanted him in the King's heart. The rivalry between these two Dutchmen was hot. In fact, Portland was soon to cast off all his offices for a ludicrous cause. Keppel in his absence abroad had installed himself at Newmarket in the rooms next to the royal apartments which Portland had long occupied; and William would not eject him. It sufficed that Portland was Marlborough's enemy for Keppel to become his advocate. Thus those obstacles against which merit and policy had so long pressed in vain were smoothly removed by the deft and tactful addresses of a youthful counsellor.

In the summer of 1698 William invited Marlborough to be governor of the boy Prince. When he kissed hands upon his appointment William uttered the gracious but discriminating words, "My lord, teach him but to know [? be] what you are, and my nephew cannot want for accomplishments." At the same time Marlborough was restored to his rank in the Army and to the Privy Council. The King announced his decision in remarkable terms in the *Gazette* of June 16, 1698:

> His Majesty has been pleased to appoint the Right Honourable the Earl of Marlborough to be Governor of His Highness the Duke of Gloucester, as a mark of the good opinion His Majesty has of his lordship's zeal for his service and his qualifications for the employment of so great a trust. . . .

The miniature Court of the Duke of Gloucester was formed with expedition in the summer of 1698. His parents and the Marlboroughs had their own ideas about its composition. The King shied at their clear-cut plans. "The Princess Anne," he exclaimed petulantly, on the eve of sailing to The Hague, "should not be Queen before her time." Marlborough made no difficulties. He sought only to know the royal pleasure; and Keppel, who was inseparable from his master, promised to guide it into proper channels. In the end the list was accepted very much as it had been planned. William had chosen Bishop Burnet to be the young Prince's spiritual guide, and in addition to educate him in history, politics, and the lesser arts. A Tory governor must be balanced by a Whig preceptor. William may also have been glad to get Burnet, "the blabbing Bishop," of whom he was tired, out of his way. However, Marlborough and Burnet became close friends. The Bishop yielded himself to the charm and courtesy of his chief. He fell so much under his attraction that he even rewrote the passages in his history dealing with Churchill's desertion of James. Improvidently he forgot to destroy the original version, which has been unearthed to his posthumous mockery. Lord Churchill, Marlborough's only surviving son, aged twelve, was appointed Master of the Horse and no doubt 'playmate in chief.' A son of Bishop Burnet became a page, and an impoverished gentlewoman named Hill was put in charge of the laundry.

Among fleeting shadows the name of Hill is significant. In 1689, shortly after the Revolution, Sarah discovered that she had poor relations. Her grandfather, Sir John Jennings, had produced no fewer than twenty-two children. His estate, though substantial, could not bear such subdivision. One of his daughters, with hardly £500 for her dowry, had married a Levant merchant named Hill. Having prospered for some years, he was ultimately ruined by speculation. When Mr and Mrs Hill died they left four children, two sons and two daughters.

> The elder daughter [Abigail] . . . [writes Sarah] was a grown woman. I took her to St Albans, where she lived with me and my children, and I treated her with as great kindness as if she had been my sister. . . . As for the younger daughter (who is still living) I engaged my Lord Marlborough, when the Duke of Gloucester's family was settled, to make her laundress to him, which was a good provision for her. And when the Duke of Gloucester died, I obtained for her a pension of £200 a year, which I paid her out of the Privy Purse. . . . The Queen was pleased to allow the money for that purchase [an annuity] and it is very probable that Mrs Hill has the annuity to this day, and perhaps nothing else, unless she saved money

after her sister had made her Deputy to the Privy Purse, which she did as soon as she had supplanted me.

The elder son was at my request put by my Lord Godolphin into a place in the custom-house; and when, in order to his advancement to a better, it was necessary to give security for his good behaviour, I got a relation of the Duke of Marlborough's to be bound for him in two thousand pounds.

His brother (whom the bottle-men afterwards called "honest Jack Hill") was a tall boy whom I clothed (for he was all in rags) and put to school at St Albans. . . . After he had learnt what he could there, a vacancy happening of Page of Honour to the Prince of Denmark, his Highness was pleased at my request to take him. I afterwards got my Lord Marlborough to make him Groom of the Bedchamber to the Duke of Gloucester. And though my Lord always said that Jack Hill was good for nothing, yet to oblige me he made him his aide-de-camp and afterwards gave him a regiment. But it was his sister's interest that raised him to be a General and to command in that ever memorable expedition to Quebec; I had no share in doing him these honours. To finish what I have to say upon this subject:—when Mr Harley thought it useful to attack the Duke of Marlborough in Parliament, this Quebec General, this honest Jack Hill, this once ragged boy whom I clothed, happening to be sick in bed, was nevertheless persuaded by his sister to get up, wrap himself in warmer clothes than those I had given him, and go to the House to vote against the Duke.

Here, then, is a succinct account of the Abigail Hill who afterwards, as Mrs Masham and Harley's confidante, saved France from destruction as surely, though scarcely as gloriously, as Joan of Arc. It was an annoyance of peculiar rankle to Sarah to the end of her long life that she, by indulging her most generous sentiments of compassion, should have prepared her own undoing and her husband's fall at the moment when the consummation of all his victories and toils seemed so near. In her strong, domineering, bustling life Sarah did many actions both bad and good, but her charity to the Hills was her special benevolence. She was, indeed, for many years their patron saint. Nepotism apart, her kindliness to them shines brightly. Yet this was one of the traceable causes of her catastrophe.

Thus we see Marlborough picking his steps warily and with foresight through all the perplexities and hazards of the times, while at the same time his devoted wife by one of the best deeds in her life sets in train, all unwitting, the series of events which amid his glories shall lay him low.

> The young disease, that must subdue at length,
> Grows with his growth, and strengthens with his strength.

It is a classic instance of how far romance lags behind reality.

CHAPTER TWENTY-TWO

Marlborough in Politics

ᘓ 1698-1700 ᘔ

MEANWHILE Marlborough's family had grown up, and in the years 1698 and 1699 his two eldest daughters both married. The eldest, Henrietta, became engaged to Francis, Lord Godolphin's son. The lifelong friendship between both the Marlboroughs and Godolphin is a factor in history; but this was no marriage of political or worldly calculation. It was a love-match between very young people—Francis was only twenty and Henrietta eighteen—who were thrown together by the intimacies of their parents, to whom it gave the keenest pleasure. Godolphin's wife had died after giving birth to Francis a generation earlier. The Treasurer was too deeply attached to her memory ever to marry again. In that corrupt age, when public office was almost the only road to riches, Godolphin was for more than thirty years and in four reigns in control of the national finances. He was, however, a man of stainless integrity in money matters. At his death in 1712 he left but £14,000, somewhat less than what he had inherited forty years before. He could therefore at this time give only the smallest competence to his son. But the fabulous avarice of John and Sarah seems to have slumbered on this occasion, as it had when they themselves plighted their penniless troth. Marlborough's notorious greed for lucre had so far left him at forty-five the poorest of his rank. Nevertheless he provided a dowry of £5000. The Princess Anne, whose enthusiasm was kindled by this cementing of friendship in her circle, wished to bestow £10,000 upon the young couple. But the Marlboroughs, no doubt from some base motive, would only accept £5000. The marriage took place on March 24, 1698.

The bride was beautiful and accomplished. Her graces were the theme for the rhymesters of the day. The union was lasting.

The marriage of Marlborough's second daughter, Anne, in January 1700, was a theme of greater importance. We have seen how long and varied had been the relations of Marlborough and Sunderland and the political association that had always subsisted between them. A close friendship had grown between their wives.

Sunderland's heir, Lord Spencer, who was a widower, was a remarkable personality. He had none of the insinuating charm and genial courtesy of his incomprehensible father. He was an ultra-Whig of the straitest and most unbending type. He did not trouble to conceal his republican opinions. He was so conscious of the rights of his order and of Parliament against the Crown that he had little sympathy left for the commonalty. According to his philosophy, citizens of the worst republic were free, while subjects of the best king were slaves. He was a keen book-lover, and the Sunderland Library remained for many generations his monument. The Whig Party took a lively interest in the development of his mind. It was thought that experience would mellow his orthodox severity, and they already saluted him as the future champion of the cause for which "Hampden had died in the field and Sidney on the scaffold."

Sarah, that sturdy Whig, may have shared these hopes; but Marlborough's temperamental Toryism was repulsed by the harshness alike of Lord Spencer's doctrine and disposition. Anne was his favourite daughter, and by every account was a brilliant and fascinating creature. Intimate and subtle as were his relations with Sunderland in State affairs, important as were the reciprocal services which might be rendered, magnificent as was the inheritance, he was disinclined to mingle that wayward blood with his own, or to countenance a marriage which might not bring his daughter happiness. He was therefore very hard to persuade. However, he gradually yielded to Sarah's persuasions, and, being at length convinced of Lord Spencer's sincerity, he finally consented. Once again Princess Anne, who was the girl's godmother, matched the family dowry with a gift of £5000. Sunderland, who seems to have longed for the marriage, wrote in a remarkable letter:

If I see him so settled I shall desire nothing more in this world but to die in peace if it please God. I must add this that if he can be thus happy he will be governed in everything public and private by my lord Marlborough. I have particularly talked to him of that and he is sensible how advantageous it will be to him to be so. I need not I am sure desire that all this may be a secret to everybody but Lady Marlborough.

These expectations were not fulfilled, and Spencer's personality and conduct were to become after his father's death a cause of serious political embarrassment. It is, however, by this marriage that the Marlborough blood, titles, and estates have descended to posterity, for his only surviving son, Lord Churchill, Master of the Horse in the Duke of Gloucester's household, had almost as short a span to live as the little Prince he served.

The ice of a long frost being broken, the King felt the comfort in his many troubles of Marlborough's serene, practical, adaptive personality, which no difficulties found without resource, which no dangers disturbed. In July 1698, when the royal departure for Holland rendered a Council of Regency necessary, Marlborough was nominated one of the nine Lords Justices to exercise the sovereign power. From this time forth William seemed to turn increasingly, if without personal friendship, towards the man of whose aid he had deprived himself during the most critical years of his reign. He used in peace the soldier he had neglected in war; and Marlborough, though his prime bent was military, though stamped from his youth with the profession of arms, became in the closing years of the reign a shrewd and powerful politician.

This new relationship of William and Marlborough requires close examination. The King seemed speedily inclined to trust him implicitly and to make common cause with him in great matters. We have Somers' letter of December 29, 1698, to prove that in his grief and wrath upon the dismissal of the Dutch Guards he confided to Marlborough, although he was not in the Cabinet, his secret resolve, withheld from some of his Ministers, to abdicate the Crown.

We have no record of what Marlborough advised; but there can be little doubt he urged the King to abandon his design. William's abdication at such a juncture might as easily have been followed by a republic as by the accession of the Princess Anne. He must surely have counselled upon the King the patience he practised himself. His comprehension of Europe at this time was second only to that of William.

Both regarded with much detachment, both viewed with a distaste which it was politic to conceal, the violent passions and prejudices of the English political parties, and both were prone to use them alternately for their own purposes, which included also the greatest purposes of the age. Thus for the next two years, if he did not wholly trust Marlborough, William leaned on him. Marlborough felt the weight, and understood and discounted the cause. He did not give himself wholly to the King. The royal confidence was only half-confidence: the rest was the need of help. Hence he preserved his independence and carefully guarded the sources of his own personal power.

Lord Wolseley has not comprehended Marlborough's conduct during the closing years of William III. He is shocked to find his hero, although employed by the King in many great matters while war drew nearer, voting on all test party issues with the Tories in their savage faction fight.

If Marlborough had cut himself adrift from the Tory Party and become a mere adherent of the Court he would soon have lost all influence upon events. His own power would have been reduced to his own personal ability, while at the same time his usefulness to the King would have vanished. William knew England almost as well as he knew Europe, but he despised the ignoble strife of its parties, and underrated the factor of party as an element in his vast problem. In his embarrassments he would turn from Whig Ministers who could not manage and would not face the House of Commons to the turbulent Tories, only to find them ignorant of world facts and with a view of national interests which was at that time wrong-headed and utterly at variance with his own purposes. The Whigs at least saw what was coming, and would help him to meet it. Marlborough, who understood the public interest as clearly as his own, knew that the Whigs could never carry England through the approaching ordeal in the teeth of Tory opposition: he knew that the Tories were by far the strongest faction in the State. Except in the most general way he did not share their prejudices, but he knew their power and that the credit he had with them was one of the main foundations of his own position. Marlborough was in close friendly relations with Harley, and through him with the House of Commons. He wielded himself great influence in the House of Lords. Through Sunderland, now linked to him by the marriage of their children, and through Sarah, he was in contact with the

Whigs. And always he stood by the Princess Anne, dominated and inspired her circle, and championed her interests, in which also the future lay.

These incomplete relationships were the King's own fault, and a misfortune to his reign. If in 1689 and 1690 William, with two kingdoms to govern and the diplomacy of half Europe in his hands, had treated Marlborough fairly and had not denied him his rightful opportunity upon the battlefields, he might have found that talisman of victory without which all his painstaking, adroit combinations and noble exertions could but achieve a mediocre result. He might have found across the differences of rank that same comradeship, never disturbed by doubt or jealousy, true to the supreme tests of war and fortune, which later shone between Marlborough and Eugene.

A tragical event supervened. The little Duke of Gloucester was now eleven. King William's interest in this child casts a pleasing light on his somewhat forbidding character. He saw and petted him repeatedly. At the time of the Fenwick trial, Gloucester, when but seven years old, caused one of his boy soldiers to write out the following address which he signed: "I, your Majesty's most dutiful subject, had rather lose my life in your majesty's cause than in any man's else, and I hope it will not be long ere you conquer France." To which his juvenile army and household appended, "We, your majesty's subjects, will stand by you while we have a drop of blood." In this same year he went with his mother to Tonbridge in order to study fortification "under the care of his clerical tutor." We may readily believe that with such propensities the young Prince rejoiced to have so martial a governor. It is, however, probable that Marlborough, far from encouraging this precocious militarism, inculcated habits of courtesy, gravity, and above all a judicious care of pounds, shillings, and pence.

The hearts of Englishmen and the eyes of Europe were turned towards this child. The Whigs drew from his games the hope of a sovereign who would make valiant head against France. The Tories, on the other hand, repeated with gusto some of his alleged disrespectful interruptions to Burnet's constitutional discourses. A warrior prince, an English prince, a prince with Plantagenet blood and the necessary Parliamentary education—a good match for any warming-pan impostor, however clad with Divine Right!

These hopes were blasted; other solutions awaited the problems of the English people. On July 30, 1700, the Duke of Gloucester died of smallpox so swiftly that his governor reached his bedside only as he breathed his last. His playmate Churchill survived but three years, before he fell beneath the same fatal scourge.

Immense, far-reaching interests were opened by this new gap in the succession. Anne's health amid her repeated miscarriages and stillborn births was precarious. William's days were plainly drawing to a close. The Crown of England, and with it not only all those issues of religion and Constitution which obsessed men's minds, but also the part which the British Isles would play in the destiny of Europe, was once again adrift on a dark, tempestuous ocean. There were many alternatives and many weighty objections to all of them. No one seems to have hankered for James II; but naturally many thoughts turned to the Prince of Wales. The warming-pan myth had lost its primal power. Why should he not be brought up under William's care in Holland? A Protestant, if possible; a Catholic, if it must be, but none the less with his constitutional duties engrained in him.

Historians have debated whether William did not at this time of amity with France dwell upon this solution. He certainly played with it. Had James II died one year earlier and the rightful heir been left alone, freed from the antagonisms which centred upon his father, our affairs might have decided themselves differently. Then there were the children of Victor Amadeus of Savoy, who had married the daughter of Charles II's sister, the famous 'Minette.' But the house of Savoy was under a cloud. Its Duke had so recently deserted the Grand Alliance in the face of the enemy. Thirdly there were the rights of the house of Hanover, at this time represented by the aged Electress Sophia. This solution seemed likely to renew all the difficulties which had arisen in England through the importation of a foreign king. All monarchical sentiment longed for a prince of island character and English speech. But there was another sentiment which suddenly surged up stark and logical. Why should the nation be tormented by these riddles of a disputed succession? Why should not William III be the last King in England? The expense of a Court was in those days sufficient to maintain powerful additions to the Navy or afford longed-for reliefs of taxation. The sudden advance of the republican idea made it imperative that a decision should be reached without delay. This mood dictated the Act of Settlement, and gave the Crown to the house of Hanover in a statute which was virtually a reproach upon the reign of King William. The sovereign must be an Anglican—neither a Catholic nor a Calvinist. He must never leave the country without the permission of Parliament (as some had done so often). He must be advised not by any secret Cabinet or closet about his person, but by the Privy Council as a whole; and the Privy Council must be governed by the preponderating authority of an elected assembly wielding the money power. Thus the reign of Anne would be an interlude; and all would be in readiness at her death to give a dutiful and chilling reception to a Hanoverian prince.

We have no doubt where the Marlboroughs stood in these dominant matters. They must have been unswervingly hostile to any plan of the Prince of Wales intervening between Anne and her declared rights of succession. After Anne they felt themselves free to choose. It was unwise to peer too far ahead.

The untimely death of the Duke of Gloucester deprived Marlborough of his office; but he was by now so strongly established in the centre of English politics that, in spite of his recent difference with the King, his personal position was unimpaired.

In October 1700 Brydges, who had called upon him, noted down in his diary, "My Lord [Marlborough] told me, he believed the Parl: would not be dissolved, and that for Secretary of State the King had not disposed of it, not denying it might be given to himself." A Dutch envoy reported home, "On dit toujours que le comte de Marlborough sera fait secrétaire d'état et le Lord Godolphin, premier commissaire de la trésorerie, mais ces deux icy ne sont pas encore declarez." These anticipations were reduced to irrelevance by wider events.

The Earl of Godolphin. BY PERMISSION OF THE DUKE OF MARLBOROUGH.

King William the 3d.
1650 - 1702.

William III: The Last Phase, by Godfrey Schalcken.
BY PERMISSION OF THE DUKE OF MARLBOROUGH.

CHAPTER TWENTY-THREE

The Spanish Succession

ᘒ 1698-1701 ᘓ

No great war was ever entered upon with so much reluctance on both sides as the War of the Spanish Succession. Europe was exhausted and disillusioned. The bitter aftermath of eight years' desultory conflict had turned all men's minds to peace, or at least to a change of experience, and to economic instead of military expansion. The new-found contacts which had sprung up between William and Louis expressed the heartfelt wishes of the peoples both of the Maritime Powers and of France.

There is no doubt about the sincerity of William III in the peace effort. It did not only arise from his own nature. He could not conceive how England could be brought again into the field. She seemed to have shot her bolt for at least a generation. He saw the turbulent pacifism of the Parliament; he bowed to the irresistible pressure of disarmament; he understood, while he resented, the insularity and detachment of his acquired subjects. Holland might yet resist any menace to her frontier; but England was cloyed with the Continent, and saw in a strong navy and a strict neutrality a sure escape from the deadly labyrinth. Without the aid of England the States-General must submit to almost anything short of subjugation. War against France without the power of Britain was impossible. Therefore William was in earnest. He must keep peace at almost any price.

The feeble life-candle of the childless Spanish King, known to his country as Charles the Sufferer, flickered, smoked, guttered, but still burned. At any moment it might have gone out. Yet it kept alight for nearly a third of a century, and one by one the great statesmen of Europe who had watched for its extinction had themselves been overtaken by the darkness of night. But now the candle burned low in the socket. To the ravages of deformity and disease were added the most griev- ous afflictions of the mind. The royal victim believed himself to be pos- sessed by the devil. Every sign and symptom betokened the end. What then was to happen to half the world, and what would the other half do with it? A score of claimants, ranging from a successful usurper in Portugal to the Emperor Leopold, confident in his vague, but to his mind paramount, dynastic right, would come forward to demand a greater or lesser share of the mighty heritage. But could not William and Louis, incomparably the most skilled and experienced diplomatists in Europe, lords of the strongest armies and fleets in existence, both of whom saw and shrank from the danger of a renewal of the European conflict, devise some solution to which every candidate would be forced to bow?

England and Holland, who lived by seaborne trade and dreamed of colonies and wealth beyond the oceans, could not bear that the control of Spain, the Indies, Mexico, South America, and the Mediterranean should fall into the competent hands of France. They saw themselves shut out by prohibitive tariffs, mercantile laws, and indefinite naval ex- pansion, alike from their daily bread and their future. The inde- pendence of Belgium from France was a vital interest which England and Holland shared in common. The Protestant states shivered at the prospect of the Government that had revoked the Edict of Nantes be- ing united with the Government that had devised and enforced the Holy Inquisition. The Emperor, that Catholic despot without whose aid Protestantism and Parliamentary institutions would be imperilled, advanced proud and impracticable claims. Unless a settlement could be reached between him and France there must be general war. Still, if Louis and William could agree upon a settlement, they would together have the power to impose their will on all concerned.

The peace so earnestly desired could only take the form of a new partition of the Spanish Empire. Very secretly—breathing not a word to Spain nor to the Emperor—the two leading princes set about this task. There were three claimants, each of whom could advance impor- tant pretensions. The first was France, represented by the Dauphin. Next there was the Emperor, who, as the widower of the younger

Spanish princess, claimed as much as he could, but was willing to transfer his claims to the second son of his own second wife, the Archduke Charles. Thirdly there was the Emperor's grandson by his first marriage, the Electoral Prince of Bavaria.

Only one conviction dominated the Castilian aristocracy—the Spanish Empire must not be divided. It was intolerable to their patriotism —indeed, to their good sense—that the empire their ancestors had gathered should be parcelled out in fragments. Accordingly Spain plumped for the Electoral Prince. Where the trunk of their empire was, there the limbs should also go. On November 14 Charles signed and declared a will by which the whole of the Spanish domains passed intact to the Electoral Prince.

But now a startling event occurred. The will of Charles II was made public on November 14. On February 6 the little Prince of Bavaria, the heir to these prodigious domains, the child in whose chubby hands the greatest states had resolved to place the most splendid prize, suddenly died. Why did he die, how did he die? A coincidence so extraordinary could not fail to excite dark suspicions. But the fact glared grimly upon the world. All these elaborate, perilous conversations must be begun over again.

Ultimately William and Louis arranged a second Treaty of Partition on June 11, 1699. To the disgust of Harcourt, his Ambassador at Madrid, Louis consented to the Archduke Charles being heir-in-chief. To him were assigned Spain, the overseas colonies, and Belgium, on the condition that they should never be united with the Empire. The Dauphin was to have Naples and Sicily, the Milanese, which was to be exchanged for Lorraine, and certain other Italian possessions. The terms of this provisional treaty allowed the Emperor two months in which to decide whether he would or would not be a party to it. But his heart was set upon Italy; and he finally refused.

On March 13, 1700, therefore, the treaty was ratified only by France and the Maritime Powers.

From this point onward the guile of Louis becomes obvious. During the greater part of 1700, while he was negotiating with William, his Ambassador in Madrid was using every resource, especially money, to win the Spanish Court to the interests of a French prince. At one and the same time he was signing with William the treaty which favoured the Archduke Charles, fomenting a party in Madrid in favour of his grandson, the second son of the Dauphin, Philip, Duke of Anjou, and gradually moving a considerable army towards the Spanish frontier. Since the Emperor would not accept the Partition Treaty, and war between France and the Empire seemed certain, it was natural that, if he must fight anyhow, Louis should fight for the maximum rather than for the minimum claims of his dynasty. Moreover, the weakness of England's pacific mood and the consequent incoherence of the Maritime Powers became continually more apparent. He therefore soothed William with his treaty, and shook Madrid with his propaganda, resolving to seize what fortune should offer.

The event was decisive. Charles II was on his deathbed. Within that diseased frame, that clouded mind, that superstitious soul, trembling on the verge of eternity, there glowed one imperial thought—unity. He was determined as he lay prostrate, scarcely able to utter a word or stir a finger, with his last gasp to proclaim that his vast dominions should pass intact and entire to one prince and to one alone. In the nick of time the French gold in Madrid and the French bayonets beyond the Pyrenees triumphed. The influence of the Holy See under the new Pope was transferred to the side of France. A palace revolution occurred. The Archbishop of Toledo, with a few other priests, established himself in the sick-room and forbade the Queen to enter. The King was then persuaded to sign a will leaving his throne to the Duke of Anjou. The will was completed on October 7, and couriers galloped with the news from the Escurial to Paris. On November 1, Charles II expired.

Louis XIV had now reached one of the great turning-points in the history of France. Should he stand by the treaty, reject the will, and face a single war with the Empire? Should he repudiate the treaty, endorse the will, and defend his grandson's claims in the field against all comers? Apart from good faith and solemnly signed agreements upon which the ink was barely dry, the choice, like so many momentous choices, was nicely balanced.

The news of the death of Charles II reached Paris on November 8, and no further delay was possible. A conference was held in Madame de Maintenon's rooms at which the King, his brother, Pontchartrain (the Chancellor), the Duc de Beauvilliers, and Torcy were present. The will had it. On November 12 Louis wrote to Madrid accordingly.

On November 16 a famous scene was enacted at Versailles. After the

Great King's levee he brought his grandson and the Spanish Ambassador, Castel des Rios, into his Cabinet. To the latter he said, indicating the Duke of Anjou, "You may salute him as your King."

We must now return to England. William was dining at Hampton Court when the news arrived. He bent his head in vain attempt to conceal his feelings. He saw the work of his lifetime was to be shattered, yet he was powerless. He knew it would be futile to appeal to Parliament. King William bowed to the awful logic of circumstances. On December 22 Tallard was able to report that the English and the Dutch would recognize Philip V. They would merely demand certain safeguards. William could only trust that from the discussion of these safeguards a Grand Alliance against France would emerge.

But now Parliament began to realize that the language and attitude of the French King about the essential separation of the Crowns of France and Spain was, at the very least, ambiguous. In February 1701, indeed, Louis XIV had expressly reserved his grandson's right of succession to the French throne, an action which seemed fatally significant to the Maritime Powers. Then came the news—keenly disturbing to all the British commercial interests represented by the Whig Party as the champions of civil and religious liberty—that the Spaniards had handed over to a French company the entire right of importing negro slaves into South America. But the supreme event which roused all England to an understanding of what had actually happened in the virtual union of the Crowns of France and Spain was a tremendous military operation effected under the guise of brazen legality. Philip V had been received with acclamation in Madrid. The Spanish Netherlands rejoiced in his accession. The bonfires blazed in the streets of Brussels in honour of their new sovereign. The fortresses of Belgium constituted the main barrier of the Dutch against the French invasion. After the Peace of Nimwegen * the most important had been occupied by Dutch garrisons who shared with their then Spanish allies the guardianship of these vital strongholds. But now the position was reversed. The Spaniards were the allies of France, joined not by a scrap of paper, but by

---

* The various treaties constituting the Peace of Nimwegen were signed during the autumn of 1678. Louis had come off with solid advantages; nevertheless, Nimwegen registered in his mind an unmistakable sense of being checked. He had widely extended the boundaries of France; but he had felt the thrust of definite and formidable resistances to his onward career.

kindred Crowns. The European states which had fought against France in the late war were still undecided. But everywhere the storm signal had been hoisted. Preparations were being made; officers and soldiers were being recalled from penury to their old formations. Louis, knowing that his enemies would fight if they could muster strength and courage, resolved to make sure of the barrier fortresses.

Citadels defended during all the years of general war, the loss or capture of any one of which would have been boasted as the fruits of a hard campaign, were swept away while a moon waxed and waned. Every one of these fortresses had to be retaken by Marlborough before he could even reach the position established at the Peace of Nimwegen. Only Maestricht, by the accident of an exceptionally strong Dutch garrison which guarded enormous supply depots, escaped the general landslide. Thus all that the Grand Alliance of 1689 had achieved in the Low Countries in eight years of war melted like snow at Easter.

Europe was roused, and at last England was staggered. Some of Louis's admirers condemn him for this violent measure. They argue that when all was going so well for his designs, when his grandson had been accepted as rightful King by every part of the Spanish Empire in the Old World and the New, when his adversaries in their lack of union seemed utterly impotent, he should have displayed all the virtues of quiescence and restraint. But, like William, he knew that the storm was gathering. He had launched himself upon an audacious voyage; and he knew the value of the fortresses. The nations were now arming fast, and we may imagine with what a glow of hope and salvation all those poor, neglected, despised, professional soldiers saw again the certainty of employment, of pay, of food, of shelter, and the chance of fame. Once more fighting men would come into their own. Once more the drums would beat, and the regiments in their brilliant uniforms would march along the highways. Once more the smug merchants and crafty politicians would find they could not do without 'popinjays.' Once more they would flatter the martial class and beg—though so lately ungrateful—for its renewed protection.

In the early summer of 1701 the Whig Party, a minority in the House of Commons, mobilized its pamphleteers to convert the electorate. But the Tories were slow. They were still hunting William III and planning retrenchment. They were still dreaming of detachment from Europe when the nation awoke beneath them. On May 8, 1701, the freeholders of Kent presented a petition to the Commons, begging the House to grant supplies to enable the King to help his allies "before it is too late." The militant pacifists were for punishing the freeholders for the presumption. They actually imprisoned their leaders; but the ground crumbled beneath their feet. The insular structure in which they sought to dwell crashed about their ears. The mass of the Tory Parliament had already moved some distance. On June 12, when they had extorted from the King his assent to the Act of Settlement, Parliament had also authorized him to "seek allies." Ten thousand men, at any rate, should be guaranteed to Holland. William felt the tide had set in his favour, and on the flow he prorogued Parliament, well knowing that their hour had passed.

The same processes which undermined the Tory factions and all their reasonings, so weighty to modern minds, united William and Marlborough. They joined forces, nor was their partnership unequal. For while King William now saw that he could once again draw the sword of England, he felt the melancholy conviction that he himself would never more wield it. This was no time on either side for half-confidences or old griefs. Some one must carry on. In his bones the King knew there was but one man. On May 31 he proclaimed Marlborough Commander-in-Chief of the English forces assembling in Holland. On June 28—the day of the Prorogation—he appointed him Ambassador Extraordinary to the United Provinces. The instructions to Marlborough show the far-reaching character of his powers. Discretion was given him not only to frame, but to conclude treaties without reference, if need be, to King or Parliament. But the King would be at hand and would maintain the closest contact possible. On July 1 the royal yacht carried them both to Holland. Though the opportunities of the reign had been marred or missed by their quarrels and misunderstandings, the two warrior-statesmen were at last united. Though much was lost, all might be retrieved. The formation of the Grand Alliance had begun.

CHAPTER TWENTY-FOUR

The Grand Alliance

ᚠᚦ 1701-2 ᚦᚠ

THE duties at length confided to Marlborough were of supreme importance. He was to make one last effort to avert the war. If that failed, he
was to make an offensive and defensive alliance against France between
the three great Powers, England, Holland, and the Empire; thereafter
to draw into the confederacy by subsidiary treaties Prussia, Denmark,
and as many of the German states and principalities as possible, and to
make a treaty with Sweden ensuring at least her friendly neutrality.
The King was at hand, usually at Loo, but in practice everything was left
to Marlborough and settled by him. Meanwhile through Godolphin he
vigilantly watched the tempestuous Parliamentary situation at home,
the movement of English opinion, and the reactions which these produced upon King William. In this press of affairs he passed the next
four months, and for the first time we see him extended upon a task
equal to his capacity.

At this moment also two men who were to be his closest intimates
and to continue at his side in unfailing loyalty through the whole period make their appearance. They were already his old friends. William
Cadogan, the son of a Dublin lawyer, had won Marlborough's confidence at the taking of Cork and Kinsale. He was now serving in Ireland as a major of the Royal Irish Dragoons. Marlborough appointed
him Quartermaster-General in the Low Countries, and he came to
Holland with the twelve battalions transported thither from Ireland.
He was in the van of all the battles and in numberless operations.
Nothing disturbed his fidelity to his chief or the mutual comprehen-

sion between them. He shared Marlborough's fall, refusing to separate himself from "the great man to whom I am under such infinite obligations." "I would be a monster," he added, "if I did otherwise."

The second was his military and political secretary. Adam de Cardonnel, the son of a French Protestant, had entered the War Office at an early age, rose to be a Chief Clerk, and came in contact with Marlborough at the beginning of William's reign. From the early part of 1692 he had acted as his secretary, and was in his closest personal friendship and confidence. He too made all the campaigns with Marlborough. He conducted the whole of his correspondence with the sovereigns, princes, and commanders of the Grand Alliance and with the English political leaders, drafting the letters himself, writing from Marlborough's dictation, or copying what his chief had written, to the very great advantage of its grammar and spelling. Thus when the occasion came to Marlborough he was not only ready himself, but he had at his disposal both a military and a civilian instrument which he had long selected and prepared, and which were so perfectly adapted to his needs that they were never changed.

At this moment also appears upon our scene Marlborough's famous comrade. During the spring the Emperor, with the encouragement of King William, had gathered an army of thirty thousand men in the Southern Tyrol. At the head of this stood Prince Eugene.

Prince François Eugene of Savoy was born at Paris in 1663, but from the age of twenty, for just over fifty years and in more than thirty campaigns, he commanded the armies and fought the battles of Austria on all the fronts of the Empire. When he was not fighting the French, he was fighting the Turks. A colonel at twenty, a major-general at twenty-one, he was made a general of cavalry at twenty-six. He was a commander-in-chief ten years before Marlborough. He was still a commander-in-chief, fighting always in the van, more than twenty years after Marlborough's work was done. At the end of his life of innumerable and almost unceasing perils, toils, checks, and triumphs, his skinny body scarred with many wounds, he could still revel in his military duties. He never married, and although he was a discerning patron of art, his only passion was warfare. His decisive victory over the Turks at Zenta in 1697 made him at this moment in our story "the most renowned commander in Europe."

Eugene was a grandson of Duke Charles Emmanuel of Savoy and

son of Olympe Mancini, a niece of Cardinal Mazarin and one of the most beautiful women at the Court of Louis XIV. As a youth, his weakly frame, turned-up nose, and short upper lip gave him, despite his fine eyes, a vacant appearance and caused him to be considered unfit for a soldier. Against his will he was forced to enter the Church, and the King nicknamed him *le petit abbé*. Intrigue at Court twice brought about his father's exile. His mother's grief at this misfortune weighed deeply upon the young mind of the Prince, and he is said to have sworn to leave France and never to return except with his sword in his hand. He became the persistent enemy of France throughout his life. After the early death of his father, Eugene, with two of his brothers, migrated to Vienna. His lack of frivolity, which had injured him at Versailles, was a positive advantage to him at the sombre Court of Leopold I. His earliest experience of war was in the fateful year of 1683, when the Turks reached the gates of Vienna. Here his eldest brother was killed. But Eugene made his mark in a strange land. The Emperor liked and admired him. He saw warfare in its most ruthless forms, and fought under the leadership of the famous Charles of Lorraine. After he had become a colonel Eugene abandoned his desire for a principality in Italy, and fixed as his sole ambition the command of the Imperial Army.

In essence the second Grand Alliance was bound to become another Partition Treaty. Hard pressure had to be put upon the Emperor to reconcile his extortionate demands with the claims of Holland, and thereafter English interests had to be sustained against both Powers. Marlborough, with the angry debates upon William's Partitions in his ears, was intent to study the susceptibilities of the House of Commons, and also to secure due prominence for the particular kind of buccaneering warfare on the sea and across the oceans which was alone acceptable to Tory hearts. In the end he presented results which reconciled the pride of the Empire, the cautious obstinacy of the Dutch, and the commercial and colonizing appetites of the English.

Although French and Austrian troops were already fighting fiercely in Italy, the last hopes of a general peace were not abandoned. Marlborough had been given a separate set of instructions to enter into negotiations with the Ministers of France and Spain at The Hague. He demanded once again on behalf of the Maritime Powers the withdrawal of the French garrisons from the barrier fortresses, the surrender

of "cautionary towns" by the Spaniards to Anglo-Dutch control, and
the guarantee of "a reasonable satisfaction" for the Emperor out of the
Spanish heritage. He seems to have thought it just possible that
Eugene's victories in Italy, the process of forming the Grand Alliance
at The Hague, and the evident resolve of the Allies to proceed to ex-
tremities would oblige Louis to agree in August to the terms he had rejected in March. The French King refused to consider the Emperor's
demands, or even to admit to a conference the Ambassador of a Power
with whom, though not formally at war, his troops were already engaged.

When, on the 18th, Marlborough learned that Villeroy had left for
Italy he felt sure that France had abandoned any thought of opening a
campaign in Flanders during the autumn of 1701. Forthwith he allowed Sarah to come over for the greatest day his life had yet seen. On
September 7, 1701, he signed alone for England the main treaty with
the Empire and Holland by which the three Powers bound themselves
to exact their terms from France by negotiations or arms. Sarah was
present at his side in his hour of triumph. She was fêted by the bril
liant throng assembled for the famous event.

Great moderation characterized the stipulations of the allies. They
acquiesced in the rule of Philip V over Spain and the Spanish Indies,
provided that the Crowns of France and Spain should never be united.
The Emperor was to secure Milan, Naples, Sicily, the Spanish Mediterranean islands, together with Belgium and Luxembourg. But these last
two, under the sovereignty of Austria, were to be so organized as to
serve "as a fence and rampart, commonly called a barrier, separating
and keeping off France from the United Provinces." This basis being
settled, the minor states were urged by subsidies provided by England
and Holland and by other inducements to join the alliance, and with
each a separate agreement was made. The recognition of the Elector of
Brandenburg as King of Prussia was the price reluctantly paid by the
Emperor in return for his adhesion.

The territorial objectives of the war having been at length agreed,
the three principals proceeded to discuss the *dénombrement*. It was
finally settled that the Empire should bring into the field against
France 82,000 men, the Dutch 100,000, and the English 40,000, together with an equal number for the fleet.

It will be seen that Marlborough's fear of offending Parliament by finally deciding the treaties without their approval was even more acute where the quota of British troops was concerned.

On October 3 he writes to Godolphin:

*. . . You will excuse me that I trouble you again about the *dénombrement*. I have made use of the argument, that is very natural for England, which is that their [England's] expense at sea must be great. This argument is of more use to me when I speak to the Imperialists, than with the Pensioner; for the latter tells me, that they shall be willing to furnish at sea the same proportions as they did the last war, which was three in eight; and since their land forces are greater than they were the last war, the people here might reasonably expect that ours might not be less. I continue still of the opinion that it would be fatal to have this settled anywhere but in Parliament; but on the other hand I ought to say some thing to them, and I should be glad to know if I might not endeavour to make them not expect more than one half of what they had the last war. For aught I know, this may be more than England will care to do; but I hear no other language here, than that this war must be carried with more vigour than the last, if we ever hope to see a good end of it; and I confess it is so much my own opinion, that I hope we shall do our utmost; what that is, you and 16 [Hedges?] are much properer judges than I am. When the King speaks to you of this matter, I beg you will be positive in the opinion that it is of the last consequence [not] to do any thing in it, but in Parliament. That which makes me the more pressing in this of the *dénombrement* is that the Pensioner is inclined to have it done before the Parl meets; which I think would be destruction.

While all these preparations resounded upon the anvil of Europe, both sides, though yielding nothing further, nevertheless still hoped against hope for peace. As so often happens in world affairs, and particularly in English affairs, a sense of dire necessity grows in men's minds and yet they shrink from action. The atmosphere is loaded with inflammable gas: but a flash is needed to produce the explosion.

On September 16, 1701, James II died. Louis visited in state his deathbed at Saint-Germains. While the unhappy exile was in the stertorous breathing which often precedes the flight of the soul, the Grand Monarch announced to the shadow Court that he recognized his son as King of England and would ever sustain his rights. Chivalry, vanity, and a recklessness born of the prolonged suspense had impelled Louis to this most imprudent act. He upheld it in face of the solid opposition of his Cabinet. Its consequences surprised him beyond measure. All England was roused by the insult to her independence. The Act of Settlement had decreed the succession of the Crown. The Treaty of Ryswick had bound Louis not only in formal terms, but by a gentleman's agreement, to recognize and not to molest William III as King. The domestic law of England was outraged by the arrogance, and her treaty rights violated by the perfidy, of the French despot. Whigs and Tories vied with one another in Parliament in resenting the affront. Was England, then, a vassal of France on whom a king could be imposed and despite all plighted faith? The whole nation became resolute for war. Marlborough's treaties, shaped and presented with so much Parliamentary understanding, were acclaimed; ample supplies were tendered to the Crown. King William saw his moment had come. Forthwith upon the news he recalled his Ambassador from Paris and dismissed Tallard from St James's. Now also was the time to rid himself of the Tory Party, which had used him so ill and in their purblind folly had tied his hands till all seemed ruined. Now was the time to hale before the bar of an awakened nation those truculent, pigheaded Commoners who had so provedly misjudged the public interest. The King saw his way to a sound Whig Parliament for the vigorous waging of war. Whispers of Dissolution pervaded the high circles of Court and politics.

Marlborough watched the King attentively. He read his mind and dreaded his purpose. The expulsion of the Tories in a disastrous war-fever election would undermine all the power and credit he had acquired in these spacious months. Moreover, he judged better than the King the inherent strength of Tory England. Even taken at so great a disadvantage, the Tories would be strong enough to wreck, if they could not rule. Only the peace party could draw the sword of England. A Whig triumph at the polls threatened a divided nation in the war. He used all his arts to dissuade William from the course upon which he saw him bent. The King, though filled with admiration at the capacity of his lieutenant, discounted his advice as interested, and held to his design.

He did not mean to be persuaded. "I have but just time to tell you," wrote Marlborough about September 18, "that as the king went into his coach he told me that he would write to me, by which I understand that I am not to stir from hence till I hear from him. . . ." The King quitted Holland suddenly, leaving Marlborough thus chained to his post. Several weeks passed before the efforts of Godolphin and Albemarle secured him permission to come home. On the very day his letter of recall arrived Marlborough learned that Parliament was dissolved and that Godolphin had resolved to resign.

The election belied King William's hopes. Although a cluster of his personal assailants and many Jacobites lost their seats in the Whig attack, the Tories were found to have, as Marlborough had predicted, a very solid core. They actually carried Harley back to the Speaker's chair in the new Parliament by a majority of four. The two parties were so even that, for all their hatred, they could scarcely maul one another. This in itself was a gain; but, on the other hand, the Tory rage against the King was mortal. They held that he had flung them to the country wrongfully within a year of their return at a time when they were giving him loyal and resolute support. He had played a party trick upon them, and the trick had failed. They never forgave him; they longed for his death. Nevertheless they joined with the Whigs in supporting his war.

The turn of affairs had brought about a sensible change in Marlborough's political position. In spite of Godolphin's demand to resign, the Tory Ministry had been kept by the King till he could see the election results. From his point of view this half-measure was a mistake, for the party in power had great influence upon the poll. After the results were known, the King felt himself strong enough to get rid of the Tories. He sent Rochester packing and released Godolphin. Marlborough's case was that of a man all of whose colleagues had been dismissed, but who has himself become detached from their fortunes by the importance of a foreign mission for which all parties judge him supremely fitted. Moreover, although he had worked consistently in the Tory interest and kept all his labels unchanged, he had become in fact the mainspring of the Whig policy in Europe. Thus both parties looked to him with regard and recognized, however grudgingly, that he was above their warfare. This was not the result of calculation on his part, for the happenings had been often contrary to his wishes and almost entirely beyond his control. Events had detached him from his party and left him, without partisan reproach, independent on the hub of affairs. Henceforward he ceased gradually to be a party man, though still of Tory hue. We shall see him try long and hard to keep this neutral footing until he is driven through coalition to the Whigs and finally destroyed by the revengeful Tories.

The gathering together of so many threads and resources in the hands of a single man of known abilities and ambition aroused fierce jealousies in that world of proud magnates; and all foresaw that the King's death and the accession of Anne would make Marlborough virtual master of England. To the Tories this was not unwelcome. They thought they saw in it the ascendancy of their party. For this very reason the Whigs were alarmed. Although they realized that Marlborough held the Whig view of foreign policy, although his wife was an ardent Whig, although Sunderland probably laboured to reassure them, yet the Whigs could not regard the arrival of Marlborough at the supreme direction of affairs as other than the triumph of a Tory chief serving a Tory Queen. Some of their leaders entertained the idea of passing over the Princess Anne and of bringing the Elector of Hanover to the throne. Marlborough, whose sources of information were extensive, heard of this. He questioned Dartmouth, who replied that he knew of the proposal, but did not regard it seriously. Marlborough declared that the plot existed, and, with a fierce flash unusual in him, exclaimed, "But, by God, if ever they attempt it, we would walk over their bellies!" This unwonted violence may well have been calculated. He was so situated that he could certainly have used the Army as well as the Tory Party to resist any such design, and he no doubt wished this to be well understood. The prize long awaited was near, and he would not be baulked of it.

The second Grand Alliance now formed must have seemed a desperate venture to those whose minds were seared by the ill-fortune of William's eight-years war. How vain had been that struggle! How hard to gain any advantage over the mighty central power of France! Hardly a trophy had been won from all that bitter toil. France, single-handed, had fought Europe and emerged wearied but unbeaten. In the six years of peace she had regained without a shot fired all the fortresses and territory so stubbornly disputed. But now the widest empire in the world was withdrawn from the Alliance and added to the resources of its antagonists. Spain had changed sides, and with Spain not only the Indies, South America, and the whole of Italy, but the cockpit of Europe—

Belgium and Luxembourg—and even Portugal. Savoy, the deserter, still rested with France. Cologne was also now a French ally. Bavaria, constant to the end of the last war, was to be with France in the new struggle. The Maritime Powers had scarcely a friendly port beyond their coasts. The New World was almost barred against them. The Mediterranean had become in effect a French lake. South of Plymouth no fortified harbour lay open to their ships. They had their superior fleets, but no bases which would carry them to the inland sea. On land the whole Dutch barrier had passed into French hands. Instead of being the rampart of Holland, it had become the sallyport of France. Louis, occupying the Archbishoprics of Cologne and Trèves, was master of the Meuse and of the Lower Rhine. He held all the Channel ports, and had entrenched himself from Namur through Antwerp to the sea. His armies ranged through the region east of the Meuse to the Dutch frontier. His winter dispositions disclosed his intention in the spring campaign to renew the invasion of Holland along the same routes which had led almost to its subjugation in 1672. A terrible front of fortresses, bristling with cannon, crammed with troops and supplies, betokened the approaching onslaught. The Dutch cowered behind inundations and their remaining strongholds. Lastly, the transference of Bavaria to the side of France laid the very heart of the Empire open to French invasion. In every element of strategy by sea or by land, as well as in the extent of territory and population, Louis was twice as strong at the beginning of the War of the Spanish Succession as he had been at the Peace of Ryswick. One final adverse contrast must be noticed. The Papacy had changed sides. Clement XI had abandoned the policy of Innocent XI. He espoused the cause of the Great King. He sent his congratulations to Philip V, and granted him subsidies from Spanish ecclesiastical property. He lived to repent his error. The scale of the new war was turned by the genius of one man. One single will outweighed all these fearful inequalities, and built out of the halved and defeated fragments of William's wars a structure of surpassing success under the leadership of England.

"The little gentleman in black velvet," the hero for a spell of so many enthusiastic toasts, now intervened. On February 20, William was riding in the park round Hampton Court on Sorrel, a favourite horse said to have once belonged to Sir John Fenwick. Sorrel stumbled in the new workings of a mole, and the King was thrown. The broken collarbone might well have mended, but in his failing health the accident opened the door to a troop of lurking foes. Complications set in, and after a fortnight it was evident to him and to all who saw him that death was at hand. He transacted business to the end. His interest in the world drama for which he had set the stage, on which the curtain was about to rise, lighted his mind as the shadows closed upon him. He received the reports of his gathering armies and followed the business of both his Parliaments. He grieved to quit the themes and combinations which had been the labour and the passion of his life. They were now approaching their dread climax. But he must go. He had his consolation. He saw with eagle eye the approach of a reign and Government in England which would maintain the cause in which his strength had been spent. He saw the only man to whom in war or policy, in the intricate convolutions of European diplomacy, in the party turmoil of England, or amid the hazards of the battlefield, he could bequeath the awful yet unescapable task. He had made his preparations deliberately to pass his leadership to a new champion of the Protestant faith and the liberties of Europe. In his last years he had woven Marlborough into the whole texture of his combinations and policy. In his last hours he commended him to his successor as the fittest man in the realm to guide her councils and lead her armies. William died at fifty-two worn out by his labours. Marlborough at the same age strode forward upon those ten years of unbroken victory with which our future chapters will be mainly concerned.

Sarah Countess of Marlborough. BY PERMISSION OF EARL SPENCER.